Charles Haddon Spurgeon

The Present Truth

A collection of sermons preached at the Metropolitan Tabernacle

Charles Haddon Spurgeon

The Present Truth
A collection of sermons preached at the Metropolitan Tabernacle

ISBN/EAN: 9783337114602

Printed in Europe, USA, Canada, Australia, Japan

Cover: Foto ©Lupo / pixelio.de

More available books at **www.hansebooks.com**

THE

PRESENT TRUTH

A Collection of Sermons

PREACHED AT

THE METROPOLITAN TABERNACLE

BY

C. H. SPURGEON

" I will not be negligent to put you always in remembrance of these things,
though ye know them, and be established in the present truth."—2 PETER I. 12

NEW YORK
ROBERT CARTER & BROTHERS
530 BROADWAY
1883

St. Johnland
Stereotype Foundry,
Suffolk Co., N. Y.

New York:
Press of
Jenkins & Thomas.

CONTENTS.

MR. SPURGEON AS A POPULAR AUTHOR.

From the Pall Mall Gazette.

Of Mr. Spurgeon's personal popularity nothing need be said here. The old north countrywoman who declared that before she died she must go to London "to see Madame Tussaud's and hear Spurgeon," was by no means so rare a type as some superfine people are inclined to think. But although every one would admit the personal popularity, or, if they prefer it, the notoriety, of Mr. Spurgeon, comparatively few are aware of the enormous sale of the productions of his pen. His sermons are regularly reported by a professional shorthand writer, whose "copy" undergoes revision by Mr. Spurgeon. Every week of the past twenty-nine years has seen a sermon of Mr. Spurgeon's issued to the public. The regular weekly sale of the sermon (counting in the numbers put into monthly covers) is now above twenty-five thousand. Mr. Spurgeon's sermons have been translated into nearly all the languages of the world. His volumes of "Readings," either for the family or the closet, are meeting with a very rapid sale. But by far the most popular of Mr. Spurgeon's books is his racy "John Ploughman's Talk." The "Talk" (published in 1868) is in its three hundred and twentieth thousand; and of the Sequel, which was issued only four years ago, one hundred thousand copies have been sold. In many parts of Scotland, Mr. Spurgeon is venerated beyond all other men. "We English," said a Southron once to the old lady who takes visitors round the ruins of Melrose Abbey, "have had many famous men, but we have had no John Knox." "True," said the old dame; "you have had no John Knox, but then you have Mr. Spurgeon!" From a Scotch Presbyterian what tribute could be more extravagant?

ADVERTISEMENT.

The wide popularity Mr. Spurgeon's Sermons have enjoyed for many years may preclude the supposition that "*a new series*" will be hailed by the public as a startling novelty, yet must warrant the expectation that it will be greeted with a friendly welcome. The natural freshness and spiritual force of the Preacher are generally admitted: but the marvel is that the discourses should retain so much of their original grace and glow, after passing through the hands of reporters and printers. "The Present Truth" is a sequel to "Types and Emblems" being collated from the Sunday evening and Thursday evening Sermons; and quite distinct from the "Metropolitan Tabernacle Pulpit," which contains, for the most part, week by week, the Sermon of the previous Sunday morning.

That this little volume may meet with God-speed wherever it goes is the fervent hope of

THE PUBLISHERS.

THE PRESENT TRUTH.

𝔄 𝔐𝔞𝔫𝔶-𝔖𝔦𝔡𝔢𝔡 𝔐𝔬𝔱𝔱𝔬.

One thing is needful.—LUKE x. 42.
One thing I know.—JOHN ix. 25.
One thing I do.—PHILIPPIANS iii. 13.

I HAVE "one thing" in view—"*one thing*" on which I want to rivet your attention. Forbear with me if I detain you a few minutes before announcing a text. It has been said that a man of one book is terrible in the force of his convictions. He has studied it so well, digested it so thoroughly, and understands it so profoundly, that it is perilous to encounter him in controversy. No man becomes eminent in any pursuit unless he gives himself up to it with all the powers and passions of his nature—body and soul. Michael Angelo had never been so great a painter if his love of art had not become so enthusiastic that he frequently did not take off his garments to sleep by the week together; nor had Handel ever been such a great musician if his ardor for sounds celestial had not led him to use the keys of his harpsichord till, by constant fingering, they became the

(9)

shape of spoons. A man must have one pursuit, and consecrate all his powers to one purpose, if he would excel or rise to eminence among his fellows.

When streams of water divide themselves into innumerable rills, they usually create a morass, which proves dangerous to the inhabitants of the neighborhood. Could all those streams be dammed up into one channel, and made to flow in one direction, they might resolve themselves into a navigable river bearing commerce to the ocean, and enriching the people who dwell upon its banks. To obtain one thing, one comprehensive boon from heaven, has been the object of many a saintly prayer, like that of David,—" Unite my heart to fear Thy name." The advice of Paul was—" Set not your affection upon things on the earth," not "your affections," as it is often misquoted. The Apostle would have all the affections tied up into one affection, and that one concentrated affection not set upon earthly things, but upon things above, where Christ sitteth at the right hand of God. The concurrence of all our powers and capacities with one single impulse, to obtain one object, and to produce one result, is one great aim of the Gospel of Jesus Christ.

The "one thing" concerning which I am now about to talk very seriously to you will require three texts to elucidate it. There are three pithy passages of Holy Scripture which I shall endeavor to press home on your heart and conscience.

Our first text is to be found in the Gospel according to St. Luke x. 42,—"ONE THING IS NEEDFUL."

This one thing, according to this passage, is *faith in Christ Jesus*, the sitting down at the Master's feet, the drinking in His Word. If I may expand for a minute the "one thing," without seeming to make twenty things of that which is but one, I will refer it to the possession of a new life. This life is given to us when by the power of the Holy Ghost we are created anew in Christ Jesus, and it develops itself in a simple confidence in Jesus, in a hearty obedience to Jesus, in a desire to be like Jesus, and in a constant yearning to be near to Jesus. "One thing is needful;" that one thing is salvation, wrought in us by the Holy Ghost, through faith which is in Jesus Christ our Lord. The new heart, the right spirit, a filial fear of God, love to Jesus—this is the "one thing needful."

Now I trust you all know how to distinguish things essential from things convenient, and that you are more concerned about needful things than about things merely attractive, or, at most, but accessory to your welfare. The little child may admire the field which is covered with red and blue flowers; the husbandman cares nothing for these flowerets; he delights in the wheat that is ripening for the sickle. So our childish minds are often fascinated with the flaunting flowers of fortune and fashion; craving after wealth and fame and worldly distinction; but our better reason, if it be allowed to speak, will prefer the necessary things, the things which we must have or else must perish. We may do without earthly goods, for thousands have been happy in life and triumphant in death without any of the luxury which riches can purchase. The heart's love of his fellow-creatures has been fairly won by many a humble man who never courted popular applause. The patience of the poor has often counted for fine gold, while the pride of the affluent has passed for nothing but foul dross. Even lack of health, which is heaven's priceless boon to mortals here below, has not hindered some precious sufferers from serving their generation, glorifying God in a martyrdom of pain, and bequeathing treasures of piety to a grateful posterity. Ten thousand things are convenient; thousands of things are desirable; hundreds of things are to be sought for; but there is one thing, one only thing, the one thing we have described to you, of which our Saviour speaks as the "one thing needful." And oh how needful this one thing is! Needful for your children—they are growing up about you; and much joy they give you; for you can see in them many budding excellences. To your partial eyes they give promise of goodness, if not of greatness. They will be the comfort of your declining years. You have carefully watched their education. Not a whit of their moral habits have you failed to overlook. To give them a fair start in the world has been your fond desire till their portion is the fruit of your providence. From perils you would protect them. Lest they should have to rough it, perhaps, as much as their father before them, you would pilot them through the straits. Good! but, dear parents, do recollect that "one thing is needful." For your children, that they may commence life, continue in life, and close life honorably, it is well that they should be educated; it is well that morality should be instilled into them, but this is not enough. Alas! we have seen many leave the purest parental influences to plunge into the foulest sins; their education has become but a tool for iniquity, and the money with which they might have helped themselves to competence has been squandered away in vice. "One thing is needful" for that bright-eyed boy. Oh! if you can take him to the Saviour, and if the blessing of the Good Shepherd shall alight on him and renew him while yet a child, the best will have been done for him—yea, his one chief need supplied. And if that dear girl, before she comes to womanhood, shall be led to that blessed Saviour who rejecteth none that come to him, she will have received all she shall want for time and for eternity.

Quicken your prayers, then, dear parents. Think of your children, to seek their welfare more intelligently. Be more importunate in intercession on their behalf. Truly, this is the one thing needful for them. One thing, too, is needful for that young man just leaving home to go out as an apprentice and learn his trade. That is a trying time for an untried hand. The heart may well flutter as one young and inexperienced reflects that he is now about to sail, not on a coasting voyage, but to put fairly out to sea. Ere long it will be seen whether those fair professions had truth as a foundation. He will get to London—many of you have passed through this ordeal. The metropolis; what a maze it seemed to you at first, and with what amazement you surveyed it! Appalling propensities lurk within your breast, and profuse attractions without lure your ears and dazzle your eyes, till by temptation you are spell-bound. What could not be done in the village, what you dared not think of in the little market-town, seems easy to be done unobserved in the great city. Hundreds of fingers point you to the haunts of pleasure, the home of vice, the path to hell. Ah, mother and father! you present the Bible as your parting gift; you write the youth's name on the fly-leaf. You offer your prayers, and you shed your tears for him. Steals there not over you the conviction that the one thing he needs you cannot pack in his trunk, nor can you send it up to him by a post-office order. The one thing needful is that Christ should be formed in his heart the hope of glory. With that he would begin life well. A sword of the true Jerusalem metal that will not break in the heat of the conflict will be serviceable all his journey through. Do I address some young man who has not forgotten his mother's kind remarks when he left home? Let me just echo them, and say to him, One thing thou lackest; oh seek it, seek it now! Before going

out of this house seek till, through grace, you obtain this one thing needful which shall bear thee
safely to the skies.

But "one thing is needful," not merely for those
youngsters at home, or for those about to go
abroad in the world. One thing is needful *for the
business* man. "Ah!" saith he, "I want a great
many things." But what, I ask, is the one thing?
You speak of "*the needful.*" You call ready cash
"*the indispensable.*" "Give me this," says the man
of the world, "and I don't care about anything
else. Recommend your religion to whom you
please, but let me have solid gold and silver and
I will be well content." Ah, sirs! ye delude yourselves with phantoms. You fondly dream that
wealth in your hands would count for more than
it has ever done for your fellows. You must have
seen some men make large fortunes whom you
knew to be very miserable. They have retired
from business to get a little rest, and yet they
could find no rest in their retirement. You must
have known others who the more they have got
the more they have wanted, for they have swallowed a horse-leech, and it has cried, "Give, give!"
Of course you never suspected that the money did
the mischief, or that the precious metal poisoned
the heart. But are you in quest of happiness?
It lies not in investments, whether in consols or
mortgages, stocks or debentures, gold or silver.
These properties are profitable. They can be used
to promote happiness. As accessories to our wel-

fare they may often prove to be blessings, but if accredited with intrinsic worth they will eat as doth a canker. Money circulated is a medium of public benefit, while money hoarded is a means of private discomfort. A man may make a muck-raker of himself if he is forever seeking to scrape everything to himself. A miser is bound to be miserable. Before high heaven, he is an object to make the angels weep.

One thing is needful for you merchants, brokers, and warehousemen, to keep you from sinking under your anxieties and losses, cr to preserve you from becoming sordid and selfish through your successes, and lest your greed should increase with your gains. One thing is needful that your life may be a true life, or else, when it comes to its end, all that can be said of you will amount to this,—"He died worth so much." Must that be your only memorial? When you depart from this world the poor and needy will not miss you; widow and orphan will not grieve for you; the Church militant will not mourn; the bright spirits above will not be waiting to greet you. The grand climax of your career a will! a testament sworn under a very large sum! What shall it profit any man what fortune soever he may have amassed, if he lose his soul? Think ye that riches possessed in this world will procure any respect in the nether regions? I have heard that in the old Fleet Prison the *swell* who was put in jail for ten thousand pounds thought himself a gentleman in comparison with those common fellows who were put in for some paltry debt of twenty or five-and-twenty pounds. There are no such distinctions in hell. You who can boast your talents of gold and talents of silver, if ye are cast away, shall be as complete wrecks as those who never had doit or stiver, but lived and died in privation and poverty. You want one thing, and if you get this one thing your wealth shall prove a blessing; otherwise it will be a curse. With this one thing your sufficiency for the day guaranteed to you by promise shall make you as one of heaven's favorites, fed by the hand of God; ever needy, but never neglected.

Ye aged sires,—there are some such here—shall I have to remind any of you that one thing is needful—ay, most needful to you? Death has already put his bony palm upon your head and frozen your hair to the whiteness of that winter in which all your strength must fail and all your beauty fade. Oh how sad, if *you* have no Saviour! You will soon have to quit these transitory scenes. The young may die, but the old *must*. To die without a Saviour will be dreary and dreadful. Then after death the judgment. Brave old man, how will your courage stand that outlook if so be you have none to plead your cause? Oh, aged woman, you will soon be in the scales; very soon must your character be weighed. If it be said of you, "Tekel: she is weighed in the balances and found wanting," there will be no opportunity to get right or adjust your relations to God or to your fellow-creatures. Your lamp will have gone out. There will be no chance of rekindling it. If lost, that means forever lost; forever in the dark; forever cast away! Little enough will it avail you then that you have nourished and brought up children. It will not suffice you then that you paid your debts honestly. Vain the plea that you attended a place of worship, and were always respected in the neighborhood. One thing is needful; lacking that, thou wilt turn out to have been a fool. Notwithstanding many opportunities and repeated invitations, to have rejected the one thing—the one only thing—what an irreparable mistake. Oh, how thou wilt weep as one disappointed! How thou wilt gnash thy teeth as they do who upbraid themselves! Thou wilt mourn forever, and thy self-reproach shall know no end.

I wish I could move you, as I desire, to feel as I feel myself, that this one thing is needful to every unconverted person here present. Some of you have already got this one choice thing that is so needful. Hold it fast; never let it go. Grace gave it to you; grace will keep it for you; grace will hold you true to it. Never be ashamed of it. Prize it beyond all cost. But as for you who have it not—I think I hear your funeral knell pealing in my ears, and as you speed away, your spirits made to fly for very fear, right into the arms of justice; methinks I hear your bitter cry, "The harvest is past, the summer is ended, and we are not saved!" I would fain pluck you by the skirts, if I could, and say to you, "Why not seek the one thing needful without more ado? Get it now. It will not in any way hurt you. It will make you happy here and blessed hereafter. It is as needful for this life as for the next, as needful for the exchange as for the sick chamber, as needful for the street and for the shop as for the dying bed and for the day of judgment. One thing—one thing is needful."

II. And now suffer me to halt before taking you a stage further. Allow me, as it were, to change horses. I must take another text. It is in the Gospel according to John, the ninth chapter, and the twenty-fifth verse, and these are the words: " ONE THING I KNOW."

The man who was born blind, whose eyes were opened at the pool of Siloam, said, "One thing I know." This simple statement I want to turn into a pointed question. Among the many things, dear friends, that you are acquainted with, do you know the one thing that this poor man knew, "Whereas I was blind, now I see?" There is a wealth of self-knowledge in this single avowal. Little enough, I daresay, he knew about other people, but he knew a great deal about himself. He was well aware that he once was blind, and he was quite positive that he now could see. Oh! can you say it with sincerity—"I know that I was once blind; I could see no beauty in Christ, though I thought I saw great beauties in the world. Then I could not love God; I did not hate sin; I had no repentance, nor had I any faith; I was blind; but now—oh, blessed change—now I see my sin, and weep over it; now I see a Saviour and I trust him; now I see his beauties and I admire him; now I see his service, and I delight to spend my strength in it. One thing I know." What a marvellous experience of a marvellous change this implies!

Nor can its importance be overrated. There is no going to heaven unless you undergo a change which shall make you entirely new, and make all things entirely new to you. A young convert once said, "I do not know how it is: either the world is changed, or else I am, for nothing seems to me to be the same as it once was." Ah! this old Bible, what a dry book it used to be; but oh, how it abounds in marrow and fatness now! Prayer —what a tedious duty once, but what a delightful exercise now! The going up to God's house on the Sabbath—used it not to be a weariness of the flesh? How much better to be in the fields? Yet now, how delightful we feel it to assemble with the Lord's saints! With what pleasure we hail the festal morn! All things are altered. Behold, all things are become new. What we once hated we love, and what we loved we hate. Is it so, dear hearer—is it so with you? Do not, I prythee, be content with mere reformation. Were you aforetime a drunkard, and are you now a teetotaler? Good—very good; yet, good as it is, it will not save your soul. Dishonest and knavish you once

were, but truthful and trustworthy you may now
be; yet rely not upon it for salvation. In former
days unchaste, by stern resolve you may have
given up the favorite lust, but even that will not
save you. Those who never fell into your foul
sloughs need the change. "Ye must be born
again." You must have an entire renewal—a
radical change. It is not cutting off the limbs
of a tree, nor shifting it to another place that will
convert a bramble into a vine. The sap must be
changed. The heart must be renewed. The inner
man must be made completely new. Is it so with
you? Why, I think if some of us were to meet
our old selves walking down the street we should
hardly know ourselves. 'Tis true our old self has
taken good care to knock at our door pretty often
since. Of all the knocks we hear, not even ex-
cepting that of the devil, there is none we dread
so much. The knock of the old man when he
says, "Let me in with my corruptions and lusts,
and let me reign and have my own way." Nay,
old man, you were once ourselves, but go your
way, for we have put off the old man with his
deeds, and put on the new man; we cannot know
you, for one thing we know now that we knew not
before—whereas we were blind, now we see.

Need I linger any longer upon this point. Let
it suffice if I leave it as a kind of awakening question
upon the heart and conscience. There are not
twenty things, but there is one thing you have to
inquire about. Do you know of a surety this one

thing: that you are not now what you used to be? Do you know that Jesus has made the difference—that Jesus has opened the eye that was once without sight—that you now see Jesus, and seeing, you love him?

III. Our third text is in the third chapter of the Epistle to the Philippians, at the thirteenth verse. There the Apostle Paul says—"ONE THING I DO."

Pray observe that I did not introduce *"doing"* first. That would not answer. We do not begin with doing. The one thing needful is not doing. Coming to Christ, and trusting to him, must take the lead. Not until after you have got the one thing needful, and know that you have got it, and are conscious that, whereas you were blind now you see, can you be fit to take the next step—"One thing I do." And what is that one thing? "Forgetting the things which are behind, and reaching forth unto those things which are before, I press toward the mark for the prize of the high calling of God in Christ Jesus." It seems, then, that the Apostle gave his whole mind up to the glorifying of God by his spiritual life. He was never content with what he was. If he had a little faith, he sought for more. If he had a little hope, he aimed to obtain more. If he had some degree of virtue, he coveted more. Oh, Christians, never be satisfied with being merely saved. Up with you! Away, off! Go onward to the high mountains, to the clearer light, to the brighter joy! If saved, and brought like the shipwrecked mariner to shore, is that enough? Yes, for the moment it is enough to warrant the purest satisfaction and the warmest congratulations. But the mariner must seek a livelihood as long as he lives. He must put forth his energies. Whatever avocations open up before him, he must vigorously seek such favors of fortune as may possibly be within his reach. Just so let it be with you. Saved from the deep which threatened to swallow you up, rejoice that you are preserved from death, but resolve that the life vouchsafed to you shall be active, earnest, vigorous, fruitful in every good work. Be diligent as your traders are. See how they wake their servants up in the morning, how they scold them if they are not up betimes. This man must be hurried to one place, and that man to another. How sharp they speak! How quickly they move about! They will do their business; and they spare no pains to increase it. Oh! that we were half as diligent in the service of God. Here we are drivelling away our time. We do not put out all our talents, augment our faith, and enlarge our coast. Why are we so tenacious of going to that great Giver of every good and perfect gift for fresh supplies? Why do we not wait upon him to be enriched? Would to God that we were as diligent in spiritual as we are in temporal things! Oh! that we were avaricious with a holy covetousness for the best gifts God can bestow, and the choicest blessings saints can receive!

Paul was anxious to do more good, to get more good, to be more good. He sought to win souls.

He wanted to make Christ's name known. An ardent passion inflamed him; a high enthusiasm inspired him. Tent-making, it is true, was his trade, but tent-making did not monopolize quite all his heart and soul and strength. Does your secular vocation absorb all your thoughts? Though Paul was proud of his industry, and could say conscientiously, "My own hands have ministered to my necessities," yet preaching the Gospel was the one thing he pursued as his life-work. He was a workman just as many of you are; but where were his tools? They were ready to hand when he wanted them. And did they, think you, ever creep up into his heart? I trow never. "For us to live," said he, "is Christ." That was as true, I will warrant you, when he was tent-making, or picking up sticks on the island of Malta, as when he was talking heavenly wisdom to the worldly-wise, addressing the Athenians on Mar's Hill, or when he discoursed touching the resurrection of the dead to the Jews, or when he expounded the way of justification to the Gentiles. He was a man of one idea, and that one idea had entirely possessed him. In the old pictures they put a halo round the heads of the saints. But, in fact, that halo encircles their hearts and penetrates every member of their bodies. The halo of disinterested consecration to Christ should not be about their brows alone to adorn their portraits, for it encompassed their entire being, their spirit, soul and body. It environed them and encircled their whole being. "This one thing I do," was the motto of early saints. Let it be your motto. Beloved, I address you as the saints of this generation. My earnest desire is that you should not come behind in grace or in gifts. When the believers of all ages muster, and are marshalled, may you be found among the faithful and true. If not among the first or second-class of worthies in the army of the Son of David, yet good soldiers of Jesus Christ. Our God is a loving Father. He likes to praise his people. To this end do be clear about the one thing you need, the one thing you know, and the one thing you do; so will you stand well in that day. "For what is our hope, or joy, or crown of rejoicing? Are not even ye in the presence of our Lord Jesus Christ at his coming?" Amen.

A Distinct Message.

I have a message from God unto thee.—JUDGES iii. 20.

CAN there be a person here present to whom God has never sent a message? Possibly the question may startle you. The very thought of the great invisible God sending such a message seems to you strange and unlikely. To me it is far more surprising that any one should imagine he has never done so. Is he your Creator? And has he who made you launched you forth on the tempestuous sea of life to drift in solitude without compass or guide? We know that he has made you immortal, and is it possible that during that short life which is a preface to eternity, upon which that never-ending period depends—is it possible that he has left you without any sort of communication? Does it seem likely? You call him "Father," because he is the author of your being; can he be your Father and yet have no concern for your well-being; never have spoken to you; never have sent a message from his great throne to your hearts? How improbable this sounds. Is not the question open to another solution? The truth of the matter,

(26)

methinks, is that you have been deaf to God's messages; he has often desired to correspond with you, nay, he has sent some communications to you, but you have resented and rejected them? Is it not likely that he has often spoken when you have not heard, and that he has drawn near to you, and called to you when you would not listen to him? I think, from the analogy of nature, this looks like a correct statement of the case. It cannot be that God has left the world; it must be that the world has left God. It is not possible that God has ceased to speak to the soul. Surely the soul has ceased to hearken to God; to acknowledge his messages; or to reply to them. I believe, my dear hearers, and I especially address my remarks to those of you who have not yet received Christ by faith and love into your hearts—I believe that the most of you, although still without God and without Christ, have had many messages from him. Let me remind you of some of them. Then, let me admonish you that the gospel itself is a distinct and direct message to you. And, finally, let us occupy a few minutes in endeavoring to consider how we ought to treat that message.

1. That you have not been without MESSAGES FROM GOD I am quite sure.

This Bible is in the house of every Englishman. You can scarcely find a cot so poor that it does not now contain a copy of the Word of God. If your Bible could speak to you—or rather, if you would listen to what it does say to you—you would hear

in the chamber where that Bible lies the words, "I
have a message from God unto thee."   Do but open
it; look down its pages; let your eye glance along
its sacred verses, and I think it would not be long
before it would have communion with your spirit,
and this would be its voice, "I have a message
from God unto thee."   Sure I am that each one of
you would read some verse that is personally applicable to yourself, perhaps more applicable to you
than to any other man.   There is some one special
nook in Scripture which was prepared specially
for you; there is an arrow there that was intended
for your heart; some oil and wine fitted to assuage
your pain and heal your wounds.   Whether your
case be that of carelessness or of despondency that
Book says, "I have a message from God unto thee."
Shall I chide the indifference which neglects the
Book?   Shall I rebuke the levity which had rather
turn to any novel, or to any frivolous magazine,
than to this momentous volume, which appeals to
you as with the voice of God?   Scarcely need I do
so.   Each man must be conscious that it is the
height of guilt to slight the King's proclamation,
and pursue the common and ordinary things of
everyday life as if no Royal mandate had been issued.
How much more when it is the voice of him that
speaketh from heaven!   Your unread Bible shall
rise up in judgment to condemn you.   Attempt to
alight from the railway car while the train is in
motion you are liable to a penalty of forty shillings.
Do not say you are ignorant of the law.   It was

posted in the carriage that conveyed you. The Angel of Time might surely write with his finger upon the dust of your Bibles the sentence of your condemnation. Beware, ye who refuse to listen to Moses and the Prophets. If ye will not hear them, ye would not be converted though one should rise from the dead and admonish you of your peril.

Other messengers you have had. Some of them have come to you in golden type; their words have been sweet as honey. I should call them a bountiful Providence. I know not what you would call them. Perhaps a vein of luck. Have you been favored with success in business? A prosperous wind has filled your sails. In your families you have had welcome mercies. Children have been given you. Those children have been restored from beds of sickness when your heart has been sore with anxiety. In your own health of body you have not been strangers to God's choice favors. Moreover, you have had times of gladness and of merry-making. Your hearts have held their festivals; the streets of Mansoul were illuminated, the houses decked with fair colors, and the streets of your mind strewn with flowers. On those days did not these mercies seem to say, as they came trooping along down the streets of your soul, " We have a message from God unto thee?" Oh, if you would but listen, each one of these parental gifts would have said, " My son, give me thy heart." Surely such mercies should have been like the bonds of love and the cords of a man to have drawn you.

Ought not the kindness and compassion extended to you in Providence to have led you to say, "How can I grieve such a God? How can I provoke him to anger? Does he not deal with me generously, and lavish His treasures at my feet? How shall I forget him? I will celebrate His favor with sacrifices of thanksgiving; I will bind my offerings to the horns of the altar."

Other messengers have come to you draped in black; their garments have been rent, sackcloth has been about their loins, and ashes on their heads. They have spoken in hoarse notes, but solemn were their tones, and though they have not led you to repentance, their admonitions have stilled your pulse, chilled your blood, and constrained you to pause and think. That sickness—fever or ague, cholera or diphtheria—which prostrated your strength, disqualified you for your daily labor or your ordinary business, and summoned you in the quiet of your chamber to look back upon the past and look forward to the future. Can you forget the season when life trembled in the scale, and the physician knew not which way it would turn; that hour, that silent hour, when they trod the room with gentle footsteps, and the nurse closed not her eyes through all the still hours of the night; then the noisy watch uttered the only sound that broke the silence of that room. Do you not remember it? Those diseases that laid hold of your vitals said, "We have a message from God unto thee." And some of you have escaped from manifold perils by sea and by land, from shipwreck and from fire; you have been preserved in accidents and catastrophes by which others have died. All these strange, these terrible things were spoken to you in righteousness when you were careless and unconcerned; they had a message from God for you. Oh, deaf ears that will not listen when God speaks to you in such solemn tones, and strikes you while he speaks that he may compel you to listen!

Another dark messenger has come to you. Death has bereaved you of friends and comrades. Those with whom you were most familiar have been suddenly carried away. Have you not been startled by the news that a neighbor or acquaintance, with whom you chatted a day or two ago, is dead? "Dead!" you said. "Why, he was in my shop only a few days ago! Dead! Why, he seemed to be in good health, strong in body, vigorous in mind, full of plans and projects; I should have thought of any man being dead sooner than he!" Do not you recollect the time when you heard the bell toll for a near relative, and when you stood over the open grave? Ah, then, when the dust fell upon the coffin-lid, and the words were uttered, "Dust to dust, ashes to ashes," each of those thundering morsels said, "I have a message from God unto thee." Walk the cemetery, and, while every grave tells of our common mortality, how some graves speak to us of the precarious tenure by which our frail life is held. In all, what a warning-message we may hear. Turn over the list of the friends of your youth, the companions of your hale manhood, and you who have grown gray, call to remembrance the names of those old acquaintances of yours who have passed from this land of shadows to the bar of God; let the ghosts of the departed start up before you and pass in solemn procession before your eyes; then, let each one say, with all the pathos of their final exit, "I have a message from God unto thee." Among them all is there one who learned aught of vice or scoffing from you, young man? Is there a soul among the lost that you first led astray? Man, you who have blasphemed, are there some now ruing their bitter doom whose ruin you helped to precipitate? Oh, thou base deceiver, are there those whom thou didst delude? Are there those whom thou didst ensnare who have gone their way before thee to feel the terrible remorse, and are waiting for the grim time when they shall look on thee with eyes of fire, and curse thee because thou didst lure them on to their eternal destruction? Those ghosts, of all others, must be the most startling, and their fingers of fire must point the most fearfully, and make one feel that they have indeed a message from God to us from the place of torment. Let the remembrance of them make you pause and think and turn from your sins to the living and true God.

But though these messages have too often been unheard, the Lord, who desireth not the death of a sinner, hath sent to us by other and equally useful messengers. Oh! in what kind ways has he been pleased to select the persons who should bring the tidings to us. The first messenger that some of us had was that fond woman, upon whose breast in infancy we hung. We should never breathe the word "mother" without grateful emotions. How can we forget that tearful eye when she warned us to escape from the wrath to come? We thought her lips right eloquent; others might not think so, but they certainly were eloquent to us. How can we ever forget when she bowed her knee, and with her arms about our neck, prayed for us: "Oh! that my son might live before Thee." Nor can her frown be effaced from our memory, that solemn, loving frown when she rebuked our budding iniquities; and her smiles have never faded from our recollection, the beaming of her countenance when she rejoiced to see some good thing in us toward the Lord God of Israel. Mothers often become potent messengers from God, and I think each Christian mother should ask herself in secret whether the Lord hath not a message to give through her to her sons and to her daughters. And did you despise that messenger? Had you the hardihood to reject God when he spoke in this way, when he selected one so near and so dear, who could speak so well, and could talk to that tender instinct, which respects and hallows a mother's love? Could it be? Ah! thus it has been up till now with some of you. God has spoken with other messengers to you. Was it your sister? Did she not write a note to you, because her timidity would scarcely let her speak? Or perhaps it was a friend. It may have been that young man you ridiculed and called fanatical; but you know how soon you shook off the impressions which those pointed remarks of his seemed to make upon you at the time. Or possibly it was a tract that met your eyes; or a book like Doddridge's *Rise and Progress*, or Baxter's *Call to the Unconverted*, or Alleine's *Alarm*. Through these printed appeals God spoke to you.

Yet, again, it might have been through some preacher of the gospel. God's minister's have been God's messengers to many thousands of immortal souls. Within this house of prayer, sometimes, there are many who hardly know how to keep their seats when we try to ply the conscience with all the arguments of the truth, and seek to move torpid souls by some of the thunderbolts of the Almighty. Oh, how many men here have been rebuked and rebuked, times without number, but still they go on in their old sins. Take heed, take heed, men, for if ye refuse God when he speaketh by his servants, and by his providence, and by your friends, he will one day speak to you by a bony preacher, who will deliver his message so that you must hear him. You know where my text comes. "Ehud said, I have a message from God unto thee." It was a dagger which found its way to Eglon's heart, and he fell dead. So shall death deliver his message to you.

"I have a message from God unto thee," he will say, and ere you shall have time to answer you shall find that this was the message: "Because I the Lord will do this, prepare to meet thy God, O Israel—Thus saith the Lord, cut it down; why cumbereth it the ground?—Set thy house in order, for thou shalt die, and not live." Oh! may you hear the other messengers of God before he sends this last most urgent one, from whom ye cannot turn away.

II. I have thus sought to refresh your memory, by reminding you of the many warnings you have received. The intent of them all has been to arouse your conscience. But now, in the second place, we admonish you that the gospel of the grace of God is in itself a message from God to you.

Oh, how passing strange are the reasons, the extraordinary reasons, why many people attend our churches and chapels! Some people go merely because everybody else goes. Others go because—well, perhaps it helps their business a bit! Some go when they happen to have fashionable clothes, in which they like to make an appearance. Ask the large majority of men and women what they go for. Even among the best of people, were they to be candid, how many would tell you that they suppose it is the right thing to do; it is their duty. But how few go with the idea that God will speak to them there, and that the gospel preached there will be a message from God to their souls! And,

I am afraid, there are some ministers who hardly think that the gospel is intended to come personally home to the people. They talk, as I read of one the other day, who said, that when he preached to sinners he did not like to look the congregation in the face, for fear they should think he meant to be personal, so he looked up at the ventilator, because there was no fear then of any individual catching his eye. Oh! that fear of man has been the ruin of many ministers. They never dared to preach right at the people. We have heard of sermons being preached before this and that honorable company; but preaching sermons before people is not God's way; we must preach sermons at the people, directly to them, to show that it is not the waving of a sword in the air like a juggler's sport, but it is the getting the sword right into the conscience and the heart. This, I take it, is the true mission of every minister of Christ. It is said of Whitefield, that if you were the farthest away from him in a throng, where you could but hear the sound of his voice, you felt persuaded that he meant to speak to you; and of Rowland Hill it is said, that if you got into Surrey Chapel you could not hide in a corner there; though you should manage to get into a back seat, or were squeezed tight into the windows, you would still feel persuaded that Mr. Hill was addressing you, and that he had singled you out for his expostulations. Surely this is the perfection of preaching. Ought it not to be our aim to find men out, and make them feel that at the present moment they are themselves addressed; that there is a message from God to the soul.

Now, my friend, the gospel is a distinct message directed to you. I know it speaks to your neighbor and tells him that he is fallen. That is for him, not for you, to think of. Your portion is that which singles you out and tells you that you were in Adam when he sinned; that you fell in him, and that as the result your nature is corrupt, you are born in sin and prone to commit sin; there is no good thing in your natural disposition; whatever seems good in your own eyes or in the eyes of others is so tainted by the inherent vice of your own depravity that it cannot be acceptable in the sight of God. When we preach to sinners, never think that we mean the riff-raff in the streets. The gospel, which saves a sinner, is a message from God to you. Think of your own sins and the naughtiness of your own heart.

I have heard of a woman who affected to believe that she was a sinner, and her minister, convinced that she did not know what she meant, thus exposed her folly. He said to her, " Well, if you are a sinner, of course you have broken God's laws; let us read the ten commandments, and see which you have broken." So turning to the decalogue he began to read: "Thou shalt have none other God before me;" "Did you ever break that?" " Oh, no; not that she knew of." He proceeded, " Thou shalt not make to thyself any graven image," and so on;

"Did you ever break that?"   "Never, sir," said she.
Then "Thou shalt not take the name of the Lord
thy God in vain."   "Oh, dear no; she had been
very particular on that point; she did not know
that she had ever offended in that respect in her
life."   "Remember the seventh day to keep it holy."
"Oh," said she, "I never do any work on a Sunday; everybody knows how particular I am about
that."   "Honor thy father and thy mother."   "Yes,"
she replied, "she had been quite perfect in this
matter; you might ask her friends if she had not
been."   "Thou shalt not kill."   "Kill anybody!
She wondered how the minister could ask her that."
Of course, "Thou shalt not commit adultery," must
be passed without a question.   "Thou shalt not bear
false witness."   Much of a gossip though she was,
she protested she never did backbite anybody in all
her life.   And as to the idea of coveting, well,
she might sometimes have wished that she was
a little better off, but she never wanted any of any
body else's goods, she only wanted a little more of
her own.   So it turned out as the minister suspected,
that she really was not a sinner at all in her own
estimation.   It is marvellous how people who indulge in general confessions of sin attempt to exculpate themselves of each and every particular
offence.   Whatever the indictment is, they plead
"Not Guilty."   But the condemnation which the
gospel pronounces upon all who have transgressed
the law is a message from God to you.   Oh! I would
have those of you that have not fled to Christ feel

and realize the terrors of the law. How stern its precepts! How dreadful its penalties! How divine its sanctity!

And remember it is a message from God to you. Where is the possibility of escape from the justice it metes out, the judgment it pronounces? Methinks I see the fire; the pile of Tophet; the burning wood and the much smoke; the breath of the Lord doth kindle it. Methinks I hear the cry of spirits lost without hope; mark the worm that never dies, and witness the agonies of conscience never appeased, while the remembrance of opportunities haunts them, and the wrath of God stirs the fire that never shall be quenched. Of that appalling spectacle I might speak at length to you, but I will not. Oh, my dear hearers, I would have you remember that this is a message from God to you. As sure as you live, except you repent, the everlasting burning must be your portion. You must make your bed in hell, if you continue in unbelief. Do, I pray you, forget your neighbor for awhile. Think not of anything that is applicable to the person sitting next to you. To you, to your own self, is the thunder of God's threatening sent. "If ye repent not, ye shall all likewise perish." If ye turn not from the error of your ways, God will not turn from his righteous indignation. Your destruction slumbereth not, though ye be never so drowsy. His wrath will burn like coals of juniper, forever and forever it will abide on you.

But the gospel tells of a Substitute. It informs

you that Jesus came and suffered in the place of the sinner. It says he died for those who trust him. It assures you that whosoever believes on him shall not perish but have everlasting life. Have you no anxiety that the Gospel should be a message from God to you? It will be of no use to you that Jesus died unless he died for you. If he took your sin and carried your sorrows it is all well, but though he should have died for all mankind except you, by that omission you would perish. We know that he died for believers. " Whosoever believeth on him shall not perish, but have everlasting life." The vital question is, " Do I believe in Jesus? Have I unfeignedly trusted in him? Do I depend now upon his finished work? Having no other refuge, do I trust in Jesus, sink or swim? Do I commit myself to the tide, relying on his merits, expecting thereby to be borne on safe to the haven of his glory?" If so, then there is evidence that he died for me. I am free from condemnation, he paid my debts; I am clear from the charges of the law, for he bore my punishment; I am acquitted by his mediation, therefore being justified freely I may go on my way rejoicing. But of what use is the gospel unless it thus becomes a message from God for me? Oh, the delight, dear friends, of those who recognize the promise of God as a message of love to them! Hundreds of times did I hear the gospel preached; I heard of pardon: full and free; I heard of a righteousness complete,

that wrapped the sinner from head to foot; I
heard of full deliverance from the penal sentence
of the law; I heard of adoption, of communion
with Christ, of the sanctification which the Spirit
gives, but what were all these privileges to me
when I had no interest in them. It was as
though one should take up the title-deed of an
estate and begin reading it in a social party by
way of interesting them. What more dull—what
more heavy reading? How the words are multi-
plied! How these lawyers do seek to say the
same thing over twenty times, till no flesh living
can endure them. Ah! but, my friend, if that
title-deed refers to an estate which has been bequeathed to you, all those words delight you; their
repetition seems to clench your title. You like to
have the thing made out in proper legal form.
Your eyes sparkle over that little sketch in the
corner. You take notice of the stamps, and you
are specially taken up with the signatures. Matters that would be of no interest at all under other
circumstances seem to be exceedingly precious to
you viewed in the light of your heirship. It is
just so with regard to the word of God. When
we come to read the Book, and know that it
confers blessings on us, our joy is full to overflowing. To us the message is sent. By us the
message is received. The complete salvation it
announces is ours. We are wholly saved from
every peril, through Jesus' blood. We are delivered from sin. We are endowed with a right-

cousness, not of our own performing, but of his imputing. Thereby we are adorned—

> " With the Saviour's garments on,
>   Holy as the Holy One."

With what ineffable joy does this message from God make glad our spirit!

Be sure of this, my friends, let our case be what it may, the gospel preached is a message from God to our souls. The hypocrite cannot long attend upon the means of grace without finding that its doctrines are very heart-searching. They pierce his thoughts: they hold a candle up to him, and if he would but look they would expose his desperate condition. The formalists, the men who delight in ceremonies, cannot long frequent God's hallowed courts, where his true ministers proclaim his name, without perceiving that there is a message from God to them. The most careless spirit will find in the word a looking-glass held up to his face in which he can see a reflection of himself. There have been divers messages like circulars from God to us, but the gospel, faithfully preached, is a private and personal communication.

A minister once sent his deacon to attend a certain anniversary service. The discourse turned upon Diotrephes, who loved the pre-eminence. The deacon's character was aptly described. He did not, however, agree with the preacher. He was himself a Diotrephes, though he failed to detect his own portrait; or at least, with apparent indifference, he asked a friend of his if he supposed there were such persons existing as those who had been described in the discourse? "I cannot think," said he, " who the preacher could have been aiming at?" So his friend said, "Well, I think he must have been intending you and me." No better answer could have been given. I like each hearer to make the application to himself.

But Mrs. Jones thinks sometimes that Mrs. Brown must have felt very queer in one part of the sermon; and Mrs. Brown thinks that if Mrs. Smith had looked at home she must have known that what was said was meant for her, whereas the real truth was that it suited all three of them, and there was something meant for each as well as for all. Take heed to yourselves, my beloved. Be like the young lad, who when he was asked why he attended so earnestly, said, " Because I am in hopes that one of these days the truth I hear will be blessed to my own salvation."

Brethren, if you were thirsty, you would not stand by the rippling brook and think how it flowed on to the river, and the river onward to the sea. You would not let your meditations be wandering to the meadows which it made verdant, or the mills which it turned, or the cities which employed it in mercantile industry. No, you would just stoop down and drink, and then meditate on those grand uses it served afterwards. When there is a cry for bread in the streets it is of no use telling the people that there is a large stock of corn in the Baltic, and that there has been a fine crop of wheat in the United States. Each man wants bread in his own hands, and bread in his own mouth. It is amazing how personal people become when the thing has anything to do with money. I never knew a man short of cash who was relieved by the intelligence that there were millions of bullion in the Bank. A little in his pocket cheered him more than the much that had accumulated at the fountain head. How is it that people are not personal with religion? Why are they not looking to get every man a full share in the capital it represents? How is it they do not turn everything that comes in their way to good account when the gospel is preached? Why, when good tidings are published, do they not say, " Lord, is this a message from God unto me?"

III. My last point is this—If there be such a message as this from God to us, HOW SHOULD WE TREAT IT?

Let the minister entertain this question. He ought to deliver it very earnestly. God's message is not to be delivered with marble lips; it must not drop from an icy tongue. It ought to be spoken very affectionately. God's message is not to be announced unkindly. The kindling of human passion is nothing to the purpose. Rather let the Divine flame of God-like affection burn within our souls. It should be proclaimed very boldly. It is not for the minister of God to smooth the stones, or pare down any of the angles of the gospel. He should be tender as a lamb, but yet bold as a lion. It is as much as his soul is worth to keep back a single word. He may have to answer for the blood of souls if he trims in the slightest particular. The withholding of any part of a message committed to him in trust, should he refrain himself lest he offend any one, may bring down upon him a condemnation that he knows not how to escape, and he may have throughout eternity to bewail that he had been entrusted with God's message and did not deliver it. I always feel quite easy in my own conscience if I have preached what I believe to be the truth. Do you send a servant to the door of a neighbor with a message? If the person at the door should be angry, the servant would say, " It is of no use being angry with me; you must be angry with my master, for I have given you the message just as he gave it to me." And if they should be angry with him, he would say, " I would much rather that the stranger at the door should be angry with me for telling the message than that my master should be angry with me for keeping it back, for to my master I stand or fall." I think the minister of God, if he has preached faithfully, may say, " Well, I have delivered only what my Master told me; if you are angry with me you must remember that you ought to be angry with my Master, for it was my Master's message, and it is better for *you* to be angry with me than for *my Master* to be angry with me." Baxter said, " I never rebuke myself for not having used fine flowery language when I am preaching, but I have rebuked myself full often for want of earnestness in what I have delivered." So we each of us must humble ourselves before the Lord on account of our coldness in this matter. Yet we must not handle the Lord's message deceitfully, but go on boldly to deliver the message which God has given us, remembering that we only have to give an account to him. There lives not a man under the cope of heaven that should be so free from the fear of his fellow-creatures as God's minister. To him, prince or peasant, peer or beggar must be alike. To him kings have no crowns, and queens no thrones. He speaks to men as men, going into all the world and preaching the Gospel to every creature, and being God's ambassador to men, he must go right on and speak as he gets utterances from his Lord.

Yes, but if this be God's message the minister has not only to think how he should treat it, but you have to think how you should treat it, and I have to ask those who are unconverted what they mean to do with it. What do you mean to do with God's message? Of all the bad things to do, do not do this one—do not say, " Go thy way for this time, when I have a more convenient season I will send for thee." Do not say that. Better to say—" I despise the message, and I will not obey it." Talk not like the procrastinators, for procrastinators are the most hardened of men. To promise they will do it quiets men's consciences, whereas, if they deliberately said, " I will not," perhaps conscience would be aroused, and they might be led to do it. No, say either the one thing or the other. If it were possible for you to meet an angel on your way home—the thing will not occur—but if you could meet an angel, and he should stop you, and should say, " Now, man, not a step further until you have given me an answer; God commands you to believe in Jesus Christ; he tells you to trust him with your soul; will you or will you not?" Suppose yourself placed in the same position as King Antiochus. When the Roman ambassador met him and asked him whether it was to be peace or war, he said he must have time to consider. The ambassador with his sword drew a circle in the sand. "Give an answer," he said, " before you move out of that circle, or if you step out of it your answer is war." I think there is such a phase in a man's life, when he must give a prompt reply. I know what that answer will be unless God the Holy Ghost makes you give the right one, but you must give it one way or the other, and if the man saith, " No, I will give no answer," yet if he stop beyond that appointed hour, it is war between him and God forever, and the sword shall never be sheathed, nor go back into its scabbard. He hath thrown down the gauntlet, by refusing to give a decisive pledge of obedience. The Lord hath declared eternal war against him; peace shall not be made forever. Before you go farther, which shall it be? Do you say, " I love my sins; I love the world; I love its pleasures; I love my own righteousness; I will not trust Christ?" That shows your depravity; think of the consequences and tremble! But if from the depths of your soul you say, "God be merciful to me a sinner; I would be saved!" then trust Christ and you are saved now. Believe on him; believe on him now, and you are now forgiven. Oh, may the Saviour of his own grace give us your salvation as a seal to our ministry, and to him shall be glory for ever and ever.

A Divine Mission.

Even as the Son of man came not to be ministered unto, but to minister, and to give his life a ransom for many.—MATT. xx. 28.

THE mission of Christ to our world was distinct and definite. The ministry of the gospel should be alike trustworthy and transparent. It was but the other day I read a letter from the deacon of a church in which, speaking of his minister, he said,—" We ought to understand geology thoroughly, for we usually hear something of it, at least, once every Sunday; there is one thing, however, we shall never be likely to understand under our present friend's ministry; the doctrine of the atonement he seems utterly to ignore; I have not heard him allude to it for the past three months; nor do I know, for certain, whether he believes it or not. Though he sometimes alludes to Jesus Christ as an example, I have neither heard of Christ dying, nor Christ buried, of Christ risen, or Christ pleading in heaven at all. In fact, it seems to me I might as well attend a Socinian chapel." Well, God forbid that such a reflection should ever be cast on me. Is it not my constant endeavor to bring you back, Sabbath after Sabbath, to the same old, old story of the Cross, and of the redemption by blood which was there and then wrought? This bell has but one note. It may be repeated, I sometimes fear, with too much monotony. Still the tone is clear. I know that Jesus Christ came into the world to save sinners. There is salvation in none other name under heaven. The propitiation which God has set forth for human sin is alone efficacious. There is no remission without blood. Full salvation is to be procured only through the wounds of Jesus slain. There is no salvation in heaven or earth beside. We are coming to that selfsame story again. It never wearies the believer's ear; nor does it ever fail to be the power of God unto salvation to every one that believeth. I want my text to speak. Let me, then, begin by expounding it word by word; and after that let me explain the doctrine to which it gives most distinct prominence.

"The Son of man!" So doth our Lord Jesus Christ speak of himself. In relation to our fallen humanity it sounds humble; but in the light of prophecy it is full of dignity. "The Son of man." This is none other than the true Messiah—the Son of God, infinite, eternal, co-equal with the Father, and yet he chooses to call himself full often "the Son of man," perhaps because as it was man that committed sin, it is man who must make an atonement for sin to the injured law of God. Man was the offender, man must suffer the penalty. As in one man the whole family died, in another man they must be made alive, if made alive at all. Jesus tells us that he is a man; thoroughly a man; one like to ourselves. The *Son* of man, a man among men, bone of our bone and flesh of our flesh; not wearing a fictitious manhood, but a real humanity like our own. This we must always bear in mind; for without it there could be no atonement at all. Jesus is not merely *a* Son of man, but he is pre-eminently *the* Son of man foretold in the prophecy of Daniel, and predicted on the threshold of Paradise in the language of the first promise—"The seed of the woman shall bruise the serpent's head." He is the Man, the second Adam in whom men are made alive. Being thus found in fashion as a man, and having taken upon himself the federal headship of man, he was qualified to become man's substitute and to make an atonement for human guilt. Dwell on this blessed truth, my dear hearers; dwell upon it, those of you who are not saved; look wistfully at it for the encouragement it offers you. The Person in whom you are admonished to trust is not only God—or his unclouded glory might strike you with awe, and his terrors might justly make you afraid—but he is also man, and this ought to attract you to him, for he is akin to yourselves in nature and sympathy. Sin excepted, he is in no wise different from you. Oh! may you not well draw near to him without appalling dread, and with inspiring confidence, since he calls himself the Son of man, and bids the sons of men come and put their trust under the shadow of his wings?

He "*came*"; that is the next word in our text. "The Son of man came." Strange the errand, and unique as the blessed Person who undertook it. Thus to come he stooped from the highest throne in glory down to the manger of Bethlehem; and on his part it was voluntary. We are, as it were, thrust upon the stage of action; it is not of our will that we have come to live on this earth. But Jesus had no need to have been born of the virgin. It was his own consent, his choice, his strong desire, that made him take upon himself our nature, of the seed of Abraham. He came voluntarily on an errand of mercy to the sons of men. Dwell upon this thought for a moment; let it sink into your mind; he who was King of kings and Lord of lords, the Mighty God, the Everlasting Father, the Prince of Peace, voluntarily, cheerfully descended that he might dwell among the sons of men, share their sorrows, and bear their sins, and yield himself up a sacrifice on their behalf, the innocent victim of their intolerable guilt. If the angels burst out in song on that first Christmas night, if they made heaven and earth ring with their sweet harmonies, much more may we who have a share in the redemptive work of the incarnate God burst out into song as the news greets us that heaven descends to earth, that God comes down to man, that the Infinite becomes an infant, that the

Eternal, who hath life in himself, deigns to dwell amongst the dying sons of men. Surely a way from earth to heaven will now be opened up since there is a way from heaven to earth, so sacred yet so simple. The same golden ladder that brings the blessed Visitant down to our humanity will take us up also to the divinity of God, to see him as our reconciled Father. "The Son of man came."

The next words are startling; for they reveal a singular intention, far different from the usual aim and end of messages and errands. " The Son of man came *not to be ministered unto, but to minister*." Let me give you the exact translation—"Not to be served, but to serve." That is the nearest approach to a literal rendering I can supply. He came not to be served, but to serve. He had not a selfish thought in his soul. Though he had set his heart upon being the incarnate God, he had nothing whatever to gain by it. Gain! What could the Infinite God gain? Splendor? Behold the stars; far away they glitter beyond all mortal count. Servants! Does hê want servants? Behold angels in their squadrons; twenty thousand, even thousands of angels are the chariots of the Almighty. Honor! Nay; the trump of fame forever proclaims him King of kings and Lord of lords. Who can add to the lustre of that diadem that makes sun and moon grow pale by comparison? Who can add to the riches or the wealth of him who hath all things at his disposal?

He comes, then, not to be ministered unto, but

to minister. And you see him in the workshop serving his reputed parent. You see him in his home honoring his blessed mother with all filial obedience. You see him at the noontide of his wonderful career in the midst of his disciples, much more their servant than their master; though he always maintained precedence by his own sovereign counsel, and by their weak apprehensions. As he takes the basin, and the ewer, and the towel, and washes his disciples' feet, you can see the meekness of his disposition. And soon after this you see him giving up himself, his body, his soul, and his spirit, in order that he might serve us. And what if I say that, even at this very moment, as the Son of man in heaven, he continues a kind of service of his people! For Zion's sake he doth not hold his peace, and for Jerusalem's sake he doth not rest, but continues still to intercede for those whose names he bears upon his heart. Hear it, then, all ye people, and let every one that heareth hail the gracious fact. Be ye saints or sinners, be ye saved already, or athirst for the knowledge of salvation, the thought that Christ's errand was not to aggrandize himself, but to benefit us, must be welcome. He does not come to be served, but to serve. Does not this suit you, poor sinner—you who never did serve him, you who could not, as you are, minister to him? Well, he did not come to get your service; he came to give you his services; not that you might first do him honor, but that he might show you mercy. Oh! you need him so very much.

And since he has come, not to look for treasures, but to bestow unsearchable riches, not to find specimens of health, but instances of sickness upon which the healing art of his grace may operate, surely there is hope for you. Methinks were I just now seeking Christ, and sorely cast down in spirit, it would make my heart beat for joy to think that Jesus came to serve, and not to be served. Peradventure I would say, he knows my case, and he has come to serve me, poor me. Do I not want washing? Why should he not wash me? The dying thief rejoiced to see in his day the fountain which Jesus had opened; why should not I see it too, and have a washing from that precious One who comes to serve the vilest and the meanest of the sons of men? Behold! Behold and wonder! Behold and love! Behold and trust! Jesus comes from the right hand of God to the manger, to the cross, to the sepulchre, not to be served, but that he might serve the sons of men.

Pass on to the next words—"*And to give his life,*" or, more correctly,—"and to give his soul." We have no lives to give. Our lives are forfeited; they are due to Divine justice. Christ had a life of his own which was by no means due to God on account of any obligations. He had not sinned, but he gave his life. The death of Christ was perfectly voluntary. As he was free to come or not, so he was not under any constraint to give his life, but he did so, and that of his own accord. The grand object of his coming to this earth was to give his life. Read the text again. "The Son of man came not to be ministered unto, but to minister, and to give his life." Our Lord Jesus Christ did not come into this world merely to be an example, or merely to reveal the Godhead to the sons of men. He came to make a substitutionary sacrifice. He came to give his soul as a ransom. If you do not believe this doctrine, you do not believe Christianity. The very pith and marrow, the very sum and substance of the mission of Jesus Christ is his coming to give his life that he might stand in the place of those for whom he died. He came on purpose to give his life. Now, to give the soul is something more than to give the life. He died, 'tis true; yet he did more than die; he died by an outpouring of all his life floods, by the endurance of an anguish such as no ordinary mortal could ever have borne. Of old 'twas the blood that made atonement. The animal was presented in sacrifice, but the animal was no sacrifice till it was slain, and then when the purple stream smoked down the altar's side, and the bowels of it were cast upon the altar, then it was that the sacrifice was truly presented. Jesus Christ gave up the very essence of his humanity to be a substitutionary sacrifice for us. His spirit was tortured with pangs that are past conception, much more past description. He said—"My soul is exceeding sorrowful, even unto death." He was like a splendid cluster put into the winepress, and the feet of eternal vengeance trod upon him till the sacred wine of his atoning blood streamed forth to save the sons of men. He gave his very self, his entire self, his soul, his life, his essential being, to be a ransom for the sons of Adam. Oh that I could turn your eyes to that great sight! Behold how he gave his life! Would to God that for a moment your thoughts were fixed on those five streaming wounds, those sacred founts of life, and health, of pardon and peace, to dying souls! Oh! that your eyes could but gaze within the wounds, into that heart boiling like a cauldron with the wrath of God, tossed to and fro, heaving within itself, oppressed, burdened, tormented, and filled with very anguish. Oh that you could see it! oh that you could understand that he came from heaven to suffer all this, to give himself up thus, that he might be instead of us the victim of a vengeance we deserved; that his griefs might avert our ruin, that his pangs might rescue us from destruction! He drank the cup of condemnation dry; not a dreg was left; and, in so doing, he poured out his soul unto death.

Moreover, his death is our ransom. So it is written, he came to give his life "*a ransom.*" No one here, I suppose, needs to have explained to him what a ransom means. It may be fairly illustrated by the old Jewish ceremony of the redemption-money. Every male person among the Jews belonged to God, and he must be redeemed. There was a settled price. The rich were not to give more; the poor should not give less. The same amount was fixed for all. The tithe drachma was paid by every Jew. Then he was enrolled as one of the Lord's redeemed, of whom you so often read. Failing that, he would have been cut off from the congregation of Israel. That piece of money stood instead of the man—it was his ransom. He was not to die—he was to live as a redeemed person. That is just what Jesus has done for his people. He has put himself, his soul, his life devoted, his death accomplished, before God in the stead of our soul, of our death, of us; and every man who has Christ to be his substitute is a redeemed man; he is one of the Lord's ransomed people, and shall go to Zion with songs of everlasting joy upon his head. But every man who has not accepted Christ remains an unredeemed man, under the curse, and subject to the divine wrath, under the slavery of Satan, and awaiting the sentence of an utter destruction. Jesus Christ came to give his life a ransom. As a slave is redeemed by the payment of a price, so Jesus redeems us from the curse of the law under which we were by nature, having himself come under the law. He redeems us from the death which we deserved by himself enduring a death which was a full equivalent in the estimation of God. He gave his life a ransom.

Our text says, "*for many.*" We might with greater force and stricter accuracy translate it— "He gave his life a ransom in the room of many." The word "for" there has a vicarious meaning, "He gave his life instead of many." Indeed, this is the point of the sentence—One stood for many. Jesus suffered for many; he put himself into the place of many. Mark the word "many." With this we finish the exposition. It does not say "all." There are passages which speak of all. They have their special significance. None of them, however, refer to the substitutionary work of Christ. Jesus Christ did not give his life a ransom in the stead of all mankind; but a ransom in the stead of many men. Who are those many men? Bless God, they are many; for they are not a few. But who they are God knows. "The Lord knoweth them that are his." You may ascertain as much as you need to know by answering a plain question. Dost thou trust Jesus Christ with thine eternal destinies? Dost thou come, all guilty as thou art, and rely upon his blood to take that guilt away? Dost thou confide in Jesus, and in him alone? If so, he died for thee, and in thy stead; and thou shalt never die. This is thy comfort, that thou canst not die. How canst thou perish if Jesus was put into thy place? If thy debt was paid of old by Christ, can it ever be demanded of thee again? Once paid, it is fully discharged; the receipt we have gladly accepted; and now we can cry with the Apostle, "Who shall lay anything to the charge of God's elect? It is God that justifieth. Who is he that condemneth? It is Christ that died; yea rather, hath risen again, who is even at the right hand of God, who also maketh intercession for us." See here the mainstay of every believer's confidence. He knows that

Christ died for him because he hath put his trust in his blessed mediation. If Jesus died for me, then I cannot be condemned for the sins which he expiated. God cannot punish twice for the one offence. He cannot demand two payments for one debt. The believer therefore finds sweet solace in the song which Toplady composed—

> "Turn, then, my soul, unto thy rest:
> The merits of thy great High Priest
> Speak peace and liberty:
> Trust in his efficacious blood,
> Nor fear thy banishment from God,
> Since Jesus died for thee."

Thus did the Son of man give his life a ransom in the stead of many. And such do I believe to be a fair and honest exposition of the words.

Now, as for the main drift of the text—the doctrine of a vicarious or substitutionary atonement whereby Christ's ransom sufficeth in the stead of many—let me give each thought but a sentence or two. It would *seem that man is not delivered from the bondage of his sins without a price.* No one goes free by the naked mercy of God. Every captive exposed to God's vengeance must be redeemed before he is delivered, otherwise he must continue a captive. Broad as the statement may appear, I venture to assert by divine warrant that there never was beneath the cope of heaven a sin forgiven without satisfaction being rendered. No sin against God is pardoned without a propitiation. It is only forgiven through the sufferings of the Lord

Jesus Christ. It never can be remitted without the penalty having been exacted. The divine law knows of no exception or exemption. The statute is absolute—"The soul that sinneth, it shall die." Every soul that ever sinned, or ever shall sin, must die, die eternally, too, either in itself or in its substitute. The justice of the law must be vindicated. God waives none of the right of justice in order to give liberty to mercy. Oh, my hearers, if you are trusting in the unconditional mercy of God, you are trusting in a myth. Has some one buoyed you up with the thought of the infinite goodness of God, I would remind you of his infinite holiness. Hath he not declared that he will by no means spare the guilty? No debt due to God is remitted unless it be paid. It must either be paid by the transgressor in the infinite miseries of hell, or else it must be paid for him by a substitute. There must be a price for the ransom, and evidently, according to the text, *that price* must be a soul, a life. Christ did not merely give his body, nor his stainless character, nor his labors and sufferings, but he gave his soul, his life as a ransom. Oh, sinner; Almighty God will never be satisfied with anything less than thy soul. Canst thou bear the piercing thought that thy soul shall be cast from his presence forever? Wouldst thou escape the dire penalty, thou must find another soul to stand in thy soul's stead. Thy life is forfeited. The sentence is passed. Thou shalt die. Death is thy doom. Die thou must, forever die, unless thou canst find another life for a sacrifice in lieu of thy life. But know that this is just what Christ has found. He has put a soul, a life into the place of our souls, our lives. How memorable that text— "Without shedding of blood there is no remission." Why? Because "the blood is the life thereof." Until the blood flows, the soul is not divided from the body. The shedding of the blood indicated that the soul—the essence of the being—had been offered. Oh, blessed, forever blessed be the crowned head of him who once did bear the cross. He hath offered for his people a soul, a life, a matchless soul, a life unparalleled. No more can justice require; vengeance is satisfied; the price is paid; the redeemed of the Lord are completely free!

The question has been asked, "If we be redeemed by the blood of Christ, who receives the ransom?" Some have talked as if Christ paid a price to the devil. A more absurd imagination could never have crossed human mind. We never belonged to the devil. Satan has no rights in us. Christ never acknowledged that he had any, and would never pay him anything. What then? Surely the ransom price was paid to the great Judge of all. This is of course but a mystical way of speaking. A metaphor is employed to bring out the meaning. The fact is that God had sworn, and would not repent, that sin must be punished. In the very essence of things it was right that transgression should meet with its just recompense. There could be no moral government kept up, there could be no unimpeachable governor, unless conviction followed crime and retribution was exacted of the guilty. It was not right, nor could it have been righteous, on any ground, for sin to have been passed over without its having been punished, or for iniquity to have escaped without any infliction. But when Jesus Christ comes and puts his own sufferings into the place of our sufferings, the law is fully vindicated, while mercy is fitly displayed. A man dies; a soul is given; a life is offered—the just for the unjust. What if I say that instead of justice being less satisfied with the death of Christ than with the deaths of the ten thousand thousands of sinners for whom he died, it is more satisfied and it is most highly honored! Had all the sinners that ever lived in the world been consigned to hell they could not have discharged the claims of justice. They must still continue to endure the scourge of crimes they could never expiate. But the Son of God blending the infinite majesty of his deity with the perfect capacity to suffer as a man, offered an atonement of such inestimable value that he has absolutely paid the entire debt for his people. Well may justice be content since it has received more from the Surety than it could have ever exacted from the assured. Thus the debt was paid to the Eternal Father.

Once more. *What is the result of this?* The result is that the man is redeemed. He is no longer a slave. Some preachers and professors affect to believe in a redemption which I must

candidly confess I do not understand; it is so indistinct and indefinite—a redemption which does
not redeem anybody in particular, though it is
alleged to redeem everybody in general; a redemption insufficient to exempt thousands of unhappy
souls from hell after they have been redeemed by
the blood of Jesus; a redemption, indeed, which
does not actually save anybody, because it is dependent for its efficacy upon the will of the creature; a redemption that lacks intrinsic virtue and
inherent power to redeem anybody, but is entirely
dependent upon an extraneous contingency to render it effectual. With such fickle theories I have
no fellowship. That every soul for whom Christ
shed his blood as a substitute he will claim as his
own and have as his right, I firmly hold. I love
to hold and I delight to proclaim this precious
truth. Not all the powers of earth or hell, not the
obstinacy of the human will, nor the deep depravity
of the human mind, can ever prevent Christ seeing
of the travail of his soul and being satisfied. To
the last jot and tittle of his reward shall he receive
it at the Father's hand. A redemption that *does*
redeem, a redemption that redeems many, seems to
me infinitely better than a redemption that does
not actually redeem anybody, but is supposed to
have some remote influence upon the entire human
race.

Our last question I must leave with yourselves
to answer. *Did Jesus Christ redeem you?* Ah,
dear hearer, this is a serious matter. Art thou a

redeemed soul or not? It is not possible for thee to turn over the books of destiny and read between the folded leaves. Neither needest thou wish to do so. This is the Gospel of Jesus Christ which is to be preached to every creature under heaven— "He that believeth and is baptized shall be saved;" therefore every one that believeth, and is baptized, being saved, must have been redeemed, for he could not have been saved otherwise. If thou believest and art baptized thou art redeemed, thou art saved. Now for thine answer to the question —Dost thou believe? "I believe," says one, and he begins to repeat what they call the "Apostle's Creed." Hold your tongue, sir! That matters not; the devil believes that perhaps more intelligently than you do; he believes and trembles. That kind of believing saves no man. You may believe the most orthodox creed in Christendom, and perish. Dost thou trust—for that is the cream of the word "*believe*"—dost thou trust in Jesus? Dost thou lean thy whole weight on him? Hast thou that faith which the Puritans used to call "recumbency" or "leaning"? That is the faith that saves—faith that falls back into the arms of Jesus, a faith that drops from its own hanging place into those mighty arms and rests upon the tender breast of the Lord Jesus the Crucified. Oh, my soul, make sure that thou dost trust him, for thou hast made sure of everything else when thou hast made sure of that. Has God the Holy Spirit taught you, my dear hearer, that you cannot safely rely on your own good works? Has he weaned you from resting upon ceremonies? Has he brought you to look to the cross—to the cross of our Lord Jesus Christ alone? If so, Christ redeemed you; you can never be a slave again. Has he redeemed you, the liberty of the believer is yours now, and after death the glory of Christ shall be your portion too. Remember the words of the dying monk when, putting aside the extreme unction and all the paraphernalia of his Church, he lifted up his eyes and said, "*Tua vulnera, Jesu! tua vulnera, Jesu!*" "Thy wounds, oh, Jesu! Thy wounds, oh, Jesu!" This must be your refuge, poor broken-winged dove. Fly thither into the clefts of the rock, into the spear-thrust in the Saviour's heart. Fly there. Rest on him; rest on him; rest with all your weight of sin, with all your blackness and your foulness, with all your doubts and your despairs, rest on him. Jesus wants to receive you; fly to him—fly away to him now:

> "Come, guilty souls, and flee away,
>   And look to Jesu's wounds;
>   This is the accepted Gospel day,
>   Wherein free grace abounds.

> "God loved his Church, and gave his Son
>   To drink the cup of wrath;
>   And Jesus says he'll cast out none
>   Who come to him in faith."

A Double Challenge.

I will say to the north, GIVE UP; *and to the south*, KEEP NOT
BACK.—ISAIAH xliii. 6.

THESE words, no doubt, primarily refer to the
gathering together of the Jews in the latter
days. Whether they have wandered to the north,
or whether they have pitched their habitation in
the south, it matters little. By the wonderful
power of God they shall be both converted to
Christ and gathered into their own land. God
will have but to speak the word, and that miracle
of miracles will be wrought. The unbelief of
Judah and of Israel shall be taken away. They
shall look on him whom they have pierced, and
they shall mourn because of him.

The words may also be applied to those glorious
gatherings of the latter times when the Church
shall make up her full number; when the elect,
though they may be scattered hither and thither,
shall hear the call of effectual grace, and return
unto the Lord who has bought them with his
precious blood. May the Lord hasten those happy
times, when his word shall run, and have free
course, and be glorified!

But my intention is rather to utilize than to expound the text. To you, dear friends, specially to you who are not saved, I have thought that the address to the north and that to the south might prove, either or both of them, messages from God. "I will say to the north, Give up; and to the south, Keep not back."

These are two appeals from heaven to which ye do well that ye take heed. May the Eternal Spirit make them powerful, so that you may be obedient to their high behests. Here are two short, terse addresses; two simple items of serious advice. Oh that you might hearken and follow them to your soul's eternal benefit!

I. The first counsel is—GIVE UP. Give up what? Why, with some of you it is imperative that you give up your *prejudices*. So have you mis-estimated true religion, that you have been accustomed to denounce it as cant, and to declaim the professors of it as hypocrites. Now, give up this blind bias, and give the gospel a fair hearing. Should it turn out to be an imposture, you will at least be the better able to expose its fictions, after having studied its facts; but should it happen to be genuine and true, how ill will it be for you if you continue to despise it! The doctrine of Christ claims to be divine. It asserts itself to be the only true faith, and it argues all other systems to be false. It tells that "God so loved the world that he gave his only begotten Son, that whosoever believeth in him should not perish, but have everlasting life." This is a startling announcement. History or poetry has no parallel for such a wonder that the Holy God was willing to die for sinful men, that he who was offended should himself take the guilt of those who offended him upon himself, and suffer for their transgressions. Strange miracle of grace! that the Lord of life and glory should become a substitute for his enemies. Do not mock at the mention of such mercy. There must be something in it. Tens of thousands live happily upon the tidings. Millions have died exultingly on the credit of its authenticity. The trust reposed in it has been tried and tested in the prison, on the rack, and at the stake, and believers in it have triumphed over every form of infernal torture. They have held their confidence steadfast to the end, and finished their course bravely and gloriously, grasping the standard of the cross of Christ. Seal not your ears, shut not your hearts against the testimony; let it have a fair hearing. Give up your prejudices. Hear, and your souls shall live.

Give up in like manner your self-righteousness. In vain my entreaties, for unless God shall say it, no man will do it. The worst of men flatter themselves with some conceit of their own righteousness. Their companions back them up, and praise them as good fellows. However abandoned and dissolute their lives, they credit themselves with some virtues that make a fair show before men of their own type, which they fondly hope will pass

current with God at the last. But I beseech you
hearken to a brother's voice, while I assure you
that excuses for sin are unavailing and apologies
impertinent. The best labors of the human hand,
and the best dispositions of the human heart, are
so defiled through our natural depravity, that they
cannot be accepted by the Most High. Paul, the
great apostle, who during the early part of his life
had been one of the most excellent and exemplary
of men, observing the most authentic religion with
the most austere consistency, and supplementing
it with the most furious zeal, discovered the hol-
lowness of his piety, and the hideousness of his
character, when he came to see things in the right
light; so that he counted his own righteousness to
be but dross and dung, that he might win Christ,
and be found in him. Surely Paul knew as well
as you know, and much better too, what creature
righteousness may attain. I would feelingly admire, rather than foolishly disparage, all that is
honest and upright; admirable and benevolent;
sober and sensible. This is all admirable in its
way, but do not trust to such trifling charms. A
bridge that may carry you well enough over the
straits of this life, among your fellow-men, will fail
to bear the weight of your soul when you reach
the torrent of death, and are about to pass into eternity. Then every timber will creak and snap, and
down you will go, if grace prevent not, into the
gulf that is bottomless. I do beseech you to give
up all dependence on your own merit; give it up.

No man can be saved by Christ while he has any degree of reliance upon himself. One of the first requisites of genuine faith in Christ is to have a total despair of all salvation by your own efforts. How long we are haggling with God before we submit unreservedly to this self-renunciation. If we cannot be saved entirely by our own merits, we say—" Well, may we not at least do a little?" Let this snare be broken, and we soon entangle ourselves again saying, " Surely something must be required from us." To bring a man to the full assurance of understanding that " it is finished," that love's redeeming work is done, that the blood which cleanses from all sin has been shed, that the righteousness which justifies a man before God is already wrought out and completed—oh! this simple statement is the hardest lesson that a sinner has to learn. Little heed ye take when I cry, Give up your self-righteousness. Only God can so teach you that you shall be willing to cast it away as not only profitless, but utterly polluted. The confidence you feel in the rectitude of your judgment, in the resolutions of your conscience, and the reasonableness of your hope is a rotten foundation. Give it up.

Give up; again I say—give up your *sins.* You cannot be saved from their consequence if you cling to their company. Christ is willing to forgive you all your past sins, if you are willing to part with them now; but when you make a league with your lusts you are plotting against your own life. Drunkard, though you have all but killed yourself with strong drink, there is pardon for you now; but you must renounce that intoxicating cup. So long, sir, as you keep to it you are drinking down the venom of a deadly poison. What! will you ask Christ to deliver you, while you are destroying yourself? And you too, ye libertines, you who have violated the laws of chastity, foul as your offences are, there is forgiveness for them; the precious blood can make you white, but you must forsake your impurities. The Saviour of sinners will make no compromise with sin, nor will he have anything to do with you, unless you clear yourself of these abominations? Is there one here who has been dishonest? Still there is pardon for the penitent. Your transgression shall be covered if you come to Christ; but you must cease from fraud and falsehood of every kind. There must be no more trickery in trading; no short weights, no spurious articles, no cheating or shuffling henceforward. All imposture must be renounced. You must shake such villainy off your hand as Paul shook off the viper into the fire. Give up, and have done with it. A Good Physician is our great Master, and very willing is he to heal your diseases; but his treatment is not to be trifled with. You must not cling to habits that clash with health. Or should you feed the passions, and revel in the pleasures that sap your stamina and foster your sickness, then no remedy can restore you; your certain doom is death. Give up your sins. Are you loth to part with them?

Oh, fools and slow of heart, to hanker after harm, and desire your own destruction! Why, your sins, perhaps, have already begun to entail sorrows upon you. Now that you feel their bitterness, is it not time to have done with them? I have heard of one who kept a tame leopard in his house. It had been nursed from the time it was a cub, and it gambolled about like a cat. But one day, while the master was asleep, it licked his hand. As it licked a place where the skin was thin and broken, the blood began to flow. Then all the wild instincts of the beast of the forest flashed from its furious eyes. The man suddenly woke, and saw the situation. His end was near—unless he should be quick and skilful enough to destroy the animal. Do you think he paused or hesitated? No; a loaded pistol was within his reach; so he stretched out his hand quietly, grasped it firmly, aimed it steadily, fired it instantly, and the creature lay dead at his feet. It had come to this; that he must either kill it, or it would kill him. It is so with you. Your sins begin to draw blood from you already. Those stings of conscience, that empty purse, those red eyes—all are beginning to tell what sin can do. Not yet do you know all its horror. Before the leopard springs upon you and tears you in pieces, God help you to give it up! May God help you to give it up to-night, whatever it may be. Pluck it out, though it is like a right eye. Off with it, though it be like a right arm. It were better for you to enter into life having but one eye, or but one arm, than having both eyes and both arms to be cast into the fire of hell. Give up.

"Give up," says the text; and I use the expression thus—give up *delays*. Give up procrastination. Give up that constant—"To-morrow, to-morrow, to-morrow!" Give up talking, like Felix, about "a more convenient season." Give all this up. Some here are sickly and drooping. Symptoms of consumption are beginning to betray themselves. What does this mean? Is the great Landlord giving his poor tenant a notice to quit? Prepare ye, then, for the removal. Last Sabbath, and during the early days of this week, there was present with us, and busy among us, a dear sister in Christ, whom we all regard with affection and esteem. She has been suddenly paralyzed. When I looked at her just now, as she lay upon her bed, it was with much difficulty that she at last opened her eyes, recognized me, just smiled and then relapsed into unconsciousness. "Be ye also ready; for in such an hour as ye think not the Son of man cometh." She was at the beginning of the week, to all appearance, in as good health as you are. There she is now, suddenly smitten down, soon, perhaps, to be taken away. 'Tis a warning to us. Oh! take the warning to yourselves. How often do we hear of City men, who used to go up on the omnibus with us, or pass by our house regularly every morning. We miss them; and when we ask where they are, we are told that they are gone! Some who were so busy they could find no time to think of their latter end, have found out of a sudden that their time to live was spent, and their time to die had come. Scattered among this congregation are persons whose sable dress tells of recent bereavement. Ah! you have had the warning close at home. I pray you give up your supineness. May this be to you the appointed time, and this the hour of salvation, when eternal grace shall woo and win your hearts.

And I might well say to some here present, *give up quibbling.* You have never yet come to the point with your own conscience. You have always been so deft at finding out knots and raising questions. What is the good of it, man? If you are never saved till you get every problem solved, you will never be saved at all. A man is dying; there is a medicine that might restore him; he will not take it, because he does not understand the anatomy of his lungs and the various internal organs of his body. Stupid! Is it not enough that the physician understands the malady and the remedy? Take the medicine, man, and be content. Surely Christ understands every difficulty that could perplex a sinner's brain, and he has prepared a potent salvation fully adequate to secure the sinner's welfare. Why should we stammer at the difficulties, instead of solving the dilemma by accepting the grace? If a vessel were breaking in pieces on yonder shore, and the rocket apparatus had fired a rope into the middle of the vessel, would you not think the crew to be insane if they said to one another—"We do not understand how it is that the rocket apparatus manages this!" Oh, but they just twist the rope round the mast, get a hold-fast, and begin to swing themselves ashore. So would every sane man do; and may the grace of God rid you of the insanity of your sin, and may the Eternal Spirit make you wise to flee to Jesus ere the night of death comes on.

"Give up," says the text—and I shall use it once more—give up, you troubled ones; give up *despondency;* give up the thought that there is no hope; give up the suspicion that Jesus cannot forgive. Know you not that our Lord Jesus Christ is very God, though man, of the substance of his mother? Made of a woman, made under the law, he was nevertheless co-equal and co-eternal with the Father. Now, if he, being God, took upon himself the sin of his people, there must be a wonderful power in the sufferings he endured. There is, in fact, such power in the atonement of Christ that no sin was ever found too great for Christ to put away; no stain too deep for him to wash out. However black you may have been, depend upon it your sins shall never baffle the power of the Almighty Saviour. Give up your doubts, then, and believe the message of my Lord and Master. "He that believeth on him shall never perish, but have everlasting life." To despond and to despair, to doubt and to mistrust, were to insult the one Mediator and to bring swift destruction upon ourselves. Others have trusted, and none of them were rejected. They have depended upon the mercy of God in Christ, and many of them are safe in the city of the blessed, and thousands more are now happily on the road thither. Oh, troubled one! why dost thou not try it? God is speaking to thee through my lips, and I trust his effectual grace is commanding thee to "give up," and constraining thee to "give up" thy dark suspicions and thy gloomy fears. Drop into the arms of Christ. Fall into the bosom of pardoning grace; "give up; give up; give up!" You are not asked to do aught; you are not asked to feel aught; you are not asked to prepare yourselves for mercy; you are not asked to perform penance, or to pass through purgatory. Give up! This is everything. Give up your every other trust. Give up your every other thought, and come just as you are to the sinners' Saviour, who has said— "Him that cometh to me I will in no wise cast out." May this prove to be the message of God to many of you in these galleries and in that area. Give up! Give up!

II. We pass to the second address, which is this, "Keep not back."

Pray for me now, ye people of God, that during the next ten minutes I may be made God's mouth to some with this timely counsel, this solemn charge, "Keep not back."

Keep not back, my dear hearers, *from attending the means of grace.* It was with very great pleasure I heard that this afternoon at the special service for the young the Tabernacle was full. I do not doubt that if we had every Sunday three services we should have the house filled three times, for the people are, as a rule, willing to hear. Still, there are very many in London of all classes, relatively as many of the rich as of the poor, who keep back, and habitually neglect the house of God. Do you not see the penny Sunday paper handed in at many a working man's door on the Lord's-day morning? That is the sermon they are supplied with for the forenoon, I suppose. After dinner they do their devotions to the god of this world with libations of ale and fumes of the pipe; their Sabbath being a day of inactivity, if not of intemperance.

Ah! did they but know the blessedness of gospel privileges, they would not forsake the assembling of themselves in the fellowship of the house of God, but they would gather with eager haste to hear of the things that make for their soul's peace. Not that WE have ourselves any cause for complaint. It is entirely for their own interest I counsel the careless not to keep back with reckless indifference. As you all know, the crowds that throng this capacious chapel baffle all our efforts to provide them with accommodation. Should I happen, however, to be addressing any who do not go regularly to a place of worship, I offer you, friends, a cordial greeting. I am glad to see you here. But I earnestly admonish you to make the house of prayer a settled home. Let this casual visit be followed up with a continual resort to the sanctuary. Keep not back. Going to church or chapel will not make you a saint any more than going to school would make you a scholar. Still, we are told of one that, "being in the way, the Lord met with him." If you are in the fields at time of wheat harvest you may glean some ears of corn, but if you lounge about that house at the roadside, you will get nothing worth carrying away. If you are where Christ is distributing his royal bounties, it may be you will receive a boon such as you could never purchase. But oh! God forbid you should ever be content with "it may be!" Come with this firm resolve—that if true religion is taught anywhere you will know it; if pardon is to be had you will find it; if heaven is to be reached you will, by the grace of God, secure a place among its holy inhabitants. Now if this purpose of heart be wrought in you by God the Holy Spirit, your desires will not be disappointed. I beseech you, therefore, keep not back.

And when you do attend the house of the Lord, *keep not back from a simple obedience of the gospel.* How many times over have I told to this congregation the simple gospel whereby we are saved! How many times more, if God spare my life, shall I have to tell the same old, old story! It is summed up in a few syllables, God must punish sin. Sin is such a mischief that the most holy God cannot put up with it. It must be punished. But Jesus Christ put his bare shoulder under the Divine lash. He took the penalty of sin upon himself, and suffered for his people what they ought to have suffered. Who, do ye ask, are the people for whom Christ suffered? We answer, for as many as trust him. If you trust him, that is the evidence that he died for you. If you will depend upon him, and upon him alone, that is the mark that you were redeemed by the precious blood of Christ, and a sure token that you shall never perish. God cannot punish you for your sins if they were laid on your Substitute. It would be unjust, for he has already punished Christ instead of you. If you believe in Jesus, God's justice cannot demand twice over payment of the same debt; first at your bleeding Surety's hands and then again at yours. Now, sinner, Christ is lifted up in the gospel for you to know him and to trust him. Keep not back! Keep not back! The devil says that your sins are too great. He is a liar; keep not back. Your heart says you are not prepared. God is greater than your heart, and he knoweth all things—keep not back. You say you cannot pray, but a sigh is a prayer, a tear is a prayer—keep not back. You say you are afraid you are not elected. If your soul takes shelter in Christ you have conclusive evidence that your name is written in the Book of Life—keep not back. You are afraid you shall not hold on to the end. It is his covenant engagement to keep you from falling if you come and commit yourselves to his protection—keep not back. Christ Jesus, like the brazen serpent in the wilderness, is lifted high upon the pole that whosoever looks should be healed. Look! sinner, look! 'Tis the whole gospel in a word—look! Look to Jesus. Away with your good deeds. Away with your fine prayers. Away with all your self-righteousnesses. None but Jesus can do helpless sinners good. Look then; look to him, and keep not back.

And when you have looked to Christ, *keep not back from the mercy-seat.* You may ask of God, and he will give you your desires. Unworthy though you be, God is a Father to you, and you may tell him all your troubles, your sins, your doubts, and you may ask him for whatever he has promised. According to your faith, so shall it be done unto you. Keep not back, poor soul. When you get home to-night, and want to pray, you will think you must not, but I beseech you hear the word, " Keep not back." You will begin to pray, perhaps, and find yourself stammering and trembling, but keep not back. Your old sins will half choke you in the recollection of them, but keep not back. If anybody saw you trying to pray they would say, "What you, you old wretch, you trying to pray!" Oh! but keep not back. 'Tis mercy calls you; come and pray. The mercy-seat was built for sinners; it was sprinkled with blood for sinners; therefore keep not back.

When you have really trusted in Christ, and have learned to pray, then *keep not back from coming forward and making a profession of your faith in Jesus.* Your Master has told you to follow his example. The first thing he did in public life was to be baptized. He came to John, and asked him to baptize him, and this was the reason he gave, "Suffer it to be so now, for thus it becometh us to fulfil all righteousness." You know your Lord was not sprinkled. He knew nothing of infant baptism. He was a man of ripe years when he came forward and was baptized. You know how the gospel puts it, "He that believeth and is baptized shall be saved." Do not put the cart before the horse. It is not written, He that is baptized and then believes, but He that believeth and is baptized shall be saved. In the case of all the early converts, as soon as they believed, they were immediately baptized, and added to the church. If you have believed, then, keep not back; but in all your Lord's appointed ways pursue your journey to heaven. Then there is the Lord's Supper. "If ye love me," said he, "keep my commandments." Can ye overlook his dying command? "This do in remembrance of me." Keep not back, then. When you have found Christ, come forward and avow it at once. Some who negligently wait for a year, inadvertently wait for two years. And as nothing seems urgent when it has been long deferred, years multiply and conviction chills; duty becomes doubtful, and a languid heart finds excuses for all the lingering, till they wait so long they never care to come at all. Be prompt, if you would be precise in serving the Lord. "I made haste," said David, "and delayed not to keep thy commandments." Christ deserves and demands the most scrupulous homage.

He redeemed you openly; profess him openly. Christ did not come into this world with a secret, covert love to you, but with a bold, outspoken love. He emptied out his very heart upon the cross for you; be not ashamed of him. Take your place in the pillory side by side with his despised and persecuted people. Take up your cross daily and follow him, for he that confesseth him before men, him will he confess before his Father in heaven; but he that denieth Christ before men, him will Christ deny before his Father and his holy angels. Keep not back, then, keep not back.

To those who are saved, and have avowed their conversion, let me now say, Keep not back, my dear brethren and sisters, *from the Lord's service.* I entreat you young men not to keep back from preaching Christ. I hope, when the weather permits, there will be plenty of street preaching all over this region. It delights me to hear occasionally that our preachers are numerous enough to become a nuisance to the neighborhood. I hope you will increase the force tenfold. We must take the gospel to those who will not come and hear it. Occupy the street corners, police or no police. Preach the gospel wherever you have an opportunity. Throw it in the way of the wayfarer. Let the plan of salvation cross his path and greet his ears. I have known persons from Germany and France struck with nothing so much in London as with the open-air preaching. I have met too with cases, chiefly of foreigners, who had never heard our holy faith—such as Frenchmen, Germans, Poles, and Spaniards—who have mingled in the crowd, listened to what has been spoken, and learned for the first time a Saviour's love and felt the power of it in their hearts. Some of you young men may have great ability, but much bashfulness. Remember that souls are dying, and tremble at your own timidity while you contemplate this huge city perishing for lack of knowledge. How can you be cowardly and craven, and hide your light under a bushel? The Lord have mercy upon us if we have concealed the glad tidings in the past; but in the future let us publish the divine proclamation—"Keep not back!"

Those of you who could help in a ragged school, need not make vain excuses, or cultivate your own ease on Sundays, as is your wont. Turn out and go in quest of young Arabs from the streets. You, who might be useful in the Sabbath school, but prefer to have your time to yourselves, make it a matter of conscience that ye volunteer on the Lord's side. Judge ye whether you are doing right while ye stand aloof. Are you at liberty to keep a single talent unemployed? You are six days at work in the world for your own wage, cannot you dedicate one day wholly to Christ? I may be speaking to some sentimental Christians, who never seriously think of serving the Lord. We look for ripe fruit from your rich experience. By the love of souls, I pray you keep not back. Some of you are affluent in this world's currency; give up your substance;

keep not back. Aid others to do what you cannot accomplish by your own personal efforts. I am bold to beg for my Master. By the famishing millions; by the tens of thousands who know not their right hand from their left in the point of religion; by the activity of the priests of Rome; by the craftiness of the fiends of hell, who on every side are casting abroad their temptations; by the attractiveness of the gin-palace, the casino, the theatre, and the haunts of infamy, I pray you be vigilant, active, always on the alert. Give God no rest in your supplication for his favor. Cry aloud and spare not. Give sinners no rest in your deprecation of their behavior. Constrain them to see what wages await their wickedness, and to hear what salvation is proclaimed to their souls.

Would God I could speak with more fervor to you upon this point. Better is it that my text speak to you, "Keep not back." Let not any one of you skulk or hold back. Every man to the front as far as possible. In the name of God, the Eternal, the Almighty; in the faith of the precious blood; in the power of the blessed Spirit, let each man advance to the conflict; let each sister take her part in the fray. God bless you according to your faith—bless you according to your zeal. Oh, that many may "give-up," and all of you "keep not back." So shall he bless you very richly, for Jesus' sake, Amen.

A Timely Remonstrance.

Kiss the Son, lest he be angry, and ye perish from the way, when his wrath is kindled but a little. Blessed are all they that put their trust in him.—PSALM ii. 12.

NOW let us have a little quiet talk. I have known a simple, earnest conversation turn the whole current of a man's life. I recollect a good man, who lived at a certain market town in Suffolk. He was no preacher; so far as I know, he had never tried to preach; yet he was a mighty soul-winner. He had noticed how commonly it happened in that town, as in most of our smaller towns, that the lads as they grew up sought situations in London, or in some other large centre of industry, and, consequently, they left their home, their parents, guardians, and the associations amidst which they had been trained, to enter a new sphere, where they would be exposed to more temptation, while they would lack much of the oversight that had hitherto checked them when prone to wander. His watchful eye and ever-listening ear having ascertained within a little when any young man was going, he sent a polite invitation to tea, and at that tea-table the words he used to speak, the cautions he gave, and the necessity he urged of being decided for Christ before leaving, and especially the earnest prayer with which he concluded the evening—these things have been remembered by scores of young men, who, on removing to the larger towns, could never shake off the impression which his quiet, devout conversation had made. Some of them even traced their conversion to God, and their subsequent perseverance in the paths of righteousness, to the evening they had spent with that humble, but wise and earnest individual. I wonder whether any of us remember in our young days any such talk which exerted an influence upon us; I wonder more if, instead of aiming to preach anything great, which is not much in my line, I try to speak very seriously and pointedly to all present who are unconverted, whether God will not bless it by his Holy Spirit, and make it a turning point to decide the present course and eternal destiny of some of my hearers.

Our text contains some very sound advice. Let us ask—to whom was it originally addressed? and to whom the same counsel may now be appropriately given? *"Kiss the son, lest he be angry."* Look at the tenth verse—"Be wise now therefore, O ye kings: be instructed, ye judges of the earth." Thus, to monarchs and potentates of this world; to those who made and to those who administered the laws, in whose hands were the liberties, if not the lives of their subjects, were these words spoken. People make a great fuss about a sermon preached before Her Majesty. I must confess to having wasted a shilling once or twice over those productions. I could never make out why they should have been sold at such a price, for I think better sermons could have been bought for a penny. But, somehow, there is always an interest attached to anything that is preached *before* a king or a queen, and still more so if it be pointedly preached *to* a king. Now, this was a little private advice given to kings and judges. Still, it offers counsel by which persons of inferior rank may profit. You, sir, are not so great in station but this advice may be good enough for you. If it was meant for those who sat on thrones, wielded sceptres, and exercised authority, you will not have to humble yourself much to listen earnestly, and receive gratefully, this admonition of wisdom.

Let me take you now by your hand, and hold you for a minute, and say, Be wise now; this is the day for reason; exercise a little judgment; put on your considering cap; do not spurn the monition, or put it on one side with a huff and a puff, as though it were not discreet or urgent. This was language meant for kings; hearken to it; it may be a royal word to you. Mayhap—for strange things happen—it may help to make you a king, too, according to that saying, which is written, " He hath made us kings and priests unto God." The language which would command the attention of kings should certainly claim heed of such humble and obscure persons as are here assembled.

Surely, when the expostulation proceeds from the mouth of God, and when it is spoken to the highest potentates in the world, you might account it a privilege to have the matter made privy to yourselves. And as it intimately concerns you, there is the more cause that you take heed thereunto.

The words were spoken to those who had wilfully opposed the reign of our Saviour, the Son of God, the Lord's anointed. They had determined to reject him. They said, "Let us break their bands asunder, and cast away their cords from us." A terrible, a disastrous course to resolve upon in the teeth of a destiny that no plot can hinder, no confederation can avert. Hence, the caution and the counsel appeal to all or to any who have been opposers of Christ and of true religion. I do not suppose there are many such here, who are active and ostensibly revolting against the gospel, yet there may be some such; and, if there be, I would sound an alarm, and ring loudly the warning, "Be wise now, therefore; be instructed; do listen a little." It is good to be zealous in a good cause. But suppose it is a bad cause! Saul of Tarsus was vehement against Christ, but after some consideration he became quite as enthusiastic for him. It may cost you many regrets another day to have been so violent against that which you will find out to have been worthy of your full confidence rather than of your fierce opposition. Every wise man, before he commits himself to defend or withstand a policy, would make quite sure, as far as human judgment can, whether it be right or wrong; to be desired, or to be deprecated. Surely, I do not speak to any who would wilfully oppose that which is good. Or, if prejudice has prompted you, there is all the more reason why your judgment should now be impartial. Stop, therefore, and give ear. It may be thy relentings will be kindled, and wisdom will enlighten thy heart.

These words were spoken to those who ought to have been wise—to kings and judges of the earth. Those mighty ones had been mistaken, otherwise the rebuke would have been untimely and superfluous—"Be wise now therefore, O ye kings: be instructed, ye judges of the earth." It appeared they had rebelled—partly through ignorance, but mainly through jealousy and malice—they had rebelled and revolted against the Christ of God. Doubtless they did not rightly understand him. Perhaps they thought his way was hard, his laws severe, his government tyrannical. But he meets your wild rage with his mild reasoning. To the gusts of your passion he responds with the gentle voice of his mercy,—"Be wise, O ye kings: be instructed, ye judges of the earth." Learn a little more; get a little more knowledge; it may correct your vain imaginations. A ray of light shining into your minds might make you shudder at the darkness in the midst of which you dwelt. A view of the right might perhaps show you that you have been wrong. It might take the tiller of your soul, and turn the vessel round into another course. We are none of us so wise but we could profit by a little more instruction. He that cannot learn from a fool is a fool himself. When a man says, "I know enough," he knows nothing. He who thinks that his education is "finished," had need begin his schooling afresh, for a fair start he has never yet made. With a sound basis, the edifice of education may proceed satisfactorily, but it never can be completed. "Excelsior" is the student's motto. He sees higher and higher altitudes as he rises in attainment; and, so long as he sojourns in this world, fresh fields of inquiry will continue to open up before him.

Once again, I believe the words of our text have an especial reference to those who are thoughtless and careless about their best interests. The kings of the earth were deliberating how they might successfully oppose Christ; but they were strangely and culpably negligent of their own welfare. Hence the remonstrance—"Be wise now; be instructed, ye judges of the earth." The general lack of intelligence in the present day with respect to religion is, to my mind, appalling. The knowledge with which most men are content is superficial in the extreme. They do not think; they do not take the pains to make reflections and draw inferences from the facts within their reach, but they allow themselves to drift with the tide of what is called "public opinion." Were it the fashion for people to carry brains in their heads, some religions which are now very rife would soon come to an end. I have stood aghast with wonder and with awe at the sublime folly of mankind, when I have seen how eagerly and devoutly they will bow down before baubles and raree-shows, while they vainly imagine that they are worshipping God. Have they no brains within their skulls? Have they no faculty of thought? Have they no reasoning power? What singular defect can be traced to their birth, or with what fatal folly have they renounced their common sense? Ought we to pity, to chide, or to scorn them? In indictments for witchcraft, I suppose, you punish the impostor as a knave, while you laugh at the victim as a dupe. But in cases of priestcraft you divide the scandal more equally. So the Sunday theatricals must run their course, till the force of thought, the voice of conscience, and, I might add, the love of liberty, shall pronounce their doom.

People do not think. Some of them hold to the religion of their ancestors, whatever that may be. Your hear of Roman Catholic families and Quaker families. Not conviction, but tradition, shapes their ends. Others are of the religion of the circle in which they live; adopting the sentiments of those among whom they sojourn. They are good Protestants, they say; had they been born in Naples they would have been as good Papists; or had they been born at Timbuctoo, they would have been as good heathen. Just about as good in any case. Thought, reason, or judgment never entered into their reckoning. They go up to their place of worship; they pray as others do, or they say "Amen" to any collect that may fall into the service. Thought they have none. They sing without thought, hear without thought, and as the thing is to be done, I suppose, they preach without thought. Talk of preaching, I have specimens at home of sermons which can be bought for nine-pence each. They are underlined, so that the proper emphasis is apparent, and the pauses to be made between the sentences are fairly indicated. Preaching made easy! We shall be favored one of these days with preaching machines; we have already got down to hearing machines. The mass of our hearers is not much more animated than an automaton figure. Life and liveliness are wanting in both. Preaching and hearing may both perhaps be done by steam. I would it were not so. Men are evidently thoughtful about other things. Bring up a sanitary problem, and there are men that will work it out somehow. Is some new invention wanted, say a gun or torpedo, to effect a wholesale destruction of life? You shall find competitors in the arena, vying one with another in their study of the murderous science.

Man seems to think of everything but of his God; to read everything but his Bible; to feel the influence of everything but the love of Christ, and to see reason and argument in everything except in the inviolable truth of divine revelation. Oh, when will men consider? Why are they bent upon dash-

ing into eternity thoughtlessly? Is dying and
passing into another world of no more account than
passing from the parlor to the drawing-room? Is
there no hereafter? Is heaven a dream, and hell
a bugbear? Well then, cease to play with shadows;
no longer foster such delusions. Be these things
true or false, your insincerity is alike glaring.
Like honest men, repudiate the Scriptures if
you will not accept their counsel. Do not pretend to believe the solemnities of God's word,
and yet trifle with them. This is to stultify yourselves, while you insult your Maker. I appeal to
the conscience of every thoughtless person here,
if reason or common sense would justify such
vacillation?

Having thus tried to find out the people to whom
my text applies, let me now direct your attention
to the advice it gives them. The advice is this:
rebel no more against God. You have done so,
some of you actively and wilfully; others of you by
ignoring his claims and utterly neglecting his will.
It is not right to continue in this rebellious state,
To have become entangled in such iniquity is grievous enough, but to continue therein any longer
were an outrageous folly and a terrible crime.
Serve the Lord with fear, and rejoice with trembling. Do you say, " We hear the advice and are
willing to take it; our anxiety now is to find out
the way in which we can become reconciled to God.
How can we be restored to friendship with him
whom we have so bitterly wronged and so grossly

offended?" Here is the pith of the advice, "Kiss the Son, pay him homage; yield the affectionate fealty of your hearts to the Son of God." Between you and the great King there is an awful breach. You cannot obtain audience of him. So grievous has been your revolt, that he will not see you. He has shut the door, and there cannot be any communication between you and himself; he has hung up a thick veil, through which your prayers cannot penetrate. But he refers you to his Son. That Son is his other self—one with himself in essential deity, who hath condescended to become man, hath taken your nature into union with himself, and in that nature hath offered unto divine justice an expiatory sacrifice for human guilt.

Now, therefore, God will deal with you through his Son. You must have an advocate. As many a client cannot plead in court, but must have some counsellor to plead for him, who is infinitely more versed in the law and better able to defend his cause than he is, so the Lord appoints that you, if you would see the face of your God, must see it in the face of Jesus Christ. The short way of being at peace with God is not to try and mend your ways, or excuse yourself, or perform certain works, or go through certain ceremonies, but to repair to Christ, the one only Mediator, who once was fastened to the cross, being put to death in the flesh, but quickened by the Spirit. He is now at the right hand of God, and you are required to worship him, to trust in him, to love him. Thus do, and the reconciliation between you and God is effected in a moment. The blessed Jesus will wash you from your guilt, and the righteousness of Christ will cover you with beauty, which will make you acceptable in the sight of God. "Kiss the Son." It means render him homage, just as in our own country they speak of kissing hands with the Queen when certain offices are taken and homage is required. So come and kiss the Saviour. No hard work this. Some of us would fain forever kiss his blessed feet, and we would count it heaven enough to have so high an honor. Oh, come and pay your homage to him; own that Christ is your King. Give up your life to his service. Consecrate all your powers and faculties to do his will. But do trust him. "Blessed are all they that put their trust in him." That is the true kiss. Trust him, rely upon him, depend upon him; leave off depending upon yourself, and rely upon Jesus. Throw yourself flat down upon the finished work of Christ; when you have so done your faith has reconciled you to God, and you may go your way in peace. Only go your way henceforth to serve that King whose hand you have kissed, and to be the willing subject of that dear Redeemer who ought to have you, because he bought you with his precious blood.

This advice is urgent. Do it at once. I am not speaking now after the fashion of the orator, but I am talking to you as a friend. I wish I could pass along those aisles, or over the tops of those pews, and gently take the hand of each one, and say, " Friend, God would fain have thee reconciled to him, and it only needs the simple act of trusting Jesus and accepting him to be thy leader and thy king." Do it now. If it be ever worth doing, it is worth doing at once. It is a blessed thing to do. Why delay? It is a simple thing to do— why hesitate? It is the very least thing God could ask of thee, and even that he will not require thee to do in thine own strength. Art thou willing, but weak? He will help thee to do what he commands thee to do. Now, as thou sittest in thy pew, what sayest thou to this? " I will think it over," says one. Does it want any thinking over? If I had offended my father, I should wish to be at peace with him directly; and if my father said to me, " My son, I will be reconciled to you if you will go and speak to your brother about it," well, I should not think it hard, for I love my brother as well as my father, and I would go to him at once, and so all would be well. God says, " Go to Jesus; I am in him. You can reach me there—go round by his cross; you will find me reconciled there. Away from the cross I am a Judge, and my terrors will consume you. With the cross between you and me, I am a Father, and you shall behold my face beaming with love to you." " But how am I to get to Jesus?" do you ask. Why, have I not told you, simply to trust him, to rely upon him? Faith is trusting Christ. This is the gospel, " Believe in the Lord Jesus

Christ, and thou shalt be saved." Put your entire trust in him. Renounce all lordship that has ever been exercised over you by any other master, and become Christ's servant. Rely on him to land you safely at the right hand of God, and he will do it. "Kiss the Son." Oh, friend, I cannot make you do it; it must be done of thine own will. God alone can lead that will of thine to yield itself up to Christ's will; but I pray thee do it—kiss the Son, and do it now.

Pursuing our quiet talk, I come to my third point, which is—How is this advice pressed home upon us? The vanity of any other course is made palpable. Be reconciled to God, because there is no use in being at enmity with him. The kings of the earth opposed God, but while they were plotting and planning God was laughing. "Yet," saith he, "have I set my king upon my holy hill of Zion." I think if I were a king, and had the misfortune to be driven to go to war, I should not like to fight one that had ten times my own strength. I should rather engage in a somewhat equal combat, with a prospect that, by dint of valor and good generalship, victory might be gained. To contend against omnipotence is insanity. For any man, I care not who he may be, to put himself in opposition to God, is utter folly. I have often watched, as doubtless you have done, the foolish moth attracted by the glare of the candle or the gas. A plunge he makes at it, as though he would put it out, and he drops, full of exquisite pain, upon the table. He has enough wing left to make another dash at the flame, and again he is filled with another pain, and unless you mercifully kill him outright he will continue as long as he has any strength to fight with the fire which destroys him. That is an apt picture of the sinner's life, and such will be the sinner's death. Oh, do not so, dear friend—do not so. Speak I not with the voice of reason when I thus dissuade you? If you must fight, let it be with some one that you can overcome. But sit down and reckon now whether you can hope to win a victory against an Almighty God. End the quarrel, man, for the quarrel will otherwise end in your death and eternal destruction.

We are further pressed to the duty commanded by the claims of the Son. "Kiss the Son." As I read the words, they seem to me to have a force of argument in them which explains itself and vindicates its own claims. Kiss! Kiss whom? "Kiss the Son!" And who is he? Why, he is Jesus, the well-beloved of the Father, and among the sons of men the chief among ten thousand, and the altogether lovely. Surely Christ is such a princely one that he ought to receive homage of mankind. He has done such great things for us, and he has shown such good will towards us, that to pay him reverence seems not so much the call of duty as the natural impulse of love. The worship which is his due should flow spontaneously from the instincts of grace rather than be exacted by the fiat of law. Even those who have denied the authenticity of inspiration have always been charmed with the character of our Lord, and you will notice that the most astute opponents of Christianity have had little, if anything, to say against the Founder of it, so transparent his virtue, so charming his humility. Oh, kiss the Son, then. He is God—trust him. He is man, a perfect man—confide in his friendship. He has finished the work of human redemption, therefore hail him as your king, and pay your homage to him now. Oh that God's eternal Spirit may lead you so to do without hesitation or demur!

Were I talking to some of you in a quiet corner I might gather an argument from the simplicity of the promise here offered you. "Kiss the Son." Is that all? Pay Jesus homage. Is that all? The Emperor of Germany, in the olden times when popes were popes, had offended his Unholiness, and before he could be restored to favor he had to stand for three days (I think it was) outside the castle gate, in the deep snow, in the depth of winter, and do penance. I have seen, myself, in Rome and elsewhere, outside of the older churches, places uncovered and exposed to wind and rain, to the heat of summer and the frost of winter, where backsliders were made to stand, sometimes for years even, before they were restored, if they had committed some offence against ecclesiastical statutes. You will sometimes see in old country churches of England little windows that run slanting and just look towards the communion table, through which poor offenders who professed repentance, after some months of standing in the churchyard, or perhaps outside of it, were at last allowed to take a peep at the altar, at the expiration of their weary term of penance. All this is contrary to the spirit of the gospel, for the spirit of the gospel is, "Come now, and let us reason together; though thy sins be as scarlet, they shall be as wool." The spirit of my text is "Kiss the Son now;" and that is all. Though those lips were once blaspheming, let them kiss the Son. Though those lips have uttered high words and proud words, or perhaps lying and lascivious words, "Kiss the Son." Bow down at those dear pierced feet, and trust Emmanuel, and own yourself his servant, and you shall be forgiven—forgiven at once, without delay—and this night you shall be accepted in Christ. I am right glad I have got so good a message to tell. I would that you would receive it with gladness. May it drop like the snow-flakes on the sea, which sink into the wave! May each invitation sink into your soul, there to bless you henceforth and forever!

Moreover, the exhortation of our text is backed up with bright and beautiful congratulation for those who yield to it. "Blessed are all they that put their trust in him." Those of you who do not know anything about trusting in Christ must have noticed how joyously we sang that hymn just now—

> " Oh ! happy day that fixed my choice
> On Thee, my Saviour and my God;
> Well may this glowing heart rejoice,
> And tell its raptures all abroad."

Don't you think there was some fervor in our tones? Was it not sung as if we meant it? If nobody else meant it, I did; and I could see by the look of your eyes that a good many of you were stirred with grateful recollections. It was the happiest day in all our lives when Jesus washed our sins away. Far be it from us to deceive any of you by saying that to be a Christian will save you from the sorrows of the world, or from trials and tribulations, from physical pain or from natural death. Nothing of the kind. You will be liable to sickness and adversity in their manifold forms as other men are, but you will have this to comfort you in every dark distressing hour, that these light afflictions which are but for a season will come to you from a loving Father's gentle hand, with a gracious purpose, and they will be dealt out to you in weight and measure according to his judgment, while some sweet consolations will always be sent with them; and, above all, there is perpetual joy and perennial satisfaction in that man's heart who knows that he is right with God. Although his house may not be as he would have it, yet he has accepted God's way of reconciliation —he is reconciled by the blood of Christ—God loves him and he loves God; he is confident, therefore, that whether he live or die he must be blessed, because he is at peace with God. Oh! happy day, happy day, thrice happy day, when a man comes into this blessed state!

I have heard many regret that they have pursued the pleasures of sense and been fascinated with the follies of sin; but I never yet heard of one who had found the dear delights of faith pall on his taste. It has never yet fallen to my lot to attend a dying bed where I have heard a Christian regret that he put his trust in his Saviour; neither have I ever heard at any time of any who died believing in Jesus who has had to say, " Had I but served the world with half the zeal I served my God, I should have been a happier man." Oh, no! such bitter reflections on misspent time and misused talents befit the worldling, and the world's poets put it into the dying man's mouth in another form from that in which I gave it; for " what we might have been " and " what we might have done " make the sum of life's bewailing, when death in view makes such repentance unavailing. The Christian's satisfaction is, on the other hand, only shaded by the wish all feel that they had loved the Saviour more intensely, trusted him more confidently, and served him more diligently. Never have I heard any other kind of compunction and self-reproach. "Come along, then, friend, come along," they say to us, " what matters so long as you are happy?" I have often heard them say so. And let me say to you, if that is one of your mottoes, and you really do seek after happiness, you cannot do better than pay homage to the Son of God, end the awful rupture between you and your Creator, and henceforth put your trust in him.

One other motive I must mention. "Kiss the Son, lest he be angry, and ye perish from the way, when his wrath is kindled but a little." A striking expression! If Christ gets a little angry, men perish from the way. Then what must his great anger be? If his anger, kindled but a little, burns like devouring fire, and men perish from the way of life, and from all hope of salvation, what must his great wrath be! Is there a fear suggested here that anybody will provoke Christ to fiercer anger? There is; alas, there is! Shall I tell you the likeliest person to do it? Not, methinks, that abandoned sinner who has been born and bred in an immoral atmosphere, and has followed a vicious course to the present hour. To him I would say, "Come to Jesus, and he will wash you now and cleanse you from all your pollution." But the man I tremble for as most likely to make him swear in his wrath is such an one as I was, privileged with godly parents, watched with jealous eyes, scarcely ever permitted to mingle with questionable associates, warned not to listen to anything profane or licentious—taught the way of God from his youth up. In my case there came a time when the solemnities of eternity pressed upon me for a decision, and when a mother's tears and a father's supplications were offered to Heaven on my behalf. At

such a time, had I not been helped by the grace of
God, but had I been left alone to do violence to
conscience, and to struggle against conviction, I
might have been at this moment perhaps dead,
buried, and doomed, having through a course of
vice brought myself to my grave, or I might have
been as earnest a ringleader amongst the ungodly
as I now desire to be an eager champion for Christ
and his truth. When there is light given, when
one is not left to grope in darkness, when conscience is kept tender, a little provocation may
then very much anger Christ.

I am afraid some of you young people that are
growing up here stand in deep need of remonstrance. You have got good parents. You have
been instructed in the Scriptures from your infancy, and you have had a great many deep impressions while sitting in these pews listening to the
sound of the gospel; and yet you are playing with
them, you are trifling with them. Nothing bad
about you—so you think. You are not conscious
of having grossly violated any moral law. But
have you never understood that virtue is only tested
and proved by victory over temptation? Why,
even puppy dogs, however purely bred, are counted
of little value till they have endured and survived
a distemper to which they all are prone. So every
man must pass through trial before he can be accounted worthy. Talents, they tell us, are nur-
tured best in solitude, but character on life's tempestuous sea. I observe in the lessons drawn from

the life of James Nisbet, the publisher, an instance
much to the point.   Soon after he came to London
as a Scotch lad, a dissolute companion drew him
to the door of a house from which he shrunk
back with wholesome dread, nor dared to cross the
threshold.   To that fear of evil and to that refusal
to taste the pleasure of sin he traced the turning
point in the formation of a character which shed
some lustre on his generation and bequeathed some
lessons to the struggling youths who are seeking
to make headway in the workshops and warehouses
of this great metropolis.   If you once get a taste
for fleshly lusts you will be always thirsting after
them.   Then, instead of the hope we now cherish,
that we shall soon see you at your parents' side,
serving Christ—see you take your father's place,
young man, as a deacon or an elder in after years
—see you, young woman, grow up to be a matron
in the Church of God, bringing many others to the
Saviour—we may have to lament that the children
are not as the parents, and cry, " Woe is the day
that ever they were born."   I therefore want you to
decide, lest you perish from the way—from the way
of God and the way of righteousness—while his wrath
is kindled but a little, lest he say, " Let them alone,"
and throw the reins on your neck ; for if he should once
do that, woe worth the day!   Nothing can happen
worse to a man than to be left to himself.   Kiss
the Son, then.   Affectionately and earnestly do I
entreat you—not standing here *ex officio* to deliver
pious platitudes, but from my very soul, as though

I were your brother or father, I would say, young man, young woman, Kiss the Son *now.* Yield your heart up to Jesus now. Blessed are they that trust in him now. Oh! to-night, to-night, to-night—your first night in grace, or else your last night in hope! *To-night,* to-night. The clock has just struck; it seems to say, "To-night." God help you to say, "Ay, it shall be to-night, for God and for Christ!"

A Special Invitation.

All things are delivered unto me of my Father: and no man knoweth the Son, but the Father; neither knoweth any man the Father, save the Son, and he to whomsoever the Son will reveal him. Come unto me, all ye that labor and are heavy laden, and I will give you rest.—MATTHEW xi. 27, 28.

I HAVE often preached on the words—"Come unto me, all ye that labor and are heavy laden, and I will give you rest." There is such sweetness in the precept, such solace in the promise, that I could fain hope to preach from this melting invitation many times more. But I have no intention just now to repeat what I have said in any former discourse, or to follow the same vein of thought that we have previously explored. This kindly and gracious invitation needs only to be held up in different lights to give us different subjects of admiration. That it flowed like an anthem from our Saviour's lips we perceive: in what connection it was spoken we may properly inquire. He had just made some important disclosures as to the covenant relations that existed between himself and God the Father. This interesting revelation of heavenly truth becomes the basis upon which

(108)

he offers an invitation to the toiling and oppressed children of men, and he assigns it as a reason why they should immediately avail themselves of his succor. Such is the line of discourse I propose now to follow. Kindly understand me that I want to deal with the hearts and consciences of the unconverted, and, in the power of the Holy Spirit, to plead with them that they may at once go to Jesus and find rest unto their souls. I shall require no stories or anecdotes, no figures or metaphors, to illustrate the urgent necessity of the sinner and the generous bounty of the Saviour. We will make it as plain as a pikestaff and as sharp as a sword, with the intention of driving straight at our point. Time is precious, your time especially, for you may not have many days in which to seek the Lord. The matter is urgent. Oh, that every laboring, weary sinner here might at once come to Jesus and find that rest which the Saviour expresses himself as so willing to give! With all simplicity, then, let me explain to you the way of salvation, "Come unto me, all ye that labor and are heavy laden."

The way to be saved is to come to Jesus. To come to Jesus means to pray to him, to trust in him, to rely upon him. Each man who trusts in another may be said to come to that other for help. Thus to trust in Jesus is to come to him. In order to do this I must give up all reliance upon myself, or anything I could do or have done, or anything I can feel or do feel. Nor must I put the slightest dependence upon anything that a priest can do for me. I must cease from creature helps and carnal rites, to rest myself upon Jesus. That is what my Saviour means when he says, "Come unto me." The exhortation is very personal. "Come unto me," says he. He saith not, come to my ministers to consult them, nor come to my sacraments to observe them, nor come to my Bible to study its teaching—interesting and advantageous as under some circumstances any or all of these counsels might be; but he invites us in the sweetest tone of friendship, saying, "Come unto me." For a poor sinner this is the truest means of succor. Let him resort to the blessed Lord himself. To trust in a crucified Saviour is the way of salvation. Let him leave everything else and fly away to Christ, and look at his dear wounds as he hangs upon the cross. I am afraid many people are detained from Christ by becoming entangled in the meshes of doctrine. Some, with heterodox doctrine, distract themselves; others, with orthodox doctrine, content themselves. They think that they have advanced far enough. They flatter their souls that they have ascertained the truth! But the fact is, it is not the truth as a letter which saves any body. It is the truth as a person—it is Jesus Christ, who is the way, the truth, and the life, whom we need to apprehend. Our confidence must rest entirely upon him. "Come unto me," saith Jesus, "Come unto me and I will give you rest."

The exhortation is in the present tense. "Come"

now; do not wait; do not tarry; do not lie at the pool of ordinances, but come unto me; come now at once, immediately, just where you are, just as you are. Wherever the summons finds you, rise without parley, without an instant's delay. "Come." I know that the human mind is very ingenious in framing excuses and it is especially perverse when its own destruction is threatened. For some cause or other it will evade this simple call. "Surely," says one, "there must be something to do besides that." Nay, nothing else is to be done. No preliminaries are requisite. The whole way of salvation is to trust in Jesus. Trust him now. That done, you are saved. Rely upon his finished work. Know that he has mediated on your behalf. Commit thy sinful self to his saving grace. A change of heart shall then be yours. All else that you need he will supply.

> " There is life in a look at the crucified One,
> There is life at this moment for thee."

So sweet an invitation demands a spontaneous acceptance. Come just as you are. "Come unto me," saith Christ. He does not say, "Come when you have washed and cleansed yourself." Rather should you come *to be* cleansed. He does not say, "Come when you have clothed yourself and made yourself beautiful with good works." Come *to be made* beautiful in a better righteousness than you can weave. Come naked, and let him gird thee with fine linen, cover thee with silk, and deck thee with jewels. He does not say, "Come when your conscience is tender, come when your heart is penitent, when your soul is full of loathing for sin, and your mind is enlightened with knowledge and enlivened with joy. But ye that labor, ye that are heavy laden, he bids you to come as you are. Come oppressed with your burdens, begrimed with your labors, dispirited with your toils. If the load that bends you double to the earth be upon your shoulders, just come as your are. Take no plea in your mouth but this—he bids you come. That shall suffice as a warrant for your coming, and a security for your welcome. If Jesus Christ bids you, who shall say you nay?

He puts the matter very exclusively. "Come unto me, all ye that labor and are heavy laden." Do nothing else but come to him. Do you want rest; come to him for it. The old proverb hath it that "betwixt two stools we come to the ground." Certainly, if we trust partly in Christ and partly in ourselves, we shall fall lower than the ground. We shall sink into the pit of despair. "Come unto me" is the whole gospel. "Come unto *me*." Mix nothing with it. Acknowledge no other obedience. Obey Christ and him alone. "Come unto me." You cannot go in two opposite directions. Let your tottering footsteps bend their way to him alone. Mix anything with him, and the possibility of your salvation is gone. Yours be the happy resolve—

> "Nothing in my hand I bring:
> Simply to thy cross I cling."

This must be your cry if you are to be accepted at all. Come, then, ye that labor, ye horny-handed sons of toil. Come ye to Jesus. He invites you. Ye that stew and toil for wealth, ye merchants, with your many cares, laborers ye are. He bids you come. Ye students, anxious for knowledge, chary of sleep, burning out the midnight oil; ye labor with exhausted brains, therefore come. Come, ye ambitious men who have vexed your souls while vainly struggling after fame. Ye pleasure-seekers, come. Perhaps there is no harder toil than the toil of the man who courts recreation and thinks he is taking his ease. Come, ye that labor in any form or fashion; come to Jesus—to Jesus alone. And ye that are heavy laden; ye whose official duties are a burden; ye whose domestic cares are a burden; ye whose daily tasks are a burden; ye whose shame and degradation are a burden; all ye that are heavy laden, come and welcome. If I attach no exclusive spiritual signification to these terms, it is because there is nothing in the chapter that would warrant such a restriction. Had Christ said, "*some* of you that labor and are heavy laden may come," I would have said "*some*" too. Howbeit he has not said "some," but "*all* that labor and are heavy laden." It is wonderful how people twist this text about. They alter the sense by misquoting the words. They say, "Come, ye that are weary and heavy laden." After this manner some have even preached upon it. Others have attempted to prove that the words were intended

to define a character rather than to describe a condition, so they shut out some of those who labor
from the kind invitation. But let the passage stand
in its own simplicity. Doubtless any sinner here,
who can say, "I labor," though he cannot say *spiritually* labor, may come on the bare warrant of the
word as he finds it written here, and he will not
be disappointed of the mercy promised. Christ
will not reject him. Himself hath said it, " Him
that cometh to me I will in no wise cast out."
And any man that is heavy laden, even though it
may not be a spiritual burden that oppresses him,
yet if he comes heavy laden to Christ he certainly
shall find relief. That were a wonder without pre-
cedent or parallel, such as was never witnessed on
earth throughout all the generations of men, that
a soul should come to Jesus, be rebuffed, and told
by him, " I never called you; I never meant you;
you are not the character; you may not come."
Hear, O heaven! witness, O earth! such a thing
was never heard of. No, nor ever shall it be heard
of in time or in eternity. That any sinner should
come to the Saviour by mistake is preposterous.
That Jesus should say to him, " Go your way; I
never called for you," is incredible. How can ye
thus libel the sinner's friend? Come, ye needy—
come, ye helpless—come, ye simple—come, ye penitent—come, ye impenitent—come, ye who are the
very vilest of the vile. If you do but come, Jesus
Christ will receive you, welcome you, rejoice over
you, and verify to you his thrice blessed promise,

"Him that cometh to me I will in no wise cast out."

Now to the tug of war. It shall be my main endeavor to press this invitation upon you, my good friends, by the arguments which the Saviour used.

Kindly look at the text. Read the words for yourselves. Do you not see that the reason why you are solemnly bidden to come to Christ is because he is the appointed mediator? "All things are delivered unto me of my Father." God, even the Father, your Creator, against whom you have transgressed, has appointed our Lord Jesus Christ to be the way of access for a sinner to himself. He is no amateur Saviour. He has not thrust himself into the place officiously. He is officially delegated. In times of distress, every man is at liberty to do his best for the public welfare; but the officer commissioned by his sovereign is armed with a supreme right to give counsel or to exercise command. Away there in Bengal, if there are any dying of famine, and I have rice, I may distribute it of my own will at my own charge. But the commissioner of the district has a special warranty which I do not possess; he has a function to discharge; it is his business, his vocation; he is authorized by the government, and responsible to the government to do it. So the Lord Jesus Christ has not only a deep compassion of heart for the necessities of men, but he has God's authority to support him. The Father delivered all things into his hands, and appointed him to be a Saviour. All that Christ teaches has this superlative sanction. He teaches you nothing of his own conjecture. " What I have heard of the Father," he saith, "that reveal I unto you." The gospel is not a scheme of his suggestion. He reveals it fresh from the heart of God. Remember that the promises Christ makes are not merely his surmises, but they are promises with the stamp of the court of heaven upon them. Their truth is guaranteed by God. It is not possible they should fail. Sooner might heaven and earth pass away than one word of his fall flat to the ground. Your Saviour, O sinner—your only Saviour—is one whose teachings, whose invitations, and whose promises have the seal royal of the King of kings upon them. What more do you want?

Moreover, the Father has given all things into his hands in the sense of government. Christ is king everywhere. God has appointed Christ to be a mediatorial prince over all of us,—I say over us all,—not merely over those who accept his sovereignty, but even over the ungodly. He hath given him power over all flesh, that he may give eternal life to as many as he has given him. It is of no use your rebelling against Christ, and saying, " We will not have him." That is an old cry, " We will not have this man to reign over us." How read ye in the second Psalm? " Why do the heathen rage, and the people imagine a vain thing? The kings of the earth set themselves, and the rulers take counsel together, against the Lord, and against his anointed. Yet have I set my King upon my holy hill of Zion." Christ is supreme. You will have either to submit to his sceptre willingly, or else to be broken by his iron rod like a potter's vessel. Which shall it be? Thou must either bow or be broken; make your choice. You must bend or break. God help you wisely to resolve and gratefully relent. Has the Father appointed Christ to stand between him and his sinful creatures? Has he put the government upon his shoulders, and given him a name called Wonderful, Counsellor, the mighty God, the everlasting King? Is he Emmanuel, God with us, in God's stead? With what reverence are we bound to receive him! Moreover, all the treasures of wisdom and knowledge, of mercy and goodness, are laid up in Christ. You recollect when Pharaoh had corn to sell in Egypt, what reply he made to all who applied to him: "Go to Joseph." It would have been no use saying, "Go to Joseph," if Joseph had not the keys of the garner; but he had, and there was no garner that could be opened in Egypt unless Joseph lent the key. In like manner, all the garners of mercy are under the lock and key of Jesus Christ, "who openeth, and no man shutteth; who shutteth, and no man openeth." When you require any bounty or benefit of God, you must repair to Jesus for it. The Father has put all power into his hands. He has committed the entire work of mercy to his Son, that through him, as the appointed mediator, all blessings should be dispensed to the praise of the glory of his grace, wherein he hath made us accepted in the Beloved. Now, sirs, do you want to be saved? I charge you to say whether you do or not; for if you care not for salvation, why should I labor among you? If you choose your own ruin, you need no counsel; you will make sure of it by your own neglect. But if you want salvation, Christ is the only authorized person in heaven or earth who can save you. "There is no other name given among men whereby we must be saved." The Father hath delivered all things into his keeping. He is the authorized Saviour. "Come unto me," then, "all ye that labor and are heavy laden."

This argument is further developed by another consideration: Christ is a well-furnished mediator. "*All things* are delivered unto me," he said, "of my Father." Sum up all that the sinner wants, and you will find him able to supply you with all. You want pardon: it is delivered unto Christ of the Father. You want a change of heart: it is delivered unto Christ of the Father. You want righteousness in which you may be accepted: Christ has it. You want to be purged from the love of sin: Christ can do it. You want wisdom, righteousness, sanctification, and redemption. They are all in Christ. You are afraid that if you start on the road to heaven, you cannot hold on. Persevering grace is in Christ. You think you will never be perfect; but perfection is in Christ, for all believers, being saints of God and servants of

Christ, are complete in him. Between hell-gate and heaven-gate there is nothing a sinner can need that is not treasured up in his blessed person. "It pleased the Father that in him should all fulness dwell." He is "*full* of grace and truth." Oh sinner, I wish I could constrain you to feel as I do now, that, had I never come to Christ before, I must come to him now, just now. Directly I understand that "*Thou, O Christ, art all I want*," I most surely discover that "*More than all in thee I find.*" Why then should I not come? Is it because I want something before I come? Make the question your own. Where are you going to seek it? All things are delivered unto Christ. To whom should you go for aught you crave? Is there another who can aid you when Christ is in possession of all? Do you want a tender conscience—come to Christ for it. Do you want to feel the guilt of your sin—come to Christ to be made sensitive to its shame. Are you just what you ought not to be—come to Christ to be made what you ought to be, for everything is in Christ. Is there anything that can be obtained elsewhere and brought to him? The invitation to you is founded upon the explanation that accompanies it. "All things are delivered unto me of my Father:" therefore "Come unto me, all ye that labor and are heavy laden, and I will give you rest." The argument is so exclusive, that it only wants a willing mind to make it welcome. Only let God the Holy Spirit bless the word, and sinners will come to Christ; for unto him shall the gathering of the people be.

Now note the next argument. Come to Christ, ye laboring ones, because he is an inconceivably great Mediator. Where do I get that? Why, from this—that no man knows him but the Father. So great is he, so good, so full of all manner of precious store for needy sinners. No man knows him but the Father. He is too excellent for our puny understanding to estimate his worth. None but the infinite God can comprehend his value as a Saviour. Has any one here been saying, "Christ cannot save me; I am such a big sinner." You don't know him, my friend, you don't know him. You are measuring him according to your little insignificant notions. High as the heavens are above the earth, so high are his ways above your ways, and his thoughts than your thoughts. You don't know him, sinner, and no one does know him but his Father. Why, some of us who have been saved by him, thought when we saw the blessed mystery of his substitutionary sacrifice that we knew all about him; but we have found that he grows upon our view the nearer we approach, and the more we contemplate him. Some of you have now been Christians for thirty or forty years, and you know much more of him than you used to do; but you do not know him yet; your eyes are dazzled by his brightness; you do not know him. And the happy spirits before the throne who have been there, some of

them, three or four thousand years, have hardly
begun to spell the first letter of his name. He is
too grand and too good for them to comprehend.
I believe it will be the growing wonder in eternity
to find out how precious a Christ, how powerful,
how immutable—in a word, how divine a Christ
he is in whom we have trusted. Only the infinite
can understand the infinite. "God only knows
the love of God," and only the Father understands
the Son. Oh, I wish I had a week in which to
talk on this, instead of a few minutes! You want
a great Saviour? Well, here he is. Nobody can
depict him, or describe him, or even imagine him,
except the infinite God himself. Come, then, poor
sinner, sunken up to your neck in crime, black as
hell—come unto him. "Come, all ye that labor
and are heavy laden," and prove him to be your
Saviour. The fact that no one knows how great
a Saviour he is except his Father may encourage
you.

Now for another argument. Come to him because he is an infinitely wise Saviour. He is a
Mediator who understands both persons on whose
behalf he mediates. He understands you. He has
summed and reckoned you up, and he has made
you out to be a heap of sin and misery, and nothing else. The glory of it is that he understands
God whom you have offended, for it is written—
"Neither knoweth any man the Father, save the
Son," and he knows the Father. Oh, what a mercy
that is to have one to go before God for me who

knows him intimately. He knows his Father's will; he knows his Father's wrath. No man knows it but himself. He has suffered it. He knows his Father's love. He alone can feel it—such love as God felt for sinners. He knows how his Father's wrath has been turned away by his precious blood; he knows the Father as a Judge whose anger no longer burns against those for whom the atonement has been made. He knows the Father's heart. He knows the Father's secret purposes. He knows the Father's will is that whosoever seeth the Son and believeth on him shall have everlasting life. He knows the decrees of God, and yet he says, "Come unto me, all ye that labor and are heavy laden, and I will give you rest." There is nothing in that contrary to the decrees of God; for Jesus knows what the decrees are, and he would not speak in contradiction to them. He knows God's requirements. Sinner, whatever the things be that God requires of you, Christ knows what they are, and he is ready to meet them. "The law is holy, and just, and good," and Jesus knows it, for the law is in his heart. Justice is very stern, and Jesus knows it, for Jesus has felt the edge of the sword of justice, and knows all about it. He is fully equipped for the discharge of his mediatorial office, and those that put their trust in him shall find that he will bear them through. Often, when a prisoner at the bar has a barrister who understands his work, and is perfectly competent for the defence, his friends say to him—"Your case is safe, for if there is a

man in England who can get you through, it is
that man." But my Master is an advocate who
never lost a case. He has a plea at the throne of
God that never failed yet. Give him,—oh, give
him your cause to plead, nor doubt the Father's
grace. Poor sinner, he is so wise an advocate that
you may well come to him, and he will give you
rest. But I must not weary you, although there is
a fulness of matter on which I might enlarge.

With one other argument I conclude. He is an
indispensable Mediator. The only Mediator, so the
text says. "Neither knoweth any man the Father,
save the Son." Christ knows the Father; no one
else knows him, save the Son. There is none other
that can approach unto God. It is Jesus Christ for
your Saviour, or else for you there is no Saviour at
all. Salvation is in no other; and if you will not
have Christ, neither can you have salvation. Observe how that is. It is certain that no man knows
God except Christ. It is equally certain that no
man can come to God except by Christ. He says
it peremptorily: "No man cometh to the Father but
by me." Not less certain is it that no man can
please the Father except through Christ, for "without faith it is impossible to please him." No faith
is worth having except the grace that is founded
and based upon the Lord Jesus Christ, and him
only. Oh, then, souls, since you are shut up to it
by a blessed necessity, say at once, "I will to the
gracious Prince approach, and take Jesus to be my
all in all." If I might hope you would do this early,

I could go back to my home and retire to my bed, praising God for the work that was done, and the result that was achieved. Let us reiterate again and again the gospel we have to declare, the very essence of the gospel it is which we proclaim. Trust your souls with Jesus and your souls are saved. He suffered in the room, and place, and stead of all that trust him. If you rely upon him by an act of simple faith, the simplest act in all the world, immediately you so rely you are forgiven, your transgressions are blotted out for his name's sake. He stands in spirit among us at this good hour, and says, "Come unto me, all ye that labor and are heavy laden;" and he gives you these arguments, which ought to convince you. I pray they may. He is an authorized Saviour, and a well furnished Saviour. He is the friend of God and the friend of man. God grant you may accept him, and find the boon and benison which he alone can bestow.

A Merciful Embassy.

Now then we are ambassadors for Christ, as though God did beseech you by us: we pray you in Christ's stead, be ye reconciled to God."—2 CORINTHIANS v. 20.

THERE has long been war between man and his Maker. Our federal head Adam, threw down the gauntlet in the garden of Eden. The trumpet was heard to ring through the glades of Paradise, the trumpet which broke the silence of peace and disturbed the song of praise. From that day forward, until now, there has been no truce, no treaty between God and man by nature. The creature has been at variance with his Creator. His heart has been enmity towards God. He would not be reconciled to his rightful Sovereign. Never in the heart of any natural man, unless divine grace has put it there, has a desire to re-establish peace been felt or entertained. If any of you long to be at peace with your Maker, it is because his Spirit has made you long for it. Left to yourselves you would go from conflict to conflict, from struggle to struggle, and perpetuate the encounter, till it ended in your eternal destruction. But though man will not make terms with God, nor sue for peace at his hands, God shows his unwillingness any longer to be at war with man. That he anxiously desires man to be reconciled unto him, he proves, by taking the first step. He himself sends his ambassadors. He does not invite them from the other party—that indeed were grace—but he sends ambassadors, and he commands those ambassadors to be very earnest, and to plead with men, to pray them, to beseech them that they would be reconciled to God. I take this to be a sure pledge that there is love in the heart of God. Why, at the very announcement of these tidings, the rebellious sinner's ears should be open! It were enough to make him say, "I will harken diligently; I will hear what God the Lord shall speak; for if it be true that he takes the first steps towards me, and that he is willing to make up this deadly quarrel, his meekness and his majesty alike forbid that I should turn away; I will even now hear and attend to all that God shall speak to my soul." May he bless the message to you, that you may be reconciled to him without a moment's delay. John Bunyan puts it plainly enough. "If a certain king be besieging a town, and he sends out the herald with a trumpet to threaten the inhabitants that if they do not give up the town, he will hang every man of them, then straightway they come to the walls and give him back a reviling answer; they swear that they will fight it out, and will never surrender to such a tyrant. But if he sends an embassage with a white flag to tell them that if they will but surrender and yield to their lawful king, he will pardon every one of them, even the very vilest of them will relent." Then, saith honest John, "do they not come trembling over the walls, and throw their gates wide open to receive their gracious monarch." Would that such a result might be accomplished to-night! While I speak of the great grace of this Prince of Peace, who now sends his ambassadors to the rebellious, may some rebel say, "Then I will be at peace with him; I will hold out no longer. Such irresistible love as this has dissolved my heart, resolved my choice, and constrained my allegiance."

Well now, let us speak awhile of *the Ambassadors—the Commission* with which they are entrusted,—the *duty* they have to discharge,—and close with a question—*What then?*

I. First, then, we have to speak of Ambassadors. Welcome messengers are they!

All nations, with one accord, have agreed to honor ambassadors. Strange, then, that all nations and all people should have conspired to dishonor the ambassadors of God! Which of God's ambassadors in the olden time was not persecuted, rejected, or slain? Were they not stoned, beheaded, sawn asunder? How continually they were maltreated, and made to wander about in sheep-skins and goat-skins, though of them the world was not worthy! But there have been some men to whom the ambassadors of God have always been welcome. The men whom God had ordained to eternal life; those on whose behalf, from before all worlds, he had made an effectual covenant of peace. From them the ambassadors get a hearty welcome. Standing here to preach as an ambassador, I shall get but little attention from some of my audience. The proclamation of mercy will sound common-place to many. They will turn on their heel and say, there is nothing in it. But, mark you, the ambassador of God may be very welcome to some of you, who have bitterly felt your estrangement, to some whose hearts are prepared by a sense of ruin for the good tidings of redemption; to some in whom the secret mystery of predestination begins to work by the overt energy of effectual calling. These shall find their souls gently but surely drawn to hail the proclamation of mercy that shall be made, and they will say, " How beautiful upon the mountains are the feet of them that bring glad tidings of peace, that publish salvation!"

Ambassadors are always specially welcome to a people who are engaged in a war which is beyond their strength, when their resources are exhausted, and the peril of defeat is imminent. If some tiny little principality has ventured to rebel against a great empire, when it is absolutely certain that its villages will be consumed, its provinces ravaged, and that all its power will be crushed, ambassadors are pretty sure to receive a cordial welcome. Ah, man! thou hast bid defiance to the King of heaven, whose power is irresistible; by whom rocks are thrown down; whose voice breaketh the cedars of Lebanon; whose hand controlleth the great deep sea. He it is who bindeth the clouds with a cord, and girdleth the earth with a belt! Angels that excel in strength cannot stand against him. From the lofty battlements of heaven he hurled down Satan, the great archangel, and the mighty host of rebellious morning stars! How canst thou stand against him; shall the stubble contend with the fire? Shall the potter's vessel resist the rod of iron? What are they but a moth easily crushed beneath his finger! The breath is in thy nostrils, and that is not thine own; how then canst thou, poor mortal, contend with him who only hath immortality. With a puff of his mouth he can drive thee away like chaff. Thou art broken more rapidly than a sear leaf by the wind! How canst thou venture to be at war with One who has heaven and earth at his command, who holds the keys of hell and of death, and who has Tophet as his source of ammunition against thee? Listen to his thunders, and let thy blood curdle! Let his lightning flash, and how art thou amazed! How then canst thou stand against the greatness of his power, or endure the terror of his wrath? Happy for thee that terms of peace are proclaimed in your ears. God is willing to cease the warfare; he would not have thee be his adversary. Wilt thou not gladly accept what he proposeth to thee? Never, surely, was war more charged

with disaster than that into which thou hast madly
rushed. An ambassador is always welcome when
the people have begun to feel the victorious force of
the king. Yonder province has already yielded. Certain cities have been taken by the sword and given
up to be sacked. Now the poor, miserable inhabitants are glad enough to get peace. They dread
the foot of the conqueror since they have felt its
weight. Doubtless there are some here present
who have known the power of God in their conscience. Perhaps he has scared you with visions
and frightened you with dreams. Though it be
but the voice of a man that you heard, yet the law
has been very terrible to you, and now you find
no pleasure in your pleasures; no joy in your joys.
God has begun to break your bones with conviction; he has made you feel that sin is a bitter
thing; he has made you drunken with wormwood,
and broken your teeth with gravel stones. He
has brought you down, as the fool in the hundred
and seventh Psalm, by affliction and by labor, and
you are crying out in anguish, "God be merciful
to me a sinner!" Ay, doubtless, you that have
once felt the weight of God's hand upon your conscience, will rejoice to hear that there is an embassage of peace sent to you.

An ambassador is likewise always welcome to
those who are laboring under a fear of total and
speedy destruction. If none of you are in that
plight, I remember when I was, when I thought
every day it was a marvel of mercies that I was

kept alive, and wondered as I woke at morn that I was not lifting up my eyes with Dives in hell. Everything about Christ was precious to me then! I think I would have stood in the most crowded chapel, nor would I have been weary had I sat upon the hardest seat; no length of service would have wearied me, might I but have had an inkling that God would peradventure have mercy upon my soul. My eyes were full of tears. My soul was faint with watching, and I would have kissed the feet of any man who would have told me the way of salvation. But, alas, it seemed as if no man cared for my soul, till at last God blessed an humble instrument to give light to his poor dark child. Hence, I know that the news of mercy will be exceedingly welcome to you who stand upon the jaws of hell, fearing that the gates will soon be bolted upon you, and that you will be forever lost. You will be ready to cry, like our Methodist friends, "Hallelujah! Glory! Hallelujah! Bless the Lord!" whilst you hear that God still sends an embassage of peace to your soul.

Most acceptable, too, is a messenger of peace if the people know that he brings no hard terms. When a certain king sent to the inhabitants of a town that he would make peace with them provided he put out their right eyes and cut off their right hands, I am sure the tidings must have caused the utmost consternation; such an ambassador could not expect a cordial welcome. But there are no hard terms in the gospel. In fact, there are no terms, no conditions at all. It is an unconditional peace which God makes with men. It is a gospel which asks nothing of men, but gives them everything. The Lord saith: "My oxen and my fatlings are killed; all things are ready, come ye to the supper." There is nothing for man to get ready; all things are prepared. The terms—if I must use a word I do not like—are simple and easy. "Believe, and live;" not "Do, and live;" not "Feel this, and live;" but simply, "Believe, and live." With what joy should a rebellious sinner hear the voice of the ambassador who brings no hard conditions from God.

And should not the fame of the King increase the zest with which the embassage is received? Comes it not from him that cannot lie! No temporary peace is proposed that may presently be broken, but a peace that shall stand for ever and ever. No temporary armistice, no brief interlude between the deeds of battle do we herald. Peace; eternal, unbroken peace; peace that shall abide through life and outlive death, and endure throughout eternity, we testify and make known to you.

This peace is proclaimed to all men. It is proclaimed without exception. "Whosoever believeth in the Lord Jesus Christ shall be saved." None are excluded hence but those who do themselves exclude. Such an ambassador bringing such a message must surely be a welcome messenger from his God.

II. What now is the commission of peace which

God has entrusted us to proclaim? The words are concise, the sense is transparent. "To wit, that God was in Christ, reconciling the world unto himself, not imputing their trespasses unto them; and hath committed unto us the word of reconciliation." Let us open the commission. It lies in a nutshell. Thus saith the Lord of hosts, "As I live, saith the Lord God, I have no pleasure in the death of the wicked; but that the wicked turn from his way and live." "Come now, and let us reason together saith the Lord: though your sins be as scarlet, they shall be as white as snow; though they be red like crimson, they shall be as wool." Our commission begins with the announcement that God is love, that he is full of pity and compassion, that he is desirous to receive his creature back, that he willeth to forgive, and that he electeth, if it be consistent with the high attribute of his justice, to accept even the most rebellious, and to put them amongst his children. Our commission goes on to disclose the manner as well as the motive of mercy. Inasmuch as God is love, he, in order to remove all difficulties in the way of pardoning rebels, has been pleased to give his only begotten Son that he might stand in the room, place, and stead of those whom God has chosen; their sins he engaged to take; to carry their sorrows; and to make an atonement on their behalf. Thus the justice of God should be satisfied, and his love flow over to the human race. We declare, therefore, that God has given Christ, and he has made it a faithful saying, and worthy of all acceptation, that he came into the world to save sinners, even the very chief. Christ the Son of God has become man. Cheerfully and willingly he took upon himself our nature; veiled the form of Deity in a humble garb of clay; was born of the Virgin Mary, lived a life of holiness, and died a death of sacrifice. Through this marvellous death of the man, the God, Christ Jesus, God is at peace with his people. The peace is made already, for he is our peace. God is at peace with every man for whom Jesus died. Christ was punished for their sins. Justice cannot punish twice for one offence. Christ the substitute being punished, the sinner cannot be amenable for his own offences. Those for whom Jesus died go free. The proclamation is that God is willing to be reconciled, that he is reconciled. It is an announcement, not that you may have peace merely, but that peace is made with God by Jesus Christ for you—full peace, without condition, not half-made, but wholly made; the penalty being completely paid to the last doit, and the sacrifice completly slaughtered till the last drop of blood had expiated the last offence.

But the proclamation needs something more to give us any satisfaction. Are there any tidings in it for you and me? Well, our message goes on to announce that whosoever in the wide world will come to Jesus Christ, and commit his cause to him as Redeemer, Saviour, and Friend, shall forthwith be at peace with God, receive full pardon for all offences, and be welcomed as a favorite of the Most

High. He shall know that for him Jesus Christ did die in his stead, and as surety did stand for him when he appeared before God. From condemnation he is therefore free, of salvation he is therefore sure. This proclamation, I say, is to be made universally. Though every man will not be blessed by it, the preacher cannot discriminate between those who must and those who will not inherit the blessing. Though only some will accept it, the preacher is not warranted in showing any partiality. It is the Holy Spirit's work to impress the Word on the conscience, and to arouse the conscience by the Word. As for us, we are willing enough to turn our faces to the north or to the south, to the east or to the west. Gladly would we proclaim it to the red man who hunts the savannahs of America, to the swarthy man who never heard the name of Christ before, or to the white man who has often heard but never heeded it. The same message, that God has accepted Christ as a substitute for every man that will believe in Christ, and that whosoever trusts Christ to save him is in that moment saved, will suffice for all. Yea, we would tell them that before the sinner does trust Christ he is reconciled unto God by his death, because the atonement which he offered had been accepted, and there was peace forestalled between God and that sinner. What a message I have to present! What a proclamation I have to make! Nothing is necessary on your part: God expects nothing of you to merit his esteem, or to enhance the value of his gift. If repentance be indispensable, he is prepared to give it you. If a tender heart be needed, he is ready to give you a heart of flesh. If you feel that you have a heart of stone, he has engaged to take it away. Does your guilt oppress you, he says,—"I will sprinkle clean water, water of pure fountains, upon them, and they shall be cleansed from all their filthiness, and from all their uncleanness will I save them." Know all men that there is no exception made. When Charles II. came back to England there was an amnesty, except for certain persons, and these were mentioned by name —Hugh Peters and others were proscribed; but there is no exception here. I find not any traitors singled out and denounced by name. I have to proclaim an indemnity of such universal import that it is indiscriminate, "Whosoever believeth on him shall never perish, but shall have everlasting life."

Moreover, there is no exception made in my commission to any form of sin—unless it be the sin against the Holy Ghost—which carries its own evidence as well as its consequence. Those to whom I now speak, if they feel any drawing of heart towards God have not committed that mortal crime. Murder, theft, forgery, felony, fornication, adultery, and covetousness, which is idolatry—black and hideous as is the catalogue—here is pardon for the whole. Ransack the kennels, however filthy; rake the slums, however odious; drag out the abominations of the age, however degrading; here is pardon not only possible or probable, but positive. Bring a man here who has stained himself crimson all over with every sort of infamy, though it be not the lapse of an hour, but the habit of a life, yet God is still able to forgive. Jesus Christ is able to save to the uttermost them that come unto God by him.

I do not know whether you find it very good to hear the proclamation, but I do know that I feel it most gratifying to utter it. Thrice happy am I to have such an announcement to make to rebels. Unwonted hearers, listen to my voice. By what strange chance have yon reckless, heedless, unconverted souls mingled with this throng of worshippers? Not often do you darken the floor of a place of worship. You hardly know how you were led to come in hither. To what depths of sin have you run, to what extremities of iniquity you have gone! You marvel to find yourself in the company of God's people. But since you are here, give heed to the message: "Thus saith the Lord, I have blotted out like a cloud thine iniquities, and like a thick cloud thy sins. Return unto me, for I am married unto thee. I have given blood to redeem thee. Return, O wandering child of man; return, return, and I will have mercy upon thee, for I am God, and not man."

III. Having thus opened my commission, I will endeavor to perform a very solemn duty. My text supplies me with a warrant. It says:—"As though God did beseech you by us: we pray you in Christ's stead, be ye reconciled to God." Then it seems we have not merely to read our commission, but we have to beseech you to accept it. Why should we beseech you? Is it not because you are rational creatures, not automata; men, not machines? A machine might be compelled to perform functions without persuasion, but the Spirit of God often acts upon the heart of man by the sound arguments and affectionate entreaties of his servants whom he commissions. We are to beseech you because your hearts are so hard that you are prone to defy God's power, and resist his grace. There fore we pray you to put down your weapons. We are to beseech you because you are unbelieving, and will not credit the tidings. You say it is too good to be true that God will have mercy on such as you are. Therefore we are to put our hand on you, to go down on our knees to you, and to beseech you not to put away this blessed embassy. We are to beseech you because you are so proud and self-satisfied that you will sooner follow your own right-eousness and cling to your own works than accept a peace already sealed and ratified and now freely proffered to you for acceptance and acknowledgment. We are to beseech you because you are care-less. You give little heed to what is spoken. You will go your way and forget all our proclamations; therefore are we to press you urgently, instantly, importunately, and to beseech you as when a mo-ther pleadeth for her child's life, as when a condemned criminal beseeches the judge to have pity on him; so are we to beseech you.

I think I never feel so conscious of my own

weakness as when I have to ply you thus with exhortations. Oh, there have been a few times in my ministry when I could with flowing eyes beseech you to be reconciled to God, but these dry eyes of mine are not so often fountains of tears as I could wish. We need such an one as Richard Baxter to dilate upon this last part of the text. Perhaps we could handle the former part better than he, but he could handle this last far better than we can. Oh, how he would have summoned you by the terrible reality of things to come! With what glaring eyes and seething words he would say, "Oh, men! turn ye, turn ye, why will ye die? By such need of a Saviour as you will feel in the pangs of parting life, when the pulsings shall be few and feeble, till with a gasp you shall expire; by the resurrection when you will wake up, if not in his likeness, to everlasting shame and contempt; by the judgment-seat, where your sins shall be published, and you shall be called to account for the deeds done in the body; by the dread decree which casteth into the pit forever those that repent not; by the heaven you will lose, and by the hell into which you will fall; by eternity, that dread eternity whose years never waste; by the wrath to come, the burning indignation of which shall never cool; by the immortality of your own souls, by the perils you now run, by the promises you despise, by the provocations you multiply, by the penalties you accumulate, we do beseech you to be reconciled to God." Fly to Jesus. Call upon his name.

Trust him; his word; his work; his goodness and his grace. This is the way of reconciliation. Bow the knee and kiss the Son. We do conjure you to do so. Acquaint yourselves now with God and be at peace with him.

My text hangs like a crushing weight upon my soul at this moment. It is awful in its grandeur, and it is majestically full of divine love. I must read the words again in your hearing. Oh, that the sense might break on your understanding! We are to beseech you as though God did beseech you, and we are to do it in Christ's stead. You see, God speaks when his ambassadors speak. I wonder; oh I wonder; whether I have brain enough to compass the thought of how God would beseech you to be reconciled! 'Tis the Father's own self pleading with his prodigal son. Can you imagine the father in the parable going after his son, and finding him in rags feeding swine? Can you conceive him saying "My son, my dear son, come back! come back, and I will forgive you all!" You think you hear that son saying to his father, "Get you gone, I will not hear of it," till his father says,—"My dear son, why will you prefer the company of swine to your father's house? Why will you wear rags when you might be clothed in the best robe? Why will you starve in a far off country when my house shall be full of feasting on your return?" What if that son should utter some indignant word, and tell his father to his face he would never go back. Oh! I think I see the venerable, loving man falling on his son's neck and kissing him, in his filth just as he is—(for "great is the love wherewith he loved us when we were dead in trespasses and sins!")—and he says to the rebel that insults him and resents his tenderness—"My dear son, you must come back; I must have you; I cannot be without you. I must have you; come back!" In such style ought we to plead with men. Ah then, I cannot plead with you as I would. As though God himself, your offended Maker, came to you now as he did to Adam in the cool of the day, and said to you—"Oh! return to me, for I have loved thee with an everlasting love," even so, as though God spoke, would I woo you, ye chiefest sinners, to return to him.

You know, dear friends, that the great God did send another ambassador, and that great ambassador was Christ. Now, the apostle says that we, the ministers, are ambassadors for Christ in Christ's stead. Christ is no more an ambassador; he has gone to heaven; we stand in his stead to the sons of men, not to make peace, but to proclaim it. What! am I then to speak in Christ's stead! But how can I picture my Lord Jesus standing here? Alas, my imagination is not equal to the task. Would that I had sympathy enough with him to put myself in his case so as to use his words. Methinks I see him looking at this great throng as he looked at the inhabitants of Jerusalem. He turns his head round to these galleries, and about yonder aisles, and at last he bursts into a flood of tears, saying—"How often would I have gathered thy children together, even as a hen gathereth her chickens under her wings, and ye would not!" He is choked with tears, and when he has paused a moment, he cries—"Come unto me, all ye that labor and are heavy laden, and I will give you rest. Take my yoke upon you, and learn of me; for I am meek and lowly in heart: and ye shall find rest unto your souls; a bruised reed I will not break, nor quench the smoking flax."

I think I see him, as he looks at you again, and when he observes some hearts so obdurate and callous that they will not melt, he unwraps his mantle, and exclaims—"See here." Do you mark the gash in his side? As he lifts his hands and shows the nail-prints, and points downward to his pierced feet, he says—"By these, my wounds, which I endured when suffering for you, O my people, return unto me; come, bow at my feet, and take the peace which I have wrought out for you. Oh! be not faithless, but believing! Doubt no longer! God is reconciled! Tremble no more! Peace is established. Toil no more at the works of the law, cling not to your own doings. Cease to consult your feelings. It is finished. When I bowed my head upon the tree, I finished all for you. Take salvation: take it now! Come to me; come now to me just as you are." Alas, this is but a poor representation of my Lord and Master. I could wish myself laid among the clods of the valley, sleeping in my grave, rather than that I should be so poor an ambassador. But, Lord, wherefore didst thou choose thy servant, and why givest thou this people still to hear his voice, if thou wilt not more mightily enable him to plead with men. I have no more words: oh, let these tears plead with you. I feel that I could freely give my life if it would avail for the saving of your souls. Fain would I meet a martyr's death, if you would be persuaded thereby to come to Christ for life. But oh, sinners, no pleading of mine will ever prevail if the pleading of Christ prove ineffectual with you. To each one of you, a distinct proclamation of salvation is addressed. Whosoever among you will believe that Christ died, and that he is able to save you, and will trust your soul upon what he did, shall be saved. Oh! why reject him? He will not hurt or harm you. Do lay hold of this good hope, for your time is short! Death is hastening on; eternity is near! Do lay hold of it, for hell is hot, the flames thereof are terrible! Lay hold of it, for heaven is bright, and the harps of angels are sweet beyond compare! Lay hold of it! It shall make your heart glad on earth, it shall charm away your fears and remove your griefs! Lay hold of it! It shall bear you through Jordan's billows, and land you safe on Canaan's side. Oh, by the love of the Father, by the blood of Jesus, by the love of the Spirit, I beseech you, sinner, believe and live! By the cross and the five wounds, by the agony and bloody sweat, by the resurrection and by the ascension, sinner, believe and live! By every argument that would touch your nature, by every motive that can sway your reason or stir your passions, in the name of God that sent me, by the Almighty that made you, by the eternal Son that redeemed you, by the gift of the Holy Spirit, sinner I command you, with divine authority to sanction my vehemence, that ye be reconciled to God through the death of his Son.

IV. And what then? When we have answered this question we shall have done. What then? Are there not some of you with whom this peace is made at this good hour. I will go back and tell my Master so. Then there shall be fresh ratifications between you and him. The angels will hear of it, and they will strike their harps anew to sweeter lays than they have known before.

Others there are of you that will not be reconciled. I must have an answer from you. Do you hesitate? Do you delay? Do you refuse? You shall never have another warning, some of you! No tears of pity shall be wept for you again; no loving heart shall ever bid you come to Christ again—I must have your answer now. Yes or no. Wilt thou be damned or not? Wilt thou be saved or not? I will not have thee say, " When I have a more convenient season I will send for thee." Sinner, it cannot be a more convenient one than this. This is a convenient place, it is God's house. It is a convenient time, it is the Lord's day. Now, sinner, wilt thou be reconciled, restored, forgiven? "Wilt thou be made whole?" said Jesus, and I say the same to thee—"Wilt thou be made whole?" Do you say "No"? Must I take that for an answer? Mark you, sinner, I have to tell my Master. I must tell him when I seek the closet of the King to-night; I must tell him your reply that you would not. What then remains for the ambassador to do when he has spoken to you in the name of the Sovereign? If you will not turn we must shake off the dust of our feet against you. I am clear, I am clear, of the blood of you all, I am clear. If you perish, being warned, you perish wantonly. The wrath cometh upon you, not on him who, to the best of his power, has told his Master's message. Yet again, I beg you to accept it. Do you still say no? The white flag will be pulled down. It has been up long enough. Shall I pull it down, and run up the red flag now? Shall I hurl threatenings at you because you heed not entreaties?

> " If your ears refuse
>   The language of his grace,
>   And hearts grow hard like stubborn Jews,
>   That unbelieving race,
>   The Lord in anger drest,
>   Shall lift his hand and swear,
>   Ye that despised my promised rest
>   Shall have no portion there."

But no, I cannot pull it down, that white flag! My heart will not let me do so; it shall fly still there, it shall fly there as a sign and a symbol of the day of grace. Mercy is still held out to you. But there is one coming—I can hear his footsteps—who will pull that white flag down. The vision haunts my eyes. That grim heartless skeleton, whom men call Death, will rend the white flag from its place, and up will go the blood-red flag, with the black escutcheon of the thunderbolts. Where are you then, sinners? where will you be then? You shudder at the thought. He lays his hand on you. There is no escape. Oh, turn ye, turn ye, turn ye! Come and welcome, sinner, come now while you are welcome. 'Tis love invites you. Jesus stretches out his hand to you all the day long. He has stretched out his hands to a rebellious and a gainsaying generation. Do not say, "I will think of it," but yield to his love who around you now the bands of a man doth cast. Do not make a resolution, but commit yourself to the good confession. Now, even now, may sovereign grace constrain, and irresistible love draw you. May you believe with your heart, may you record your profession at once. Before you close your eyes in sleep, just as you would wish before your eyes are closed in death, may you be at peace with God. I pray God, as I entreat you, that this may come to pass, for his Son Jesus Christ's sake. Amen.

A Cheerful Prospect.

For the Lord shall comfort Zion: he will comfort all her waste places; and he will make her wilderness like Eden, and her desert like the garden of the Lord; joy and gladness shall be found therein, thanksgiving, and the voice of melody.—ISAIAH li. 3.

THE pedigree of God's chosen nation Israel may be traced back to one man and one woman—to Abraham and Sarah. Both of them were well stricken in years when the Lord who had called them verified his promise, yet, in the fulfilment of his covenant engagement, he built up of their seed a great nation, which, for number, was comparable to the stars of heaven. Take heart, brethren; these things are written for our example and for our encouragement. His church can never sink to so low an ebb that he cannot soon build her up again, nor in our own hearts can the work of grace ever decline so grievously that the same mighty power which once quickened cannot revive and restore us. Think of Abraham and Sarah, childless till they were old, then rejoicing in one son, who became their heir. Hence sprang the great multitude that peopled Palestine. With such a panorama unfolding before you there is no excuse for despair; but you may find ten thousand reasons for confidence in God.

I. Following up this preface, the Lord proceeds to unfold to his people a series of delightful promises. As we have no time to spare, and no words to waste, we shall plunge at once into the thick of the text, and observe, first, that you have before you HEAVENLY COMFORT PROMISED.

This is a promise to God's church. There are some who would have us always restrain Isaiah's prophecies to the Jews, as though this was their exclusive application. I have no objection to your so understanding them in their original and literal sense, nor have I any objection to our friends laboring for the Jews, especially, as a class; far rather would I commend them. Only, I would have them recollect that no Scripture is of private interpretation; that, in God's sight, neither Jews nor Gentiles are recognized under this dispensation of the gospel, for he has made both one in Christ Jesus. I, therefore, as a Christian minister, when I preach the gospel, know neither Jew nor Gentile, male nor female, bond nor free, but I simply know men as men, and go out into the world to "preach the gospel to every creature." It seems to me that this is the order in which God would have his church carry out every evangelical enterprise, forgetting and ignoring all fleshly distinctions, understanding that now men are either sinners or saints. As to circumcision or uncircumcision, vast as is its importance in the kingdom of Israel, it is of no account in the kingdom of God. The text, we believe, whatever may be its relation to the Jews as a people, belongs to the church of God and the disciples of Christ; for "*all things are yours.*" Zion was the stronghold of Jerusalem. Originally a fortress of the Jebusites, it was taken with a feat of arms by David and his valiant men. It became afterwards the residence of David, and there, too, was the residence of the Great King; for in it was built the temple which became the glory of all lands. Hence the church of God—captured as it has been by Christ from the world, chosen to be the palace where he dwells, builded together for a temple wherein he is worshipped—is frequently called "Zion," and the Zion of this passage, I believe, we are warranted in interpreting as the church of the living God.

We are told here, then, that the Lord will comfort his Church. Let *the object of this comfort* now engage your attention. "The Lord will comfort Zion." Well he may, for she is his chosen. "The Lord has chosen Zion." He would have those upon whom his choice is fixed be glad and happy. The elect of a great king have cause for thankfulness, but the chosen of the King of kings should rejoice continually in the God that chose them. He would have his church rejoice because he has not only chosen her, but he has cleansed her. Jesus has put away the sin of his people by his blood, and by his Spirit he is daily renewing the nature of his children. Sin is the cause of sorrow, and when sin is put away, sorrow shall be put away

too. The sanctified should be happy. The Lord
will, therefore, comfort them, because he has
cleansed them. The church of God is placed
where God dwells—

> " Where God doth dwell sure heaven is there:
>   And singing there should be."

What can ye conceive of weeping and lamenting
in the house where Jehovah dwelleth? It was a
rule with one of the old monarchs that no one
should come into his presence sad. In all our afflictions we may draw near to the Lord, but his
presence should dispel our sorrow and sighing;
for the children of Zion should be joyful in their
King. If the Lord dwelleth in the midst of his
people, there ought to be shoutings of joy. The
presence of the King of Heaven is the heaven of
their delight. Moreover, Zion enjoys her Monarch's
love, and therefore he would have her comforted.
We know not how dear to the heart of Christ his
church is, but we do know this, that for his church
he left his Father's house and came down to earth,
and was poor, that she through his poverty might
be made rich. A man leaveth father and mother,
and cleaveth to his wife, and they become one
flesh; what shall I say of the great mystery of this
glorious Lover, who left his Father's house, and did
cleave unto his church, and became.one flesh with
her that he might lift her up and set her upon his
own throne, that she might reign with him as the
Bride, the Lamb's Wife? Well therefore may the

Lord desire his church to be happy. Eternal love has betrothed her. Eternal purposes cluster around her. Eternal power is sworn to protect her. Eternal faithfulness has guaranteed eternal life to all her citizens. Why should she not be comforted? I do not wonder that the text says the Lord will comfort the people whom he has thus favored.

And the *Lord himself is the Comforter.* " *The Lord* will comfort Zion." Beloved, we make but sorry comforters for God's people unless Jehovah puts his own hand to the work. I have sometimes tried to cheer up my brethren when they have been desponding, and I hope not without success; yet I have always felt that to relieve and refresh a desponding saint, I must fetch the remedies from my Master's pharmacy. So, doubtless, those of you who have ever sought to obey the command, "Comfort ye, comfort ye my people," must have found that it was not your word that could comfort Zion, nor your sympathy, but God's truth applied by God's Spirit, for this alone can comfort Zion. Oh, blessed promise! "The Lord will comfort Zion; he will comfort her waste places." He that made the heavens will become the Comforter to his people. The Holy Ghost who brooded over chaos, and brought order out of confusion, the mighty Spirit who came down at Pentecost in tongues of fire, with a sound like a mighty rushing wind, — that same blessed Spirit will come to the hearts of the members of his church and comfort them. There are sorrows for which there is no solace within the reach of the creature; there is a ruin which it would baffle any mortal to retrieve. Happy for us that the Omnipotent comes to our aid. It is "he who telleth the number of the stars; calleth them by their names;" who also "healeth the broken in heart, and bindeth up their wounds!" There he is, rolling the stars along, filling heaven with wonder as he creates majestic orbs, and keeps them in their pathways, making the comet fling its gorgeous light across space and startle nations, holding the burning furnace of the sun in the hollow of his hand; yet he stoops down to minister to a desponding spirit, and to pour the oil and wine of heavenly comfort into a poor distracted heart! Yes, it is Zion that is to be comforted, but it is Jehovah himself who has promised to be her Comforter!

And how does the Lord propose to comfort Zion? If you read the verse through you will find it is by making her fertile. He will turn her barren deserts into fruitful gardens, and her unproductive wilderness into a blooming Eden. The true way to comfort the church is to build her synagogues, restore the desolation of former times, to sow her fields, plant her vineyards, make her soil fruitful, call out the industry of her sons and daughters, and fill them with lively, ardent zeal. There is an everlasting consolation for the church in those grand doctrines of grace revealed to us in covenant, such as election, particular redemption, effectual calling, final perseverance, and the faithfulness of God. Resting in his love, God forbid that we should ever keep these grand truths back; they are the wells of salvation from which we rejoice to draw the water of life. But there are other truths besides these, and we could not make full proof of our ministry if we overlooked the rain, even the former and the latter rain, which God gives in due season, or withholds in his chastening anger. I have often remarked that those persons who are always crying after the comfort that is to be derived from the stability of God's purpose, are strangely lacking in that present joy and jubilant song which revels in the goodness of the Lord, who clothes the pastures with flocks and covers the valleys with corn. I have also remarked that the best way to make a Christian man happy is to make him useful in ploughing the fields which God has watered, and gathering the fruits which he has ripened. A Christian church never enjoys so much concord, love, and happiness as when every member is kept hard at work for God, every soul upon the stretch of anxiety to do good and communicate, every disciple a good soldier of the Cross, fighting the common enemy. Thus the Lord will comfort Zion, and he comforts her by turning her desert into a garden, and her wilderness into an Eden. And oh! my brethren, how happy is the church when all the members are active, all the trees bearing fruit; when sinners are converted, and daily added to the fellowship of the saved; when, instead of the thorn, there

comes up the myrtle, and instead of the briar
there comes up the fir-tree; when God is turning
hard hearts, that were like rocks, into good soil,
where the corn of the Kingdom may grow. There
is no joy like it! If you can be happy in seeking
your own good, without caring for the welfare of
others, I pity you. If a minister can be content
to go on preaching without converts or baptisms,
the Lord have mercy upon his miserable soul!
Can he be a minister of Christ who does not win
souls? A man might as well be a huntsman and
never take any prey, a fisherman and always come
home with empty nets, a husbandman and never
reap a harvest! I wonder at some people's com-
placency. When God never blesses them they
never fail to bless themselves. "Divine sovereignty withholds the increase," they say. But it
really is their idleness that tends to poverty. The
promise of God is to the diligent, not the indolent.
Let Paul plant, and let Apollos water, God will
give the increase. It may not come to-day, nor
to-morrow, nor the next day, but come it must.
The word cannot return unto God void. It must
prosper in the thing whereto he has sent it. Had
God sent us on a listless, bootless errand, we
might well complain, but he doth not so. Only
let us preach Jesus Christ with the Holy Ghost
sent down from heaven, and we shall, doubtless,
come again rejoicing, bringing our sheaves with
us. Although when we went forth, we wept because of our inability and our want of confidence,
yet this is the way in which God comforts us.

The promise, you will observe, is given in words that contain an absolute pledge. He *shall* and he *will* are terms that admit of no equivocation. What an emphasis that man of God, the late Joseph Irons, used to lay on the words when he got hold of a "shall" and a "will" from the mouth of the Lord. Though some people say we must not make too much of little words, I will venture to make as much as ever I can of these two potent monosyllables. "The Lord *shall* comfort Zion; the Lord *will* comfort all her waste places." How much better and brighter this reads than an "if," or a "but," or a "perhaps," or a "peradventure!" He *shall* comfort Zion! Oh, how those dear saints, the Covenanters, when they were hunted about, and fled into dens and caves, said, "Ah, but King Jesus *will* have his own; he *shall* comfort Zion!" And our Puritan forefathers, when priests threatened to harry them out of the land, could see with prophetic eye the time when the harlot church would be driven out, and the true, legitimate children of God would take her place; they could say, "The Lord *shall* comfort Zion," and they looked forward to happier halcyon days. No less did those glorious Albigenses and Waldenses, when they stained the snows of the Alps with their blood, feel confident that the Church of Rome would not gain the day, that God would yet return and avenge the blood of his martyred saints, and give the victory to his true people. And surely you and I may take comfort too. "The Lord *shall* comfort Zion; he *will* comfort her waste places." Brethren, there are brighter days to come. The day breaketh, and the shadows flee away! Our hope is in God. Never doubt the true progress of the church. Believe that, notwithstanding every discouragement that checks our advance, the cause of God goes on; it must go on, and it *shall* go on, till King Jesus is universally acknowledged King of kings and Lord of lords. We have not to serve a master who cannot take care of his own. To your tents, ye Philistines; when the God of Israel comes to the battle, where will ye be? Your ranks are broken: ye flee like thin clouds before a Biscay gale! When God comes forth he has but by his Spirit to blow upon his enemies and they fly before him like the chaff before the wind. The Lord *shall* and the Lord *will;* who, then, shall disannul it? Though foes may hoot and fiends may howl, he will keep his word; it shall come to pass, and he will get to himself renown in fulfilling his own good pleasure.

II. Having thus enlarged upon the heavenly comfort promised, we pass on to notice the MOURNFUL CASES FAVORED.

" *He will make her wilderness like Eden, and her desert like the garden of the Lord.*" Now, are there not to be found in the visible church persons whose character is here vividly depicted? I think there are three sorts of people in such a case, to all of whom I trust the blessing will come. *There are those who once were fruitful, but are now comparably to waste.* If God should visit his church, he will be pleased to comfort the waste places. Do I not address some who must needs recognize their own portrait? You used to be church members, and then you did seem to run well; what did hinder you? You were, apparently, brave soldiers once, but you deserted and went over to the enemy. Still, if you are the Lord's people, one of the signs of God's grace to his church will be the recovery of backsliders. I remember one Monday afternoon, when we had been waiting upon the Lord in prayer ever since seven o'clock in the morning, that there came a most remarkable wave of prayer over the assembly. And then two backsliders got up and prayed one after the other. According to their own account, they had been very bad fellows indeed, and had sorely transgressed against God; but there they were, broken-hearted and fairly broken down. It was a sight to make angels rejoice as their tears flowed. Certainly their sobs and cries touched the hearts of all of us who were assembled. I thought to myself, "Then God *is* blessing us, for when backsliders come back it is a proof that God has visited his people." You recollect when it was that Naomi returned to Israel with Ruth, her daughter-in-law. They never came back during the time of famine; they stopped in Moab then, but they came back when they heard that the Lord had visited his people in giving them bread. Even then Naomi said, "Call me not Naomi." She seemed to come back from her exile groaning and full of bitterness, and yet she came back because God was with his people.   Backsliders, come back, come now, for God is with his church, and he has promised to comfort her waste places.   Oh, you who have forgotten your Lord, remember your first Husband! It was better with you then than now.   Though you have gone astray, yet the Lord saith, "Return, thou backsliding Israel, for I am married unto you, saith the Lord."   You may break the marriage bond with God, but he will not break it with you. He claims that he is married to you, and he bids you return to him.   I hope that some backslider will be encouraged by this promise to return with full purpose of heart to the God of his salvation.

Then a second department of the promise is, "He will make her wilderness like Eden."   I take the wilderness here to be a place of scanty vegetation.   The oriental wildernesses are not altogether barren sand, but there is a feeble herbage which struggles for existence.   We are told, you recollect, that "Moses kept his father's sheep in the wilderness."   Oh, how many there are in the church of God who are just like that!   They are Christians, but sorry Christians they are.   They do love the Lord Jesus Christ, but it is with a moonlight love—cold, very cold, and chill.   They have light, but it is dim and hazy.   If they do anything for Christ, their service is scanty; their contributions mean; their charity grudging.   They bring him no sweet cane with honey.   They do not fill him with the fat of their sacrifices, but they make him serve with their sins, and they weary him with their iniquities. Ah, dear friend, if thou art indeed a child of God, then there is this comfort for thee. He will make her wilderness like Eden. Even you who have borne so little for God shall yet be visited, and made fruitful, when the Lord comforts his people.

A third character is implied in the desert—the deserted places where no man dwells, where the traveller does not care to linger. How many professors of religion, how many who attend our chapels, answer to this description of the soil! They are like deserts. You not only never did bring forth fruit, but you never concerned yourself to do so. No man seems to care for you, and you appeal to yourselves as though you were like the sand, which it would be a hopeless task to plough, for the gleaner would never fill his hand from the produce, much less the reaper his bosom with the sheaves. Ah! well, but God has a word for these desert souls. He will make her desert like the garden of the Lord. I pray—nay, I know —that during the gracious season which God has given us we shall see many a desert heart made to blossom like the rose. These be they whom the Lord will specially transform — backsliders, scanty Christians, and those who have often heard, but never yet proved the power of the gospel at all.

Ask ye now, what does the Lord say he will do for them? He says (hear it and marvel!) that he will make the wilderness like Eden. You know what Eden was. It was the garden of the earth in the days of primeval purity. Fruit and flower, lofty tree and lively vegetation abounded there in profuse luxuriance. I know not how its groves and shrubberies were tenanted by graceful creatures and lovely birds, but I can well imagine that every sense of man was regaled by its unfailing charms. No thorns or thistles cursed the soil, no sweating brow with arduous toil forced the crops from barren sods. The land laughed with plenty. The river, branching into many heads, watered the garden. God himself was pleased to water it with the mists, and to make the fruit grow, to swell in rich abundance, and early come to mature perfection. So the Lord says that when he visits his church he will make these poor backsliders, these immature Christians, these nominal professors, like Eden. Oh that the Lord would do it! Oh that he would make them healthy, fruitful, prolific in fruitfulness, and spontaneously fruit-bearing, so that we should almost have need to say, "Hold Lord!" just as Moses and Aaron did when the people brought in the offerings for the Tabernacle, until there were more than enough. Oh that the church of Christ may be enriched with all spiritual gifts, with all heavenly graces, with all that can minister to the welfare of the saints, to the advantage of the world, and to the glory of him who created and redeemed us! God grant it may be so!

Moreover, as if to strengthen the volume of his

grace and of our hope, he says that he will make her desert like the garden of the Lord. He shall come to you and delight your heart and soul with his converse. If ever you should be an Eden, you shall be like to Paradise for a yet higher reason, because your fellowship shall be with the Father and with his Son Jesus Christ. There shall be upon you the smell of a field that the Lord hath blessed. The Lord shall water his church, shall water it every moment. He shall make fat our bones, and cause us to be as a watered garden, as a well of water whose waters fail not. Oh! some of you may well sigh as you think of those happy days you once enjoyed! Would you like them back again? Then plead with God the promise of the text. You were once blessed with nearness to and communion with Christ. You once prayed with fervor, and your soul prospered. Go to God with this promise, and say, "Lord, I am a desert; I am a wilderness; I am a waste place; but comfort thy church, and let me partake of the consolation by making me fruitful in every good word and work to thy glory!" The Lord will do it, for the promises of God shall certainly be fulfilled.

Who but Jehovah himself can do this? I have already noted this. "He will make her wilderness like Eden." It is he only that can perform it. The minister cannot. The church cannot, with all her efforts. Talk of getting up a revival! It were insufferable arrogance to make the attempt. It belongeth not to us to do this. Unto the Lord our

God alone doth this belong. "Not by might, nor by power, but by my Spirit, saith the Lord." If he will but visit his church, then we shall see the wilderness rejoice, but if not, we may plough, as is our duty, and we may work upon it, as is our calling, but there shall be no joy and no rejoicing.

III. We conclude with the view of CERTAIN DESIRABLE RESULTS WHICH ARE PREDICTED.

"Joy and gladness shall be found therein, thanksgiving, and the voice of melody." You notice the doubles. The parallelism of Hebrew poetry, perhaps, necessitated them. Still I am prone to remember how John Bunyan says that "all the flowers in God's garden bloom double." We are told of "manifold mercies," that is, mercies which are folded up one in another, so that you may unwrap them and find a fresh mercy enclosed in every fold. Here we have "joy and gladness, thanksgiving, and the voice of melody." Just so; the Psalmist tells us of our soul being satisfied with "marrow and fatness,"—two things. Elsewhere, he speaks of "loving-kindness and tender mercy," —two things again. The Lord multiplies his grace. He is always slow to anger, but he is always lavish of his grace. See here, then, God will give his people an overflowing joy, an inexpressible joy, a sort of double joy, as though he would give them more joy than they could hold—joy, and then gladness; thanksgiving, and the voice of melody.

Oh, *what a delightful thing must a visitation from God be to his church!* Without God all she can do is to groan. Nay, she will not always do that. She sometimes indulges a foolish conceit, and says: "I am rich and increased in goods, and have need of nothing." After that will soon be heard the hooting of dragons and the cry of owls. Let God visit his church, and there is sure to be thanksgiving and the voice of melody. It has been remarked that all revivals of true religion in ancient as well as modern times have been attended by revival of psalmody and song. The joy that makes the heart grateful, enlivens the spirits, and diffuses happiness, will seek and must find some tuneful strains. Not to speak of the Hebrew Psalter or of the Greek Hymnals, in Luther's day his translation of the Psalms and his chorales did more, perhaps, to make the Reformation popular than even his preaching. The ploughman at his field-labor, and the housewife at the cradle, would sing one of Luther's Psalms. So, too, in our own country in Wycliffe's day fresh psalms and hymns were scattered all over the land. And you know how, in the last century, Wesley and Whitefield gave a new impetus to congregational singing. The hymns were printed on little fly-sheets after each sermon, and at length these units swelled into a volume. Collections and selections of hymns were published. So fond, indeed, were the Methodists of singing, that it became a taunt and a by-word to speak of them as canting psalm-singers. But this is the mark of a revived church everywhere. New impetus is given to the service of song. When the

Bridegroom is gone we may well mourn and fast, and hang our harps on the willows: it is when the Bridegroom cometh that joy and feasting seek the aid of vocal music, and the people of God break forth into thanksgiving with the voice of melody. I do fervently hope, beloved, that we shall have this thanksgiving and this voice of melody in our midst for many a day to come! Would God that all the churches enjoyed it! Need I say that from all parts of the country there are tokens of it now? We do not desire at any time a monopoly of blessing. May every Christian denomination and every Christian community be favored with the dew of heaven, and have their roots watered by that river which is full of water. Oh that all the churches of Christ were fruitful! Instead of wishing any of them to be weak, I would say, with Moses, " Would God that all the Lord's people were prophets," and that the Lord would put his Spirit upon them! Oh that Jesus might be extolled from the uttermost parts of the earth to the highest heavens! Brethren, let us ask God to fulfil this promise to the church at large. Let us say to him: " Lord, comfort thy Zion! She has many waste places— comfort her! Thou knowest she has many barren spots—turn them into gardens of the Lord! Oh, let the heavenly rain descend, and the divine dew come from thee, that the wilderness and the solitary place may yet be glad!"

But what shall I say to those of you who are not saved? If you want to become as these gardens of the Lord, it is only the grace of God which bringeth salvation that can work in you this mighty change. Look to the Lord. He it is who must do it. He hears prayer. A negro was once sent by his master on an errand that did not suit him; he did not want to go. So when he came to a river he turned back, and said, "Master, I came to a river, and I could not swim across it." "Well, but was there not a ferry-boat?" "Yes, there was a ferry-boat, but the man was on the other side." "Well," said the master, "did you call to the ferry-man to come and take you across?" No, he did not think of doing that, for, as he did not wish to go over, he was glad to find an excuse. Now, it is true, sinner, that you cannot save yourself, but there is One who can. There is a ferry-boat and there is a Ferry-man. Cry to him! Cry to him, —"Master, across this river be pleased to take me; I cannot swim it, but thou canst bear me over it. Oh! do for me what I cannot do for myself. Make me to be accepted in the Beloved!" If you seek the Lord he will be found of you. He never did set a soul a-seeking but what he meant to bless it. But if you will not seek, what should be said of you but that on your head should lie your own blood? I know many of you to be greatly impressed this week. I hope the impression will not be blown away like smoke out of a chimney. May God make a deep work in your souls! Oh, some of you were easily impressed, but you quite as easily forgot the impression. You are like Ephraim's cake that was baked on one side; you do not get thoroughly cooked. You do not feel the power of the gospel permeating your whole nature in every part. You are like the cake not turned, and God accepts you not, because of this. Oh! that there might be a thorough work of the Spirit in your souls, a work of grace that shall bring you to Jesus to be rooted and built up in him and established in the faith, abounding therein with thanksgiving. Amen.

A Pitiful Chastisement.

Thou shalt be dumb, and not able to speak, until the day that these things shall be performed, because thou believest not my words, which shall be fulfilled in their season.—LUKE i. 20.

UNBELIEF is everywhere a great sin, and a grievous mistake. Unbelief has proved the ruin of those countless multitudes who, having heard the gospel, rejected it, and died in their sins, have been consigned to the place of torment, and await the fiercer judgment of the last day. I might ask the question concerning this innumerable host: "Who slew all these?" The answer would be: "Unbelief." And when unbelief comes into the Christian's heart, as it does at times—for the truest believer has his times of doubt; even Abraham, the father of the faithful, sometimes had his misgivings—that unbelief never assails his thoughts without withering his joys, and impairing his energies. There is nothing in the world that costs a saint so dear as doubt. If he disbelieve his God, he most assuredly robs himself of comfort, deprives himself of strength, and does himself a real injury. The case of Zacharias may be a lesson to the Lord's people. It is to them I am going to speak. Zacharias is a striking example of the ills a good man may have to suffer as the result of his unbelief.

In reviewing the character and position of Zacharias, we can hardly fail to discover some profitable lessons. He was undoubtedly a believer. He is said, in the sixth verse, to have been righteous before God. No man ever obtained such a reputation except by faith. "The just shall live by faith." No other righteousness than that which is by faith is of any esteem in God's account. Such was the righteousness of Abraham, and such was the righteousness of all the saints before the advent of our Redeemer. Such, too, has been the standard ever since. Zacharias evidently was a real believer. Yet for all that, when the angel appeared to him, and God gave him the promise of a son, he was amazed, bewildered, incredulous, and could not credit, but only question, the announcement. "How shall I know that these things shall be?"

Nor was he merely a genuine believer; he was well instructed and greatly enlightened, for he was a priest, and as a priest considered he was righteous before God, and blameless, walking in all the commandments and ordinances of the Lord. That he was well instructed in the Word of God is undeniable. He could not otherwise have discharged his duty, for the priest's lips must keep knowledge, and he must teach men. Being proficient in the one, and competent for the other, ignorance offered him no excuse. Moreover, as a man of years, he was probably to be classed among the experienced saints of his time. He had borne the burden and heat of the day, and received proof upon proof of the abundant mercy of God. Now mark this. For any of us to doubt who have been justified by faith, is a shameful delinquency. For those to doubt who have, in addition to their first convictions, a thousand confirmations of the truth they have embraced, who are acquainted with the covenant and its rich inventory of promises, who are deeply taught in the things of God—for such to doubt involves a higher degree of guilt. I do not think that had Zacharias been a mere babe in grace, or an inexperienced stripling, his unbelief would have met with so stern a rebuke. It was because he was a venerable priest, one thoroughly schooled in sacred truth, a man who for many years instructed the people of Israel in the oracles of God, that it became a crying evil for him to say, " Whereby shall I know this," when the angel told him of his prayer being heard, and of the manner of answer the Lord will vouchsafe him.

The high office that Zacharias held as a priest caused him to be looked up to. Hence his conduct was more narrowly watched, and his example had a wider influence. On a similar account we have need, all of us in our several spheres, to consider the effect of our actions upon others. The higher a man's position, the greater his re-

sponsibility; and in the event of any delinquency,
the graver his offence. For you to disbelieve, my
dear brother, who are at the head of a household,
is worse than a personal infirmity; it is a violation
of duty to your family. And you, dear friend, who
preach the gospel, for you to disbelieve who are
looked upon by many as an advanced Christian,
as a mature saint whose example may be safely
followed by those who listen to your counsels,—
this is a great and a crying evil, whereby you dishonor the Lord. I pray God that your conscience
may be tenderly sensitive, and that you may be
aroused to a sense of the dishonor you bring to
him by your faithlessness.

How peculiarly favored Zacharias was! An angel of the Lord appeared unto him. Not to any of
the other priests, when they were offering incense,
did such a heavenly visitor come. And what welcome tidings he brought! It was a wonderful message that he was to be the father of a child great
in the sight of the Lord, one who should minister
in the spirit and power of Elias, and become the
forerunner of the Messiah. This surely was a sig-
nal instance of divine favor. And mark this, beloved, our God is very jealous of those whom he
highly favors. You cannot have privileged communications from the Lord, or be admitted into
close communion with him, without finding that
he is a jealous God. The nearer we draw to him,
the more hallowed our sense of his presence will
be. But to doubt his word, or question the fulfil-

ment of his promise when he speaks kindly to us, must incur his censure. I speak after the manner of men; we do not expect from a stranger the esteem which we ought to merit from our servants. But our friends, who know us better than servants, ought to trust us more implicitly. And yet beyond common friendship, in the near relation and tender attachment of a wife to her husband, the most unqualified confidence should be reposed. Even so, my brethren, if you and I have ever been permitted to lean our heads on Jesus' bosom; if we have sat down at his banquets, and his banner over us has been love; if we have been separated from the world by peculiar fellowship with Christ, and have had choice promises given us, we cannot, like Zacharias, ask, "Whereby shall I know?" without grieving the Holy Spirit of God, and bringing upon ourselves some sad chastisement as the result.

What soothing comfort had just been administered to Zacharias by the angel of the Lord! Was not the manner of the salutation fitted to allay terror, and inspire him with trust? The troubled thoughts that perplexed him, and the fear that fell upon him when the angel appeared standing at the right hand of the altar, met with no rebuke. If it was natural that so unwonted a vision should startle him, there was a gentle sympathizing tenderness in the angel's address that might well have stilled the throbbings of his heart. "Fear not, Zacharias: for thy prayer is heard." And so is it with us when the consolations of God have been neither few nor small, and when his good will towards us has been pointedly expressed, does it not make doubt and questioning more inexcusable? Do we not thereby aggravate the sin? Some of us have lived in the very bosom of comfort. Precious promises have been brought home to our souls; we have eaten of the marrow and the fatness; we have drunk the wines on the lees well refined. We are no strangers to the blessing of his eternal and unchanging love, or to the light of his countenance, which they prove who find grace in his eyes. Oh, if we begin to doubt after these discriminating love tokens, what apology can we offer or how can we hope to escape from the chastening rod.

Moreover, the misgivings that Zacharias betrayed relate to the very subject on which his supplications were offered. It was in response to his own petition that the angel said to him, "Thy prayer is heard." I marvel at his faith that he should persevere in prayer for a boon which seemed, at his own and his wife's age, to have been out of the course of nature, and beyond the domain of hope, but I marvel a great deal more that, when the answer came to that very prayer, Zacharias could not believe it. So full often is it with us; nothing would surprise some of us more than to receive an answer to some of our own prayers. Though we believe in the efficacy of prayer, at times we believe so feebly that when the answer comes, as come it does, we are astounded and filled with amazement. We can scarcely think of it as a purpose of God; it seems rather to us like a happy coincidence. Surely this adds greatly to the sin of unbelief. If we have been asking for mercy without expecting it, and pleading promises while harboring mistrust, every prayer we have offered has been only a repetition of our secret unbelief; and it is God's faithfulness that brings our inconsistency to light.

One other reflection is suggested by the narrative. Zacharias appears to have staggered at a promise which others, whom we might well imagine to have been weaker in faith than himself, implicitly believed. The veteran falters where a babe in grace might have taken courage. And is it not always a scandal if any of us who have been conspicuously favored of God are ready to halt while our feebler brethren and sisters are animated and encouraged? No dubious thought seems to have crossed the mind of Elizabeth; no incredulous expression fell from her lips. She said, "Thus hath the Lord dealt with me."

This case was the very opposite of that of Abraham and Sarah. There Abraham believed, but Sarah doubted; here the wife believes in the face of her husband's scruples. In like manner Mary, that humble village maiden, accepts with simple faith the high and holy salutation with which she was greeted. She just asks a natural question, and that being answered, she replies, "Be it unto

me according to thy word." Her surprise was soon
exchanged for joy, and by and by she begins to sing
with a loud voice, " My soul doth magnify the Lord,
and my spirit hath rejoiced in God my Saviour."
Not a little remarkable is this opening chapter of
the Gospel according to Luke. Woman, who had
been in the background through long preceding
generations, seems suddenly to take a foremost
place. Zacharias and Joseph stand in doubt, while
Elizabeth and Mary exultingly believe. And who
knows but I may be addressing some poor woman
here who, in the depth of affliction, bodily suffering,
and poverty, nevertheless rejoices in God with all
her heart? But without a doubt, I am now speaking to many a man who is vexed with trifling
cares, murmurs bitterly because of petty annoy-
ances, and distrusts his God when clouds come
over the sky so that he sees not his way. Shame
on our unbelief. Think shame of yourselves because of it, I pray you. Never does it disgrace us
more than when the weaklings of the Lord's family
put us to the blush by the simplicity and sincerity
of their faith. The character and position of Zacharias may thus furnish a striking moral, but I do
urgently entreat each Christian to point the keen
edge of criticism at himself, and consider how much
he is personally to blame for his own unbelief.

Let us proceed to investigate the fault of Zacharias.
Whence this perilous wavering at that privileged
hour? His fault was that he looked at the difficulty.
" I am an old man," said he, " and my wife is well

stricken in years." And while he looked at the difficulty he would fain suggest a remedy; he wanted a sign. "Whereby shall I know this?" It was not enough for him that God had said so; he wanted some collateral evidence to guarantee the truth of the word of the Lord. This is a very common fault among really good people. They look for a sign. I have often trembled in my own soul when I have felt an inclination thus to tempt the Lord by looking for some minute circumstance to verify a magnificent promise. When I have thought— "Hereby shall I know whether he does hear prayer or not," a cold shiver has passed over me, the shudder has gone through my soul that ever I should think of challenging the truth of God's word, when the fact is so certain. For those of us who have often cried unto the Lord in our distresses, and been delivered out of our troubles, to raise such a question is indeed ungrateful. For a child of God who habitually prays to his Father in heaven to look upon his faithfulness as a matter of uncertainty is to degrade himself, and to dishonor his Lord. Yet there is no denying the tendency and disposition among us to want a sign. As we read a prophecy of the future, we crave a token in the present. If the Lord were pleased to give us a sign, or if he told us to ask for a sign, we should be quite right in attaching a high importance thereto, but for us to doubt a plain promise, and therefore ask a sign, is to sin against the Lord. Sometimes we have wanted signs in spiritual things.

Meet and proper is it for us to rejoice in the true delights of fellowship with Christ, but it ill becomes us to make our feelings a kind of test of our acceptance; or to say, "I will not believe God if he does not indulge me with certain manifestations of grace; unless he gives me the sweetmeats I crave, I will be sulky and sullen, and refuse to eat the children's bread." Why, such conduct is wilful and wicked; it is weak, and utterly inexcusable. Yet how many of us have been guilty of this folly?

Now, as Zacharias stood upon the threshold of the gospel dispensation, and as he was the first among those who heard the glad tidings to express unbelief, it was necessary that he should be made an example of. God would show at the very outset, even before John the Baptist was born, that unbelief could not be tolerated, nor should it go unchastened. Therefore his servant Zacharias must, as soon as he had asked for a sign, have such a sign as would make him suffer for months to come, and constrain him to be sorry that he had ever dared to proffer the request. O beloved, is our faith still so weak, and our experience still so contracted, that we cannot yet trust our God? Twenty years have we known him. Has he been a wilderness to us? Have his mercy and truth ever failed us in time of need? Shall all his tender dealings with us count for nothing? Do ye think so lightly of the gift of his Son, the gift of the Holy Ghost, of the daily providence which has guarded you, and of the hourly benediction

which has been vouchsafed to you, that ye would
fain put aside these unfailing benefits from your
grateful remembrance, while you indulge in some
paltry whim, and tempt the Lord your God by your
mistrust? That be far from any of us! We would
rather take up the position of Shadrach, Meshach,
and Abednego who, when arraigned before Neb-
uchadnezzar, and adjudged to be thrown into the
furnace of fire, said, "Our God is able to deliver us;
but," they added, "if not (though he should do
nothing of the kind) nevertheless be it known unto
thee, O king, we will not serve thy gods, nor worship the golden image which thou hast set up."
That is the spirit in which we ought to walk before God—"Though he slay me, yet will I trust
in him." What if he does not spare my mother's
precious life? What if he does not preserve my
child from the ravages of the fatal epidemic? What
if he take away the desire of mine eyes with a stroke?
What if my business should cease to thrive? What
if my health fail and my strength decay? What
if I be dishonored by the scandal of my neighbors?
Shall I therefore cast off my allegiance to God, or
betray my trust in him? Am I to engage in rebellion like this? Not flood nor flame could quench
or extinguish his love to me. Shall anxiety and
tribulation, disappointment or disaster sever my
heart from devotion to him? Nay, God give me
grace to see my cattle destroyed, and my goods
swept away, and my children cut off in their prime,
and to hear cruel taunts from the wife of my bosom;

to be covered with sore boils, and to sit on a dung-
hill and scrape myself with a potsherd, and then
to find my best friends miserable comforters; and
yet, in the midst of accumulated distresses, to be
able to say, "I know that my Redeemer liveth; he
has not failed to deliver me hitherto, and though,
after my skin, worms destroy this body, yet in my
flesh shall I see God. Though the fig-tree should
not blossom, though the flocks and herds be cut
off, yet will I trust in the Lord and glory in the
God of my salvation." If true to his high profession, the Christian's faith should not borrow its
hue from the circumstances by which he is surrounded. To hanker after signs that a promise
shall be fulfilled is obviously to show distrust of
the promiser. "Now the God of hope fill you with
all joy and peace in believing, that ye may abound
in hope through the power of the Holy Ghost."
So shall you be restrained from asking for a
petty sign to justify you in relying on his princely bounty. The Lord keep you from this great
transgression!

We pass on to observe the penalty that Zacharias
incurred. His morbid propensity was followed by
a mortifying punishment. He had doubted, and
he became dumb, and as the narrative clearly shows
us, he was deaf likewise. Such was his chastisement, and it was sent, not in anger, but in God's
own covenant love. What a salutary medicine!
Although bitter to the taste, how effective it was!
Read his song and you will see the evidence. He

had been for months silent, quiet, shut out from all
sound, and unable to make any. But well he had
occupied his months of seclusion. He had searched
the prophets—do you see that? He had been mus-
ing much upon the coming One—do you see that?
Deep humility had taken the place of arrogant
presumption. He was bowed down before the
majesty of God, yet at the same time full of peace
and blissful hope. Thus he looked into the glorious future. Oh, dear brethren, if you are prone to
doubt, this sickness of the mind will require a
strong corrective. Very likely God will give you
some sharp medicine, but it shall work for your
good. As his child, he will not chasten you so as
to injure you, but he will chasten you so as to
benefit you. I do not think children generally court
the rod, however beneficial it may be, and yet I am
quite sure there is no wise child of God who would
not shrink from the graver ills which render such
discipline essential to his soul's health.

See how judgment was tempered with mercy.
The punishment sent to Zacharias was not so severe as it might have been. Instead of being
struck deaf and dumb, he might have been struck
dead. As I read this passage, I wondered that
God had not struck me deaf and dumb when I have
spoken unbelieving words—when I have been de-
pressed in spirit, and spoken unadvisedly with my
lips. Oh, had the Lord been wroth with me, and
said, "If that is your witness about me, you shall
never speak again." That would have been most

just, and I might have been a mournful instance of his indignation against his unbelieving servants; he has not dealt so with me; glory be to his name!

Nor did this chastisement invalidate the promise. The Lord did not say, " Well, Zacharias, as you don't believe it, your wife Elizabeth shall not have a son. There shall be a John born, but he shall not come to your house." Oh no; that is a grand passage,—" If we believe not, yet he abideth faithful; he cannot deny himself." The promise still stands. God does not take advantage of our unbelief to cry off and say, " I will give thee no blessings, because thou doubtest me,"—no, but having said it, he does it, and his word does not return unto him void. Even the trembling, doubting children, though they get the rod, get the blessing too; and the promise is fulfilled, though the father is dumb when the blessing comes. Very painful, indeed, was his chastisement. One would not like to be deaf and dumb for a day; but to be deaf and dumb for the space of nine months, must have been a very painful trial to this man. Moreover, he could not bless the people; he could not speak a word; he could not instruct the people; he was useless for that part of the priest's work; and when the song went up within the hallowed walls of the temple, he could not hear it. He might know by signs that they were singing a hallelujah, yet his ears could not catch its grateful strains. That poor tongue of his was silent. He could not add a note to the volume of praise that went up to the God he loved. It must have been mournful to him to have no prayer in the family which he could hear and in which he could join, and to be as good as dead for all practical purposes.

Now, I am afraid there are many believers who have had to suffer something like this, for many days, on account of their unbelief. I think I can point out some who are unable to hear the gospel as once they did. Many years ago a friend said that he could not hear me preach, I said to him, " Buy a horn." " No," he said, " it is not your voice; I can hear that, but I don't enjoy it." My reply was: " Perhaps that is my fault, but I am far from sure that it is not your own." I fear, in such cases, it is quite as often the hearer's fault as the preacher's fault. At any rate, when others profit, and our judgment approves, though our hearts find no refreshment, there is reason to suspect that in the dulness of our senses we are compelled to bear chastisement for our unbelief. You go where others go, and find no solace. You hear what edifies and comforts them; but there is no cheer for you. You are deaf; your ears are closed to what the Lord says. Very often it has happened, I fear, to some here, that, for want of faith, they have lost their speech. Time was when they could tell of the Lord's goodness, but they seem silent now. They could sing once, but their harps are hung on the willows now. As they get with their companions, they seem as if they have lost all their pleasant conversation. If they try the old accustomed strings

of the time-worn harp, the ancient skill is gone.
They cannot praise God as once they did; and all
because on one occasion, when the promise was
clear before their eyes, they would challenge and
mistrust it. They could not rely upon their God.
Little do we know how many Fatherly chastisements come upon us as the result of our unbelief.

The lessons I gather, and with which I conclude,
are these,—First, if any of you, beloved, are weak in
faith: do not be satisfied about it. Cry to God.
Our God deserves better homage of us than a weak,
attenuated faith can render him. He deserves to
be trusted with such confidence as a child gives his
parent. Ask him to increase your faith. And you
who have faith; oh keep it jealously, exercise it
habitually; pray to the Lord to preserve it. Never
begin to walk according to the sight of the eyes.
Confer not with flesh and blood. Don't come down
from that blessed height of simple confidence in
God, but ask that you may abide there, and no
longer doubt. The church wants believers to believe for her, and to pray for her. "He that wav-
ereth is like a wave of the sea, driven by the wind
and tossed. Let not that man think that he shall
receive anything of the Lord." Art thou strong in
faith, be thou stronger still: art thou weak in faith,
be thou strong.

But let the unbeliever, the utter unbeliever, tremble. If a good man, a saved man, a noble and a
blameless man was nevertheless for months struck
dumb for unbelief, what will become of you who

have no faith at all? He that believeth not is condemned already, because he hath not believed on the Son of God. To you, unbeliever, no angel Gabriel will appear, but the destroying angel awaits you. What shall be your fearful chastisement? You will be silent: it will be eternal. Oh, you shall stand silent at the judgment seat of Christ, unable to offer any excuse for your rebellion and unbelief. Unbelief will destroy the best of us: faith will save the worst of us. He that believeth on the Lord Jesus Christ hath eternal life,—he that believeth not (whatever else his apparent excellencies), will assuredly perish. Faith, faith! this is the priceless saving thing to every one of us. The gift be yours to believe. The grace be yours to inherit the righteousness of faith. The joy be yours to believe in Jesus Christ with all your hearts. The triumph be yours to believe now to the saving of your souls. Amen.

A Serious Contrast.

He that covereth his sins shall not prosper.—PROVERBS xxviii. 13.
Thou hast covered all their sins.—PSALM lxxxv. 2.

IN these two texts we have *man's covering*, which
is worthless and culpable, and *God's covering*,
which is profitable, and worthy of all acceptation.
No sooner had man disobeyed his Maker's will in
the garden of Eden than he discovered, to his
surprise and dismay, that he was naked, and he
set about at once to make himself a covering. It
was a poor attempt which our first parents made,
and it proved a miserable failure. "They sewed
fig-leaves together." After that God came in, revealed to them yet more fully their nakedness,
made them confess their sin, brought their transgression home to them, and then it is written,
the Lord God made them coats of skin. Probably
the coats were made of the skins of animals which
had been offered in sacrifice, and, if so, they were
a fit type of him who has provided us both with
a sin offering and a robe of perfect righteousness.
Every man since the days of Adam has gone
through much of the same experience, more or

less relying on his own ingenuity to hide his own confusion of face. He has discovered that sin has made him naked, and he has set to work to clothe himself. As I shall have to show you presently, he has never succeeded. But God has been pleased to deal with his own people, according to the riches of his grace; he has covered their shame and put away their sins that they should not be remembered any more.

Let me now direct your attention, first, to man's covering, and its failure; and, then, to God's covering, and its perfection.

May the Holy Spirit be pleased to give you discernment, that you may see your destitute state in the presence of God, and understand the merciful relief that God himself has provided in the bounty of his grace!

I. There are many ways in which men try to cover their sin. Some do so by denying that they have sinned; or, admitting the fact, they deny the guilt; or else, candidly acknowledging both the sin and the guilt, they excuse and exonerate themselves on the plea of certain circumstances which render it, according to their showing, almost inevitable that they should act as they have done. By pretext and pretence, apology and self-vindication, they acquit themselves of all criminality, and put a fine gloss upon every foul delinquency. Excuse-making is the commonest trade under heaven. The slenderest materials are put to the greatest account. A man who has no valid argument in arrest of judgment, no feasible reason why he should not be condemned, will go about and bring a thousand excuses, and ten thousand circumstances of extenuation, the whole of them weak and attenuated as a spider's web. Some one here may be saying within himself, " It may be I have broken the law of God, but it was too severe. To keep so perfect a law was impossible. I have violated it, but then I am a man, endowed with passions that involve propensities, and inflamed with desires that need gratification. How could I do otherwise than I have done? Placed in peculiar circumstances, I am borne along with the current. Subject to special temptations, I yield to the fascination; this is natural." So you think; so you essay to exculpate yourself. But, in truth, you are now committing a fresh sin; for you are accusing God, you are inculpating the Almighty. You are impugning the law to vindicate yourself for breaking it. There is no small degree of criminality about such an unrighteous defence. The law is holy, just, and good. You are throwing the onus of your sins upon God. You are trying to make out that after all you are not to blame, but the fault lies with him who gave the commandment. Do you think that this will be tolerated? Shall the prisoner at the bar bring accusations against the Judge who tries him? Or shall he challenge the equity of the statute while he is arraigned for violating it? And as for the circumstances that you plead, what valid excuse can they furnish? Has it come to this—that it was not you, but your necessities, that did the wrong and are answerable for the consequence? Not you, indeed! you are a harmless, innocent victim of circumstances! I suppose, instead of being censured, you ought almost to be pitied. What is this, again, but throwing the blame upon the arrangements of Providence, and saying to God, "It is the harshness of thy discipline, not the perverseness of my actions, that involves me in sin." What, I say, is this but a high impertinence, ay, veritable treason, against the Majesty of that thrice holy God, before whom even perfect angels veil their faces, while they cry, "Holy, holy, holy, Lord God of hosts." I pray thee resort not to such a covering as this, because, while it is utterly useless, it adds sin to sin, and exposes thee to fresh shame.

In many cases persons violating the law of God have hope to cover their transgression by secrecy. They have done the deed in darkness. They hope that no ear of man heard their footfall or listened to their speech. Possibly they themselves held their tongue, and flattered themselves that no observer witnessed their movements or could divulge their action. So was it with Achan. I dare say he took the wedge of gold and the Babylonish garment, 'mid the confusion of the battle, and hid it when his comrades seemed too much engaged to notice so trivial an affair. While they were rushing over the fallen walls of Jericho, amidst the *débris* and the dust, he might be unmolested; and then, in the dead of the night, while they slept, he turned the sod of his tent, dug into the earth, and buried there his coveted treasure. All looks right, to his heart's content. He has smoothed it down, and spread his carpet over the grave of his lust. Little did he reckon of the Omniscient eye. Little did he count on the unerring lot that would come home to the tribe of Judah, to the family of the Zarhites, to the house of Zabdi, and, at last, to the son of Carmi, so that Achan himself would have to stand out confessed as a traitor—a robber of his God. Men little know the ways in which the Almighty can find them out, and bring the evidence that convicts out of the devices that were intended to cover their sin.

Do you not know that Providence is a wonderful detective? There are hounds upon the track of every thief, and murderer, and liar—in fact, upon every sinner of every kind. Each sin leaves a trail. The dogs of judgment will be sure to scent it out, and find their prey. There is no disentangling yourselves from the meshes of guilt; no possibility of evading the penalty of transgression. Very wonderful have been the ways in which persons who have committed crimes have been brought to judgment. A trifle becomes a tell-tale. The method of deceit gives a clue to the manner of discovery. Wretched the men who bury their secrets in their own bosom. Their conscience plays traitor to them. They have often been forced to betray themselves. We have read of men talking in their sleep to their fellows, and babbling out in their dreams the crime they had committed years before. God would have the secret disclosed. No eye had seen, neither could any other tongue have told, but the man turned king's evidence against himself; he has thus brought himself to judgment. It has often happened, in some form or other, that conscience has thus been witness against men. Do I address any one who is just now practicing a secret sin? You would not have me point you out for all the world, nor shall I do so. Believe me, however, the sin is known. Dexterous though you have been in the attempt to conceal it, it has been seen. As surely as you live, it has been seen. "By whom?" say you. Ah, by One who never forgets what he sees; and he will be sure to tell of it. He may commission a little bird of the air to whisper it. Certainly he will one day proclaim it by the sound of trumpet to listening worlds. You are watched, sir; you are known. You have been narrowly observed, young girl; those things you have hidden away will be brought to light, for God is the great discoverer of sin. His eye has marked you; his providence will track you. It is vain to think that ye can conceal your transgressions. Before high heaven, disguise is futile. Yea, the darkness hideth not; the night shineth as the day. I have known persons who have harbored a sin in their breast till it has preyed upon their constitution. They have been like the Spartan boy who had stolen a fox, and was ashamed to have it known, so he kept it within his garment, till it ate through his flesh, and he fell dead. He suffered the fox to gnaw his heart ere he would betray himself. There are those who have got a sin, if not a lie in their right hand, yea, a lie in their heart; and it is eating into their very life. They dare not confess it. If they would confess it to their God, and make restitution to those whom they have offended, they would soon come to peace; but they vainly hope that they can cover the sin, and hide it from the eyes of God and man. He that covereth his sin in this fashion shall not prosper.

Again, full many a time sinners have tried to cover their sin with falsehood. Indeed, this is the usual habit—to lie—to cloak their guilt by denying it. Was not this the way with Gehazi? When the prophet said, " Whence comest thou, Gehazi?" He said, "Thy servant went no whither." Then the prophet told him that the leprosy of Naaman should cleave to him all the days of his life. The sin of Ananias and Sapphira, in lying in order to hide their sin, how quickly was it discovered, and how terrible was the retribution! I wonder that men and women can lie as they do after reading that story. "Hast thou sold the land for so much?" said Peter. And Ananias said, "Yea, for so much." At that instant he fell down, and gave up the ghost. Three hours after, when his wife Sapphira said the same, the feet of the young men who had buried her husband were at the door ready to carry out her corpse, and bury her by his side. Oh, sirs, ye must weave a tangled web, indeed, when once ye begin to deceive; and when you have woven it you will have to add lie to lie, and lie to lie, and yet all to no purpose, for you will be surely found out. There is something about a lie that always deludes the man who utters it. Liars have need of good memories. They are sure to leave a little corner uncovered through which the truth escapes. Their story does not hang together. Discrepancies excite suspicions, and evasions furnish a clue to discoveries, till the naked truth is unveiled. Then the deeper the plot, the fouler is the shame. But to lie unto the God of truth, of what avail can that be? What advantageth it you to plead "not guilty," when he has witnessed your crime? That infallible Eye which never mistakes, is always watchful. He knows everything; from him no secret is hid. Why, therefore, dost thou imagine that thou canst deceive thy Maker? There are some who try to cover their sin by prevarication. With cunning subtlety they strive to evade personal responsibility. Memorable is the instance of David. I will not dwell upon his flagrant crime; but I must remind you of his sorry subterfuge, when he tried to hide the baseness of his lust by conspiring to cause the death of Uriah. There have been those who have schemed deep and long to throw the blame on others, even to the injury of their reputation, to escape the odium of their own malpractices. Who knows but in this congregation there may be some one who affects a high social position, supported by a

deep mercantile immorality? Merchants there
have been that have swollen before the public as
men of wealth, while they were falsifying their ac-
counts, abstracting money, yet making the books
tally; thus rolling in luxury, and living in jeopardy.
Have they prospered? Were they to be envied?
The detection that long haunted them at length
overtook them; could they look it in the face?
We have heard of their blank despair, their insane
suicide: at any rate, a miserable exposure has been
the melancholy climax. "Be sure your sin will
find you out." You may run the length of your
tether. It is short. The hounds of justice, swift of
scent and strong of limb, are on your trail. Rest
assured, you will be discovered. Could you escape the due reward in this life, yet certainly
your guilt is known in heaven, and you shall be
judged and condemned in that great day which
shall decide your eternal destiny. Seek not, then,
to cover up sin with such transparent cobwebs as
these.

Some people flatter themselves that their sin has
already been hidden away by the lapse of time.
"It was so very long ago," says one, "I had almost
forgotten it; I was a lad at the time." "Ay," says
another, "I am gray-headed now. It must have
been twenty or thirty years ago. Surely, you do
not think that the sin of my far-off days will be
brought out against me. The thing is gone by.
Time must have obliterated it." Not so my friend.
It may be the lapse of time will only make the dis-

covery the more clear. A boy once went into his father's orchard, and there, in his rough play, he broke a little tree which his father valued. But, rapidly putting it together again, he managed to conceal the fact, for the disunited parts of the tree took kindly to each other, and the tree stood as before. It so happened that more than forty years afterwards he went into that garden after a storm had blown across it in the night, and he found the tree had been riven in two, and it had snapped precisely in the place where he had broken it when it was but a sapling. So there may come a crash to your character precisely in that place where you sinned when yet a lad. Ah, how often the transgressions of our youth remain within our bosoms. There lie the eggs of our young sin, and they hatch when men come into riper years. Don't be so sure that the lapse of time will consign your faults and follies to oblivion. You sow your wild oats, sir; you have got to reap them. The time that has intervened has only operated to make that evil seed spring up, and you are so much the nearer to the harvest. Time does not change the hue of sin in the sight of God. If a man could live a thousand years, the sins of his first year would be as fresh in the memory of the Almighty as those of the last. Eternity itself will never wash out a sin. Flow on, ye ages; but the scarlet spot is on the sand. Flow on still in mighty streams, but the damning spot is there still. Neither time nor eternity can cleanse it. Only one thing can remove sin. The lapse of time cannot. Let not any of you be so foolish as to hope it will.

When the trumpet of resurrection sounds, there will be a resurrection of characters, as well as of men. The man who has been foully slandered will rejoice in the light that reflects his purity. But the man whose latent vices have been skilfully veneered will be brought to the light too. His acts and motives will be alike exposed. As he himself looks and sees the resuscitation of his crimes, with what horror will he face that day of judgment! "Ah! ah!" says he; "Where am I? I had forgotten these. These are the sins of my childhood, the sins of my youth, the sins of my manhood, and the sins of my old age. I thought they were dead and buried, but they start from their tombs. My memory has been quickened. How my brain reels as I think of them all! But there they are, and, like so many wolves around me, they seem all thirsting for my destruction." Beware, oh men! Ye have buried your sins, but they will rise up from their graves and accuse you before God. Time cannot cover them.

Or do any of you imagine that your tears can blot out your transgressions? That is a gross mistake. Could your tears forever flow; could you be transformed into a Niobe, and do nothing else but weep for aye, the whole flood could not wash out a single sin. Some have supposed that there may be efficacy in baptismal water, or in sacramental emblems, or in priestly incantations, or in

confession to a man ten times worse than themselves—one who has the impertinence to ask them
to disclose their secret wickedness to him, and betrays a morbid avidity to make his breast the
sewer into which all kinds of uncleanness should
be emptied. Be not deceived. There is nothing
in these ordinances of man, or these tricks of priestcraft (I had almost said of witchcraft, the two are
so much alike) to excuse the folly of those who are
beguiled by them. You need not catch at straws
when the rope is thrown out to you. There is pardon to be had; remission is to be found; forgiveness
can be procured. Turn your back on yonder shave-
lings; lend not your ear to them, neither be ye
the victims of their snares. In the street each day
it makes one's soul sick to see them. Like the
Pharisees of old, they wear their long garments to
deceive. You cannot mistake them. Their silly
conceit publishes their naked shame. Confide not
in them for a moment. Christ can forgive you.
God can blot out your sin. But they cannot ease
your conscience by their penances, or remove your
transgressions by their celebrations.

Thus I have gone through a rough, not very ac-
curate list of the ways by which men hope to cover
their sin, but they "shall not prosper." None of
these shall succeed.

II. A more joyous task devolves on me now,
while I draw your attention to my second text—
"Thou hast covered all their sin." This fact is af-
firmed concerning the people of God. All who

have trusted in the atoning sacrifice which was presented by the Lord Jesus Christ upon Calvary may accept this welcome assurance—" God has covered all their sin." How this hath come to pass I will tell you. Before ever God covers a man's sins, he unveils them. Did you ever see your sins unveiled? Did it ever seem as if the Lord put his hand upon you, and said—" Look, look at them "? Have you been led to see your sins as you never saw them before? Have you felt that their aggravations were fit to drive you to despair? As you have looked at them, has the finger of detection seemed to point out your blackness? Have you discovered in them a depth of guilt, and iniquity, and hell-desert which never struck your mind before? I recollect a time when that was a spectacle always before the eyes of my conscience. My sin was ever before me. If God thus makes you see your sin in the light of his countenance, depend upon it he has purposes of mercy toward you. When you see and confess it, he will blot it out. So soon as God, in infinite loving-kindness, makes the sinner know in truth that he is a sinner, and strips him of the rags of his self-righteousness, he grants him pardon and clothes his nakedness. While he stands shivering before the gaze of the Almighty condemned, the guilt is purged from his conscience. I do not know of a more terrible position in one's experience than to stand with an angry God gazing upon you, and to know that wherever God's eye falls upon you, it sees nothing but sin; sees nothing in you but what he must hate and utterly abhor. Yet this is the experience through which God puts those to whom he grants forgiveness. He makes them know that he sees how sinful they are, and he makes them feel how vile and leprous they are. His justice withers their pride; his judgment appals their heart. They are humbled in the very dust, and made to cry out— each man trembling for his own soul—"God be merciful to me a sinner!"

Not till this gracious work of conviction is fully wrought does the Lord appear with the glorious proclamation, that whosoever believeth in the Lord Jesus shall have his sins covered. That proclamation I have now openly to publish and personally to deliver to you. With your outward ears you may have heard it hundreds of times. It is old, yet ever new. Whosoever among you, knowing himself to be guilty, will come and put his trust in Jesus Christ, shall have his sins covered. "Can God do that?" Yes, he can. He alone can cover sin. Against him the sin was committed. It is the offended person who must pardon the offender. No one else can. He is the King. He has the right to pardon. He is the Sovereign Lord, and he can blot out sin. Beside that, he can cover it lawfully, for the Lord Jesus Christ (though ye know the story, let me tell it again—the song of redemption always rings out a charming melody), Jesus Christ, the Father's dear Son, in order that the Justice of God might be vindicated, bare his breast to its dreadful hurt, and suffered in our room and place and stead, what we ought to have suffered as the penalty of our sin. Now the sacrifice of Christ covers sin—covers it right over; and he more than conceals it, he makes it cease to be. Moreover, the Lord Jesus kept the law of God. and his obedience stands in stead of our obedience; and God accepts him and his righteousness on our behalf, imputing his merits to our souls.

Oh, the virtue of that atoning blood! Oh, the blessedness of that perfect righteousness of the Son of God, by which he covers our sins!

There are two features of covering I should like to recall to your recollection. The one was the mercy seat or propitiatory, inside the golden ark, where were the tables of stone. Those tables of stone seemed, as it were, to reflect the sins of Israel. As in a mirror, they reflected the transgression of God's people. God was above, as it were, looking down between the cherubic wings. Was he to look down upon the law defied and defiled by Israel? Ah, no; there was put over the top of the ark, as a lid which covered it all, a golden lid called the mercy seat, and when the Lord looked down he looked upon that lid which covered sin. Beloved, such is Jesus Christ, the covering for all our sins. God sees no sin in those who are hidden beneath Jesus Christ.

There was another covering at the Red Sea. On that joyous day when the Egyptians went down into the midst of the sea, pursuing the Israelites, at the motion of Moses' rod the waters that stood upright like a wall leapt back in their natural bed and swallowed up the Egyptians. Great was the victory when Miriam sang, "The depths have covered them. There is not one of them left." It is even so that Jesus Christ's atonement has covered up our sins. They are sunk in his sepulchre; they are buried in his tomb. His blood, like the Red Sea, has drowned them. "The depths have covered them. There is not one of them left." Against the believer there is not a sin in God's Book recorded. He that believeth in him is perfectly absolved. "Thou hast covered all their sin." I shall not have time to dwell upon the sweetness of this fact, but I invite you that believe to consider its preciousness; and I hope you who have not believed will feel your mouth watering after it; to know that every sin one has ever committed, known and unknown, is gone— covered by Christ. To be assured that when Jesus died he did not die for some of our sins, but for all the sins of his people; not for their sins up till now, but for all the sins they ever will commit! Well does Kent put it:

> "Here's pardon for transgressions past,
>   It matters not how black their cast;
>   And, O, my soul, with wonder view,
>   For sins to come here's pardon too."

The atonement was made before the sin was committed. The righteousness was presented even before we had lived. "Thou hast covered all their sin." It seems to me as if the Lamb of God slain from before the foundation of the world had in the purpose of God, from the foundation of the world, covered all his people's sins. Therefore we are accepted in the Beloved, and dear to the Father's heart. Oh, what a joy it is to get a hold of something like this truth, especially when the truth gets a hold of you—when you can feel by the inwrought power and witness of the Holy Ghost, that your sins are covered—that you dare stand up before a rein-trying, heart-searching God, and give thanks that every transgression you ever committed is hid from the view of those piercing eyes through Jesus Christ your Lord.

Some people think we ought not to talk thus, that it is presumptuous. But really there is more presumption in doubting than there is in believing. For a child to believe his Father's word is never presumption. I like to credit my Father's word. "He that believeth in him is not condemned." Condemned I am not, for I know I do believe in him. "Who is he that condemneth? It is Christ that died, yea rather, that is risen again, who is even at the right hand of God, who also maketh intercession for us."

Beloved, the covering is as broad as the sin. The covering completely covers, and forever covers; for as God sees to-day no sin in those who are washed in Jesus' blood, so will he never see any. You are accepted with an acceptance which nothing can change. Whom once he loves he never leaves, but loves them to the end. The reason of his love to them does not lie in their merits nor their charms; the cause of love is in himself. The ground of his acceptance of them is in the person and work of Christ. Whatever they may be, whatever their condition of heart, they are accepted, because Christ lived and died. It is not a precarious or a conditional, but an eternal acceptance.

Would you enjoy the blessedness of this complete covering? Cowering down beneath the tempest of Jehovah's wrath, which you feel in your conscience, would you obtain this full remission? Behold the gates of the City of Refuge which stand wide open. The grace of our Lord Jesus Christ is proclaimed to the thirsty, needy, laboring, weary soul. Not merely are the gates open, but the invitation to enter is given—"Come unto me, all ye that labor and are heavy laden, and I will give you rest." You are bidden to lay hold upon eternal life. The way of doing so is simple. No works of yours, no merits, no tears, no preparations are required, but trust—trust—that is all. Believe in Jesus. Rely upon him; depend upon him. I have heard of Homer's Iliad being enclosed in a nutshell, so small was it written; but here is the Plain Man's Guide to heaven in a nutshell. Here is the essence of the whole gospel in one short sentence. "Believe in the Lord Jesus Christ and thou shalt be saved." Trust him; trust him. This is the meaning of that word believe. Depend upon him, and as surely as thou doest it, neither death, nor hell, shall ever separate thee from the love of him whom thou hast embraced, from the protection of him in whose power thou hast taken shelter. So shall your present peace be the foretaste of your eternal felicity. Amen.

A Sad Confession.

We hid as it were our faces from him.—ISAIAH liii. 3.

YOU will find in the margin of some of your Bibles that this passage is rendered " He hid as it were his face from us." The literal translation of the Hebrew would be, " He was as a hiding of faces from him," or "from us." Some critical readers think these words were intended to describe our Lord as having so humbled himself, and brought himself to such a deep degradation, that he was comparable to the leper who covered his face and cried, " Unclean, unclean," hiding himself from the gaze of men. Abhorred and despised by men, he was like one put aside because of his disease and shunned by all mankind. Others suppose the meaning to be that on account of our Lord's terrible and protracted sorrow his face wore an expression so painful and grievous that men could scarcely bear to look upon him. They hid as it were their faces from him—amazed at that brow all carved with lines of anxious thought, those cheeks all ploughed with furrows of deep care, those eyes all sunk in shades of sadness, that

(203)

soul bowed down, exceeding sorrowful, even unto
death! It may be so; we cannot tell. So let it
pass. I have a plain, practical purpose to pursue.
Here is an indictment to which we must all plead
guilty. Let us make the reflection our own, as we
humbly bow at the dear pierced feet of our Lord,
and remember how cruelly we slighted our kindest
friend, when "We hid as it were our faces from
him."

At sundry times and in divers manners we may
have done this. Where shall I begin? Alas, I
fear me that contempt and contumely alone will
interpret some men's sayings and doings. Their
conversation is so profane that their crime becomes
palpable. Sometimes men hide their faces from
Jesus in cool contempt of him. How astounding!
how revolting! He, the Lord of glory, the Creator
of heaven and earth, out of compassion to the children of men, condescended to take upon himself
our nature—should we therefore slight him? Being found in fashion as a man, he was subjected to
all the pains and miseries of this mortal life, and
encountered the horrors of death itself—should we
therefore revile or should we not revere him? He
ought surely to be esteemed by all mankind. I
have sometimes felt that, had he not redeemed my
soul, I must reverence him for redeeming others.
Had I never tasted of his love at all myself, yet the
story of his love to his enemies is such that methinks
I could fall down and worship him. His character
claims our admiration and appeals to the tenderest

feelings of our heart. So disinterested was the love of Christ; so self-denying; so unwavering in its constancy; that he surpassed every instance on record, and excelled any ideal that the most gifted imagination could paint. Greater love hath no man than this, that he lay down his life for his friends. There creature generosity exhausts itself; mere human love has reached its limit. But God commends his love toward us in that while we were yet sinners Christ died for us.

And this blessed man Christ Jesus personally shows and makes evident this love to his enemies, his persecutors, his murderers. Still there are those who scorn his name while they scan his history. We can scarcely speak of him but forthwith the vials of their wrath begin to distil. Strange is it that a fame so lively and a name so altogether lovely should so commonly set a man against his fellows, and become the innocent cause of strife and persecution in the world. That name of Jesus—a name of highest heavenly glory, a name of peace profound, a name of universal good will, a name to knit all mankind in one common brotherhood—has become, by the perversity of human nature, a by-word and a reproach. Their Saviour in every age they have not known, their day of visitation they have not heeded. Hence his name has excited wrath and opposition among the sons of men, where it should have excited reverence and love. Some show their opposition by attempting to ignore or to tarnish the dignity of his person. These blatant infidels, I trust, are getting fewer and fewer. The rough, bullying speech of Tom Paine we sincerely hope will never be heard on earth again. There are *thinkers* (as they would have us account them) abroad in these days more courteous in their address and far more cautious in their language than the disbelievers of former times; but too often they are as full of malignity and deadly venom against the Christ of God as were the coarsest scoffers who uttered their blasphemy before we were born, so persistently is the person of Christ held in contempt alike by Greek and barbarian.

And are there not others who affect great admiration for Jesus of Nazareth as an example of virtue and benevolence, who nevertheless reject his mediatorial work as our Redeemer? As a substitutionary sacrifice they do not and cannot esteem him. Isaiah in the chapter before us was holding up Christ as the Lamb led to the slaughter, the victim of our transgressions, bearing our chastisement. How the anger of some men kindles at this representation of the gospel! They sneer at the doctrine of substitution, vicarious sacrifice, atonement; at the simple fact indeed that "his own self bare our sins in his own body on the tree." That he was a true philanthropist, an admirable teacher, and an inspired prophet, they will readily allow; but that our iniquities were laid on him, that he was punished in our stead, that he died the just for the unjust, they set aside as though it were an idle tale, a baseless fiction. This noblest of all doctrines, the grandest of all conceptions, is here brought down to the humblest capacity of the most simple understanding. The learned can find no flaw in the logic. But learning and logic have little enough to do with it. The heart that believes it can tell its worth. *"He loved me and gave himself for me."* Angels have but to hear of it and they sing of it. Marvel of marvels that there should be men on earth so wise that they hoot at its mention, and count it worthy of nothing but their scorn! They hide as it were their faces from the crucified Saviour. And then they will pour contempt upon the various doctrines of his gospel. Not satisfied with opposing the main and cardinal truth, they will hold up other parts of revelation to ridicule. If a man likes to laugh and wishes to scoff, he can find food for his folly in infinite wisdom. Nay, he can, if he has eyes that are full enough of falsehood, discover faults even in the immaculate God himself. Given but the desire to deride and parody, the occasions and opportunities will always be plentiful.

And with what pitiful disdain the Lord's people are slighted! The followers of Christ are, as it is commonly said, poor people, illiterate and uninstructed; and but few of the great ones of the earth or the learned men will give in their names as adherents of the Saviour! Well, so it ever has been. And yet the day shall come when the Lord shall vindicate his own election, and prove how infinitely superior it is to man's reputation. What though he choose the base things of the world and the things that are not, yet by these will he be exalted when his enemies are rolled in the dust.

Do I address anybody who has despised the Lord Jesus Christ? Ah, my friend, little do you consider what you have done. Your wantonness can offer no excuse but your ignorance. And as for your ignorance, it is without excuse. You are unacquainted with our Lord, or you would not decry him. Bethink yourselves, I pray you. Have you really studied his character? Have you looked into the proofs of his being the Messiah? Have you weighed the evidence of his Divinity? If you have not, surely you should be ashamed of your temerity. Can it be that out of mere prejudice you have condemned an unheard One who to us is all our hope, One who has lifted some of us out of despair and given us peace of mind, One who is now so dear to us that we feel we could cheerfully die for him? Do not affront him. Do not disparage his claim upon our tender regard. Do not speak ill of his blessed name. He is a friend to some of us, the like of whom we never elsewhere found. Were it not wiser and fitter every way that ye should listen to our testimony and go to him, and see whether he will not save you, and make you partakers of our joy? If he reject you, or if you find him false to his promises, then speak against him; but we beseech you, do not begin to rail before you have any reason. He that builds upon this stone builds securely, but alas for the man that falls foul of this stone, it will assuredly grind him to powder. As surely as Christ is God, those who oppose him will one day wonder and perish. The peril is looming as the day is coming. The glorious apocalypse for which saints look will bring about a total eclipse of every one that is proud and lofty, and everything that is high and lifted up. I will not linger on so dreadful a look-out, but I earnestly admonish you to lay it to heart.

A second and far more common way in which men hide their faces from Christ is by their heedlessness, their indifference, their neglect. Alas! all of us are guilty or have been guilty in this respect. Allow me to ask you, my beloved friends in Christ, to look back a little while to the period before your conversion. Was not Jesus as worthy of your love then as he is now, as glorious, as admirable? And yet for how long a time had you hid your face from him! Surely you must remember the days gone by when you did not care even to hear about him. Any kind of amusement was more fascinating for you than discourse or converse concerning you Saviour and your King. There is music in his name now: it was dull enough to you once. You heard sermons without heeding them. Perhaps some of you were constrained by force of circumstance to attend the sanctuary, though no part of the service was attuned to your taste. You. mixed with the multitude, but you did not see or draw near the Master. They were dreary hours; you were glad when they were spent, and you were liberated. You listened, but what came in at one ear went out at the other. Scarcely so much; for you did not allow it to go far enough into your brain for that. Listlessly you listened, with no desire to learn anything about that Christ who is your only true Saviour, your only rightful Sovereign. If you had been in the market and some one had been describing the prices of goods, telling you of the probabilities of a rise or fall, you would have been all attention; and you would have found no difficulty in carrying home the bulk of what you had heard, especially that part which was about your own business. But oh, in those days Christ was nothing to you. The preacher might lift him up with all his might, and tell you with tears that if you rejected him you must perish. You took no notice. You did not care whether you perished or not. You did not give Christ your thought. He was put before you, but you hid as it were your faces from him. Although the Bible was in your house, bearing witness to Jesus Christ, you never searched it. You may have taken the Book down sometimes and read a chapter here or picked out a verse there, and congratulated yourself not a little upon your good deed; but as to searching the Scriptures through, and comparing passage with passage, spiritual things with spiritual, that you might know Jesus Christ who is hidden there like a pearl in the field—oh no, you did not care to give all diligence in this matter. Why, some of you young men were studying hard years ago. You rose up early and sat up late over books professional

and profound, and truly if you were to be proficient
in your secular calling you had need to do so, but
all that while you never sat up an hour later than
usual to make search concerning your soul and the
Lord who bought it with his blood; neither did
you ever rise from your soft couch at daylight on
purpose that you might bow the knee and seek
your Lord and worship him. No, everything was
sought except the Saviour: every duty you would
scrupulously fulfil except that which you owed
your Lord; all the world was fair except the altogether lovely. And, mayhap, at that very time
there were pursuits that gratified you utterly unworthy of your preference. You had loves which
have proved bitterness to you; things that fascinated
your heart that did but degrade you. It was your
best friend; he who only meant your good; he who
elevates the man that does but look to him; he
whose very name fills the soul with refreshment;
he, the love of whose person is heaven begun,—
he was all this, while you cast him into the background.

I am not speaking of you, my friends, as if you
had a monopoly of reproach; I do speak of myself with many deep regrets of heart. I hid as
it were my face from him, and I let the years run
round—not without twitches of conscience; not
without rebukes, when I knew how much I did
need a Saviour; not without the warnings which
came from others whom I saw happy and rejoicing
in Christ, while I had no share in his salvation,

Still I put it off, as perhaps some of you are doing, from day to day, and month to month, and thought that Christ might come in some odd hour and when I had nothing else to do I might think of him whose blood could cleanse me. O my soul, I could fain smite thee now! I have heard of a minister who preached for several years before he was converted, and when converted he became a very earnest preacher of the gospel; but one day as he rode along the street he was observed to stop and cane a dog which was lying in front of a door. When they said to him, "Mr. McPhayle, why did you beat the dog?" he said, "He was so exactly like myself, lying in the sun sleeping—a dumb dog that didn't bark—that I could not but give him a touch of the rod; though I meant it all the while for myself." Truly I could lay this rod about my own heart to think that weeks and months should have rolled over my head, and I should have hid as it were my face from Christ in wilful neglect of my dear Lord whose heart has bled for me. Does not this come home to any-body here? Are there not some who might justly chastise themselves?

But we pass on to a third form of this same folly. We hid as it were our faces from him, many of us, by preferring any other mode of salvation to salvation by faith in Christ. The great gospel fact is that whosoever looks to Christ is saved. The moment faith, with her intelligent eye, beholds Christ on the cross, and depends on him, the man that exercises that faith is forgiven, rescued, saved. Now, when we were aroused to something like anxiety about our souls, we were told this. Some of us were told it very plainly, others, perhaps, not quite so clearly; but we did not like this way of being saved simply by believing. Did not we try to merit salvation by our own good works? Oh, we would do this, and that, and the other; we would correct ourselves in this department, and we would push on and make progress in the other; and we tried to do so. Oh, I could pour scorn upon myself to think of some of the good resolutions I made! I blew them up like children with their pipes and their soap. Fine bubbles they were, reflecting all the colors of the rainbow. But a touch, and they dissolved. They were good for nothing—poor stuff to built eternal hopes upon. Oh, that working of ours! What slavery it was, but what small results it produced! We came to grief whenever we began to get a little comfortable with ourselves. Just when we said, " Now my tower will stand, " there came an earthquake and it all went to a heap of ruins.

Then, if we remember well, we tried our feelings: we said, "It cannot be that if I believe in Jesus just as I am I shall be saved: I must feel something." How we resorted to sharp books, terrible sketches of death and judgment and perdition—I know I did. Baxter's *Call to the Unconverted* cut me to the quick, and harrowed up my

gloomiest apprehensions. We expected to feel
something indescribable, and when we began to
feel a little alarm and distress of mind we found
it was not the thing that brought satisfaction to
the mind or peace to the heart; for the more we
did feel the less we thought we felt; and the more
we felt, the less we considered our feelings to
be of the right kind. So, after tossing, and
toiling and rowing with feelings, we found we
had got no farther than we did with works. And
all this while there stood the Saviour with this
simple counsel—" Look unto Me, and be ye saved,
all the ends of the earth." Still we wrapped ourselves in our mantle and hid as it were our faces
from him. We kept looking at ourselves and
inquiring in the biographies of good men after
this feeling and after the other, while we hid as
it were our faces from him.

And when we were beaten off from that false
refuge we took to a fresh conceit. Thinking we
could pray ourselves into heaven, we began to
pray. This would have been quite right, had not
we put the exercise of prayer before the commandment to believe. " He that believeth and is baptized shall be saved,"—that is the gospel. We
were reluctant to surrender ourselves to an im-
plicit confidence in our Lord; so we resolved to
pray. Prayer seemed to us a proper performance;
a religious duty acceptable to God and much to be
commended. We did not understand that we
must need be quickened into life before we could

breathe freely. Looking upon daily prayer as a kind of ecclesiastical exercise, albeit there was no real heart in it, we thought some good would come of making it a habit. But no good did come. Our prayers became a form, and we disquieted ourselves in vain. We found we could not pray. Oh, what fools we were. What fools all of us are to look anywhere for salvation but to Jesus Christ! God the Father has set forth Christ to be a propitiation for sin. If God has done that, cannot I be contented? If the Lord has accepted Christ instead of me and promised that if I believe in Jesus I shall be saved, why need I gad about to find some other way of peace, pardon, and full salvation? Is not God's way good enough for me? If God accepts it, why should not I rejoice in it?

O dear friends, if we have been covering our faces, let us uncover them now, and if they are black as soot with sin, let us just look up to the cross with a black face, and say, "Saviour of sinners, I, the very chief among them, put my sole trust in thee! Hiding my eyes no more from the light, I will look to thee and trust thee with all my heart."

In yet another way we hid our faces from him. After we were quite sure that we could not be saved other than by the one Mediator, do you remember how we continued to hide our face from Jesus by persistent unbelief in him? I know it for myself. I held up the handkerchief before my eyes, saturated with my own tears. His sympathy for our sorrows I could not credit. It is the sullen sulk of sad souls. Their distress of mind has come between them and the Redeemer. Strange to tell, some men will reason against themselves. No doubt, if there were a gift to be bestowed upon all the poor people in the parish, everybody who wanted anything would try to prove himself to be in the parish. If there was a man who lived with half his house in one parish and half in another, I'll be bound to say he would try to prove he lived in the parish where the gifts were to be had; but somehow or other awakened sinners try to prove that they are not the sort of people Christ died for. They used to have in Rome when they were canonizing saints an *Advocatus Diaboli,* or advocate of the devil, who was wont to plead against the person being canonized, and offer all the objections he could. It seems strange that so many people should turn *Advocati Diaboli* against themselves. I can tell you how they argue, for I have talked to them by the hour, and this has been the fashion of their counter-pleading, " But, sir, I don't feel my need of it." We reply, " If you cannot go to Christ *with* a broken heart, go to Christ *for* a broken heart." " Oh, but, sir, I don't feel that I am fit to go." " Your unfitness is the only evidence he wants." " But I don't think I have repented enough." " Granted; and you never will repent enough, could your tears forever flow. You cannot be saved by the merit of your repentance. Jesus Christ will forgive your impenitence as well as your other sins. Certainly if you want more repentance, you must go to him for it." "Well, but, sir, do you know I cannot help fearing that perhaps I am not one of the elect?" We have replied, "Perhaps you are; and anyhow you had better go to Christ, because he has given an invitation to every creature: he says, 'Whosoever will, let him come and take of the water of life freely.'" "Ah, sir, but you don't know—I am so indifferent." "Well, but you never will be otherwise than indifferent as long as you stay away from the Saviour. If you go to him and put your trust in him, he will remove your indifference. He alone can roll away this stone from the door of your heart." One moment they will say they do not feel, and almost in the same breath they will turn round and say they feel the horrors of despair. When they tell you of the dreadful blasphemies that come into their mind, you may answer that it is written, "All manner of sin and of blasphemy shall be forgiven unto men, and whosoever believeth in him is not condemned," feel or not feel as he may.

Well, I have pursued that business till I have been pretty nearly tired of it, and then all of a sudden the person I have been trying to comfort has begun again where he commenced, as if he had never said those things before: he has gone over the same round of objections, and I have no doubt would have continued to repeat himself, had I continued to answer him, fifty times over; so did he encourage the morbid apprehension that he should not himself be saved. You see a man put into the condemned cell at Newgate, and you go in and tell him that Her Majesty presents him with a free pardon. I warrant you he will not put his hand to his brow, and say, "Well, but I think there is this or that objection to my accepting it." "No," thinks he, "if there is any objection, let those find it out that like; it is no business of mine." And so with the soul that is bidden to come to Christ; I say, let it come, objections or no objections, and if there be objections, let somebody else find them out, but as for thee, poor sinner, don't cover thy face from Jesus, but come as thou art, just as thou art, and say, "Here I am, my Saviour: if thou canst save— and I believe thou canst—save me. At any rate, if I perish, I will perish trusting in thee." Rather, sinner, shall heaven and earth pass away than even one soul perish that acts on this firm resolve. Hide not your eyes from the Saviour; it is a dreadful temptation of Satan, this mistaken notion of humility. People think, or affect to think, that it would be arrogant or presumptuous on their part to believe in Jesus. I tell you solemnly that unbelief is not humility; it is a foul conceit. Humility trusts the Saviour. Base indeed is the ingratitude which casts a slur upon his truthfulness, and refrains from venturing to accept his promises. O brethren! we once hid as it were our faces from him; let us pray for others who are hiding their faces, and beseech the Lord to incline them to turn their faces right round to his dear cross, and then let us gently take off the mantle that obscures their vision, and say to them, " Look, look through your tears; look even now; for there is life in a look at the Crucified One."

But not to tarry, I am afraid there are some of us who must plead guilty to another charge; we have hidden as it were our faces from him since he has saved us, and since we have known his love, by our silly shame and our base cowardice. Perhaps I speak to some Christians here who, though they love the Lord, have never professed his name.

Dear brother, dear sister, do you think this is right—is it loyal? Had he kept his love to you a secret, and never openly espoused your cause, and given up himself for your salvation, where would you now have been? Howbeit he boldly declared he was not ashamed to call us " brethren," and true to his word he acted a brother's part, and carried through the work of our redemption. Since Jesus Christ was not ashamed of us, surely we need never be ashamed of him. " But I think I may go to heaven by myself," says one, " for I am afraid I shall compromise other people if I dishonor Christ." And you do not think, my dear brother, that you are dishonoring him by such a suggestion? " Oh, but suppose I were to fall into sin?" Nay; do not you think that even now you are living in sin while you are refusing what he demands, that you should confess him before men? His promise is that he that with his heart believeth, and with his mouth maketh the good confession, shall be saved. Or as it is put in another form, we read, "He that believeth and is baptised" (which is the open confession of him) "shall be saved." Do not, I entreat you, play the coward! "Suppose I should fall," say you, "after I have made a profession?" Which do you think the safer place, where your Lord bids you, or where you choose to be yourself? Come forward, if you are his followers, and put on his regimentals. I wonder what our Government would say if Her Majesty's soldiers were to take off their red coats and protest, "We should be just as good soldiers, and as true, without this uniform as with it." They would be suspected of treason; they would be taken up as deserters. And are there no deserters here? I should like to send the officer round and find you out.

> "Are you the soldiers of the cross
> The followers of the Lamb:
> How can you blush to own his cause,
> Or fear to speak his name?"

Come out, brethren, come out. If you want your Master's blessing, come and join your Master's servants.

Ay; but some of us who have made a profession of our faith may nevertheless have sometimes hid our faces from Christ. Have you never been in company where religion was jested at, and felt, "Well, I had better hold my tongue here?" There are seasons when that is prudent, and even proper,

—when you are so weak a champion that you might damage the cause. At the same time, even the weakest champion had better have his lance broken than be altogether a coward. How often might we have spoken for Jesus when nothing has kept us back except cowardice! It was not prudence, it was cowardice, downright cowardice. We thought they would give us an ill-name, and so we dishonored Christ lest we should encounter a rude joke or a coarse jest from a person whose opinion was never worthy of a moment's thought. I wish there were more boldness for Christ everywhere. In the higher circles he that confesses Christ may have to run the gauntlet for it, but let him do so boldly. And amongst working men in the shop or factory there is a deal of "chaffing" going on, often of a cruel kind, against the Christian, but he who is such a feather-bed soldier that he cannot bear the reproach is not worthy of such a Lord. Our sires were not so tame that they could be intimidated with a taunt. Their cheek never blenched at the stake or in the fire. They were ready to die for the Lord Jesus. How think ye then? Should we play the craven; shall a little maid make us afraid, or shall some silly fools, who scoff at all that is holy, drive us to disown our Saviour? Oh, brethren, do not surrender your souls so cheaply. Never mind their sneers. Never hide your face from him. Come out, and have no fellowship with the profane, the profligate, or the persecutors. Is Christ in the pillory? Put me in with him, and then throw what you like at me. Is Christ's name rolled in the mire and made a by-word and a proverb? Link my name with his and make a by-word and proverb of it. Twist the two together, and let us be the object of your slanders. I will glory in it. The reproach of Christ is greater riches than all the treasures of Egypt. Hide not then your faces from him, beloved, nor shrink from espousing his cause.

I feel sure that many, if not all of us, who are believers will penitently confess that we have sometimes hidden our faces from Christ by not walking in constant fellowship with him. I once asked a brother how long it was since he had enjoyed fellowship with Jesus. His reply was remarkable. "I feel sorry," said he, "you have asked me that question, and yet I must thank you. Had you asked me whether I continued in prayer, I would have said 'Yes,' for, with more or less fervor, I do constantly pray. Had you inquired whether I endeavored to walk honestly and uprightly before my fellow creatures, I should have said, 'Yes, thank God, I hope I have not slipped with my feet;' but when you say, 'How long is it since you really have had fellowship with Jesus?' I blush to own that many a day has passed since I have known this high privilege." Is that so with you, my dear brothers and sisters in Christ? If so, it is very, very sad. Our heart, if we are Christians, is married to Christ. Say, then, would it not be strange if a wife should live with her husband and hide her face from him by the week and month together; should there be scarcely a comfortable word between them; should there only be just the decent civilities of a daily routine, without much concern or any confiding? Yet perhaps some of you pray a little every morning and every night, because you think it is proper. At special times you do your reverence to Christ; and anon you go out into the world, and there, in a measure, you estrange yourselves from him, and then you return home, far from being eager and anxious for communion with your Lord; so, not seeking his face for yourselves, you do in effect hide your face from him. There is no face-to-face fellowship. Remember, I entreat you, that his love to you is constant, although your love to Christ may grow cold. If you can dispense with his company, he delights in your company. There it stands in the Canticles—"Let me see thy face; let me hear thy voice; for sweet is thy voice, and thy countenance is comely." Now, had you said that to Christ, it might be easily understood; but when he says that to you it is most admirable. His love makes him desire to hold fellowship with you —will you refuse it; will you deny him? Surely you will say, "Dost thou think so much of me? I ought to have said to thee what thou hast said to me; thou hast ravished my heart, my sister, my spouse, with one look of thine eyes and one chain of thy neck. Nay, but these are the words of him from whom I have so often hid my face. And is this precious Christ so enamored of me? Has he, the

Prince of Life, so fixed his affections on my spirit?
does he love to hear me speak with him; does he delight in my communing with him?   Oh, then I cannot forbear; I must cry 'Come to me, my Lord, and
I will tell thee my griefs, and my joys, and thou
shalt tell me all thy heart, and we will thus confer and confide with secrets of which the world wots
not.'"   The secret of the Lord is with them that
fear him.

Let us therefore tell our heart's love to Christ.
We hid as it were our faces from him.   Say when
and how did you begin thus to act?   You used to
revel in the light of his countenance once: why did
you hide your face?   Did you get worldly?   Did
you dote too much upon some earthly object?   Did
you neglect prayer?   Did you give way to temptation?   Beloved, whatever may have been the
cause, remember Jesus Christ has not divorced
you.   He hath said, "Return, ye backsliding children; I am married unto you, saith the Lord."
Come back, then; come back now, as we meet
around the Lord's table, you that love your Lord,
but have lost fellowship with him: pray—pray
that this may be the beginning of a happier era.
Oh that we might keep looking to Jesus, and Jesus looking to us!   Oh that we might maintain
that dear fellowship, and never have it broken till
it shall melt into the yet nearer and more glorious
communion on the other side of the river, where
nothing can disturb the profound enjoyment!   Get
ye up, get ye up, believers, from your sorrows,

from your cares, from your anxieties and distractions, get ye up to the Master's feet, and sit there with Mary, and look up into his dear loving face, and listen to his gracious words of promise; hide not your face from him, he will not hide his face from you. Say, like the spouse in the Canticles, " Let him kiss me with the kisses of his mouth, for his love is better than wine," and he will answer your prayer, and make your heart burn within you with the holy ecstasy of fervent love.

A Present Pardon.

*Blessed is he whose transgression is forgiven, whose sin is
covered.*—PSALM xxxii. 1.

MEN have all of them their own ideals of
blessedness. Those ideals are often altogether contrary to the sayings which our Saviour
uttered in his Sermon on the Mount. They count
those to be blessed who are strong in health, who
are abundant in riches, who are honored with fame,
who are entrusted with command, who exercise
power—those, in fact, who are distinguished in the
eyes of their fellow-creatures. Yet I find not such
persons called " blessed " in God's Word, though I
do notice that oftentimes humble souls, who might
excite pity rather than envy, are congratulated
upon the blessings which they are heirs to, and
which they shall soon enjoy. To the penitent there
is no voice so pleasant as that of pardon. God,
who cannot lie—God, who cannot err—tells us
what it is to be blessed. Here he declares that
" Blessed is he whose transgression is forgiven,
whose sin is covered." This is an oracle not to be
disputed. Forgiven sin is better than accumulated

wealth. The remission of sin is infinitely to be preferred before all the glitter and the glare of this world's prosperity. The gratification of creature passions and earthly desires is illusive—a shadow and a fiction; but the blessedness of the justified, the blessedness of the man to whom God imputeth righteousness is substantial and true. How apt we are to say in our hearts, "Would God Adam had never fallen, for blessed must be the man who never sinned!" Could any man have attained to a perfect life, which deserved commendation at God's hands, blessedness would surely glow around him like a halo; at his feet the earth would blossom; in his nostrils the air would breathe sweet odors; and his ears would be regaled with the sweet singing of birds; "content indeed to sojourn while he must below the skies, but having there his home." Such a man would feel and find the beams of brightness playing over the entire expanse of life, and the thrill of gladness filling his heart with unbroken peace. The mountains and hills would break forth into singing, and all the trees of the field would clap their hands to multiply his inlets to happiness.

But it is not of such imaginary bliss that our sacred Psalmist loves to sing; because, however true, it would be a mere mockery to tell us who are so deeply fallen of sweet delights that those alone could know who never fell. Our time of probation is over. We of mortal race were proved, tried and condemned long ago. It is not possible now for us to have the blessedness of uncorrupted innocence.

And yet, thank God, blessedness is still possible to us, sinners though we be. We may hear the voice of the ever-blessed of God pronouncing us to be blessed. His mercy can secure to us what our merit could never have earned; for so it is written, "Blessed is he whose transgression is forgiven, whose sin is covered." May every one of us partake of this blessedness, and know and rejoice in the full assurance.

Now, the observations I address to you shall be very simple; but if they come home to us as true, and we can grasp them with a lively faith, they will be none the less gratifying to us because they seem common.

I. Evidently there is forgiveness with God: transgression may be forgiven.

It is spoken of here, not as a flight of fancy, or a poetic dream; it is not an imaginary or a possible circumstance, but it is described as a fact that does occur, and has been the happy lot of some who knew its sweet relief, and felt its strange felicity—"Blessed is he whose transgression is forgiven." Do take the words with all their weight of meaning; for though taught in our catechisms, embodied in our creeds, and admitted in our ordinary conversation on religious subjects, the belief in the forgiveness of sins is not always sincere and hearty. When the guilt of sin is felt, and the burden of sin grows heavy, and when the wound stinks and is corrupt, as the Psalmist says, we are very apt to doubt the possibility of pardon; or, at least, of our own pardon. Under deep conviction of sin, and a sense of the peculiar heinousness of our own guilt, there is a haze and more than a haze—a thick fog, which hides the light of this doctrine from our view. We think all men pardonable except ourselves. We can believe in the doctrine of forgiveness of sin for blasphemers, for thieves, for drunkards, even for murderers; but there is some particular aggravation in the sin which we have committed that appears to us to admit of no place of repentance, to find no promise of absolution. So, writing bitter things against ourselves, we become our own accusers and our own judges, and seem as if we would even become our own executioners. In our distraction we are thus prone to doubt that our transgression can be forgiven.

And, beloved, I am not sure that those of us who are saved do not sometimes have misgivings about this grand truth. Although I know that I am saved in Christ, yet at times when I look back upon my life, and especially dwell upon some dark blots which God has forgiven, but for which I can never forgive myself, the question comes across me, "Is it so? Is that really blotted out? It was so crimson, so scarlet, can it be that the spot is entirely gone?" We know that being washed in the blood of Christ we are whiter than snow, but it is not always that our faith can realize the forgiveness of sins while our heart and conscience are revolving the flagrancy of their guilt.

It should not be so. We ought to be able to bear, at one and the same time, a vision of sin in all its horror and aggravation and a full view of the sacrifice for sin in all its holiness and acceptance to God—to feel that we are guilty, weak, lost, and ruined, yet to believe that Christ is not only able to save to the very uttermost, but that he has saved us,—to confess our crimes, while we cast ourselves without a question into his blessed arms. I trust that we can do this. But, alas! a fly may find its way into the sweetest pot of ointment, a little folly may taint a good reputation, and an unworthy doubt may tarnish the purest faith; so it may be profitable to remind even the forgiven man that forgiveness of sin is possible, that forgiveness of sin is presented in the gospel as a covenant blessing, that forgiveness of sin is the possession of every believer in Jesus, that his sin has gone entirely and irreversibly, and that for him all manner of sin has been forgiven, blotted out, and put away through the precious blood of Jesus, seeing that he has believed in God's great propitiatory sacrifice.

Peradventure there has strolled into this sanctuary to-night some professing Christian who, though a true child of God, has foully stained his profession. It may be, my dear friend, that in your weakness, and to your shame and to your confusion of face, you have forsaken God, and have fallen into sin. You who knew better, you who have instructed others, you who would have denounced

such conduct with great severity in your fellow-
creatures, have fallen into the transgression yourself, and now you are conscious that both the sin
and its results are very bitter; you are smarting
under the rod, your bones have been sore broken,
and, perhaps, while I am speaking, it seems as if
my words were putting them out of joint again
where they had been a little healing. Beloved
brother or sister in Christ, if your sin be a public
sin, a grievous sin, a black and foul sin; if it be
one which conscience cannot for a moment tolerate,
and which God's people must account terrible, even
though it be committed by you who are dear to
them, let me entreat you not to suffer the deceit-
fulness of sin to drive you to despair. In the anguish of remorse do not shun the mercy-seat.
Doubt not that the Lord is still ready to pardon
you. Let not Satan persuade you that you have
sinned a sin which is unto-death. Nay, come to
the cross of Christ. The blood of Jesus was real,
and it was really shed to wash away real sin, not
sin in the abstract as we talk of it here, but sin in
the concrete as you have committed it—such sin
as yours; nay, your sin, that special sin, that degrading sin, that sin which you are ashamed to
mention, that sin which makes you now, even at
the very thought of it, hang your head and blush.
Know of a truth that your sin is pardonable.

Do you ask me why I draw this inference from
my text? I answer that it was penned by David,
when his crimes were complicated, his character

corrupted, and his case seemed beyond the possibility of a cure. Deliver me from bloodguiltiness, O God! Whatever your sin may have been, it can scarcely have exceeded his in atrocity. You know how he added sin to sin; you know how high he stood and how low he sunk; and you know how sweetly he could sing—" Blessed is he whose transgression is forgiven, whose sin is covered." It shines forth more clearly now than ever it shone before. Sin *is* pardonable: the Lord God *is* merciful and gracious. Hear the heavenly invitation— "Come now, and let us reason together: though your sins be as scarlet, they shall be as white as snow; though they be red like crimson, they shall be as wool." Hear Jehovah's voice out of heaven—" I, even I, am he that blotteth out thy transgressions for mine own sake, and will not remember thy sins." With such a peerless proclamation of perfect pardon we leave this point. We trust, however, that you will not leave it till you have proved its preciousness and its power.

II. Observe now that, the pardon being proved, the BLESSEDNESS MAY BE ENJOYED.

So much sadness comes from a sense of sin that it is not easy for a penitent to regard pleasure as within his reach, or for a criminal to imagine that cheerfulness can become his habitual condition. How have I heard a man say—" Were God to forgive me, I do not think I could be happy; such is my sin that, though it should be put away, the memory would haunt me, the disgrace would distract me; my own conscience would confound me; I never could blend my voice or chime in with the songs of the blessed ones." Is not this just what the prodigal said—"I am no more worthy to be called thy son: make me as one of thy hired servants"? He could not think so well of his father as to suppose that he could receive him again into his affections as his child; hence he would be content to take the yoke of service, and to be a hired servant of his father's; not a servant born in the house, though these were common enough among the Jews, but a hired servant, willing to be even with the lowest class of servants, so that he might but live in his father's house. I know that this is often the feeling of humble souls, but look at the text and observe the blessed truth which it teaches. You may not only be forgiven, my dear friends, but you may enjoy, notwithstanding your past sin, blessedness even on earth. Oh, look up through those tears! They can all be wiped away; or should they continue to flow in a long life of penitence, if they do but fall upon the Saviour's feet, which thou wouldest fain wash in fond affection with thy tears and wipe with the hairs of thy head, thou shalt find those tears to be precious drops that ye need not rue. Though evangelical repentance may be compared to bitter herbs in one respect, to be eaten lamenting, yet in another respect there is no grace so sweet as repentance. In heaven, it is true, they do not repent, but here on earth it well becomes the saints. It is sweet here below to sit and weep one's heart away in sorrow for sin at the foot of the cross of Christ, saying, "With my tears his feet I bathe:" and although we shall have done with it when we reach those blissful shores, until then repentance shall be the occupation of our lives.

But, dear friends, you may suppose that, as sincere repentance always leads to great searching of heart, it cannot be blessed, yet it really is so. Repentance, as we have already said, is a sweet grace. You remember that the prodigal shed his tears, his best tears, in his father's bosom, when he put his face, as it were, close to his father's heart, and sobbed out, "Father, I have sinned!" Oh, what a place for repentance is the bosom of God, when his love is shed abroad in the heart, making you contrite and moving you to say, "How could I have sinned against so good a God? How could I be an enemy to one who is so full of grace? How could I run away and spend my substance with harlots when my father had such deep care for my welfare? How could I choose their base love, when a love so pure, so true, so constant, was watching over me?" Oh, it is a holy sorrow that hath a clear life ensuing; and I tell you that, however deep your repentance may be, it shall not detract from your happiness; but it shall even prove to be one tributary stream to the blessedness of your experience.

Does the memory of your sins haunt you, and do you feel that you shall always hang your head as one whom pardon could not purge? Not thus did the apostle Paul reflect on his many sins.

Though he bewailed the wickedness of his heart and was ashamed of the evil he had done, yet his humility after he was converted took the form of gratitude, cheering his very soul with the most lively impulse. While confessing that he was the very chief of sinners, at the same time and in the same breath he said, "This is a faithful saying, and worthy of all acceptation, that Christ Jesus came into the world to save sinners." Conscious of his own infirmities he could exclaim, "O wretched man that I am! who shall deliver me from the body of this death;" yet, confident of his full redemption, he could add, "I thank God through Jesus Christ our Lord." Moreover, hurling defiance at all his accusers, he asks, "Who shall lay anything to the charge of God's elect?" No bolder or more triumphant champion of Divine grace than that apostle who was before a blasphemer and a persecutor and injurious, but now rejoices to bear record, "I obtained mercy, that in me first (being as it were a model) Jesus Christ might shew forth all long-suffering, for a pattern to them which should hereafter believe on him to life everlasting." What though your past offences be never so rank and your present shame should sting you with ever so much poignant sorrow, yet with thrills of bliss you shall prove the full blessedness of the man whose transgression is forgiven, whose sin is covered.

Methinks I hear one say, "Few men have fallen more foully into sin than I have; if converted, I might be pointed out as an illustrious monument of Divine grace; yet, what with vanities which have matured into vices, and passing follies which have grown into positive evil habits, it is not likely I should ever attain the same eminence in grace as those who were trained from childhood in the sanctuary, and never lived a dissolute life or risked a desperate death as I have done." Let me assure you that this is a great fallacy. The heights of glory are now open to those who once plunged into the depths of sin. Say not, slave of Satan, that thou canst not be a soldier of the cross. Thou canst be a heroic soldier. Thou mayest win a crown of victory. Why *needest* thou be weak in faith? Thou canst not be languid in love. Great sinner as thou art, thou hast in this a sort of advantage; thou wilt love much because thou hast had much forgiven thee. Surely, if thy love be warmer than that of others, thou hast the mainspring of zeal, the mightiest force within to mould thy future course. Instead of being less than others, thou shouldest seek to outdo them all, not out of carnal emulation, but out of holy strife. I counsel thee, poor sinner, when thou comest to Christ, do not try to hide thyself in some obscure corner; but come to the light, that thou mayest have near and intimate fellowship with thy Lord: for the love thou hast to him, show kindness to his lambs; by thy generosity to his disciples, show thy gratitude to the Master; grudge no service; be ready to spend and to be spent; yield yourself a living sacrifice to him who redeemed thee from thy sins and restored thee to his favor.

I like what one said to me to-day when I was seeing inquirers who are seeking membership with us. " By God's grace," he said, " I will try to make up for lost time." Let this be your resolve, my friends. If you are called by grace when the day is far spent, and the time in which you can hope to serve your Lord is getting brief, do not waste an opportunity, but engage with all your heart and soul in works of faith and labors of love for the Lord Jesus. Some of us were called at the first or second hour of the day, and while we were yet children we found some employment in the vineyard. Still we cannot serve Christ as we would. Oh! I wish I had a thousand tongues that I might tell out his love, and could live a thousand lives to proclaim his grace amongst the sons of men! But as for you, whose time must, in the course of nature, be so short; you who have given so much of your lives to Satan—do not let Christ now be put off with the fag end, but give him the very best of your love, the fat of your sacrifice, the strength and soul of your being.

And in the matter of enjoyment, I cannot believe for a moment that when a great sinner is blessed with a great pardon he should fail to have the fulness of joy which so divine a benefit must properly excite. My observation has been that the joy of those who have been graciously forgiven after having greatly transgressed rather exceeds than falls short of the joy of such as are more gradually brought into gospel liberty. Oh no; my Master will not adjudge you to take a second rank.

He who was by birth an alien, and in open rebellion an enemy to God shall have all the rights of citizenship, and partake of all the privileges of the saints. Not he who like Samuel was lighted to his couch in childhood by the lamps of the sanctuary is more welcome at the Father's board than the returning prodigal. Such blessedness is in store for some of you. You have fallen; you have lost your character; you have stifled the voice of your own conscience; you have forfeited all title to self-respect. But by Christ redeemed, in Christ restored, this infinite blessedness shall be your portion. Have you been put out of the Church? Have your brethren been compelled to withdraw from fellowship with you because of your flagrant sin? Have you been convicted of a crime, and suffered a term of imprisonment? There is blessedness possible to you yet. There may have strayed in here one who from the fold has wandered very far. Though you have forfeited your good name, I simply and sincerely point out to you the means whereby you may yet transform your blighted life into a blessed life. Glory to God and peace to your own soul shall immediately follow your trust in the sacrifice of Christ. "Blessed is he whose transgression is forgiven, whose sin is covered." Seemeth it not to thee that this is the very fountain of all blessings? Thou comest here to the stream-head, to the source of the great wide river of mercies. Those of you, therefore, who believe in the forgiveness of sins

should not be satisfied till you have the title-deeds,
enjoy the possession, and revel in the blessedness
of this reconciliation to God. "*If* I am a Christian," said a sister to me hesitantly; "but I do not
like that ugly 'if'; I must get rid of it." So she
prayed the Lord. "Let there be no 'if' between
me and thee." I would have you pray in like
manner. Oh, those horrible "ifs!" They are
like mosquitoes that sting and harass us; they
are like stones in the shoes, you cannot travel
with them. Hear what David says: "Blessed is
the man unto whom the Lord imputeth not iniquity, and in whose spirit there is no guile."

III. Still enlarging upon our last point rather
than venturing on to anything fresh, observe THAT
THE STATE OF FORGIVENESS IS EVIDENTLY A STATE OF
BLESSEDNESS IF WE REMEMBER THE CONTRAST IT INVOLVES.

Ask the sinner conscious of his guilt and its
penalty, who is bemoaning himself and crying out,
"God be merciful to me a sinner!" what wouldest
thou think if thy condition could be changed and
thy conscience cleansed by one line of the pen or by
one word of the lips that can pronounce a pardon?
Would not that be blessed beyond wishful thought
or wakeful dream? "Oh!" say you, "I would
count no penance too severe, no sacrifice too costly,
if I might but get my sins cancelled, forgiven, and
completely obliterated." Look at poor Christian,
wringing his hands, sighing and crying. Why
was it? He wanted to have his burden taken off.
Had you spoken to him, he would have told you

he was willing to go through floods and flames if he could get relief from his burden, and be clean rid of it. Seeing how every anxious soul longs for forgiveness, clearly it must be a state to be greatly desired, and those who do attain it find it to be full of gladness, delight, and rejoicing. It is indeed blessed to have sin forgiven; but oh, how wretched to face its infamy, to feel its malignity, to fear its terrible penalty! Witness a soul in despair; that is a dreadful sight; I think I would sooner walk fifty miles than see a despairing soul; I have seen several such, shut up in the iron cage. You may talk, talk, talk, and try to give some cheer, but it is of no use. No promise can comfort; the gospel itself seems to have no charm. Were you to put the question to a despairing soul, "Would it be a blessed thing to have sin forgiven?" sharp, quick, and decided would the answer be. Not the lips only—the heart would express itself in every muscle of the face, in every limb of the body—the nerves all tingling with joy, the eyes shining with gleams of heaven.

Ask dying sinners, stung with remorse at the memory of their lives and filled with dread at the prospect of the future, whether it is not a blessed thing to have sins forgiven. Though they may have trifled hitherto, the death-hour forbids dissembling. Now the vanities of time pass like a shadow, and the realities of eternity come up like a sceptre. "Too late!" they cry, "too late! Had we but fled to Christ before! Had we but turned our eyes to him in years gone by, then hope would have cheered us in this extremity!" But it is not death they dread so much as the after death; not present dissolution, but (shall I say it?) the damnation that may follow. Unforgiven sin! Who can paint the sentence it must meet? Could we peer into that world where wicked spirits are tormented ever and anon, and there ask the question, "Would it be a blessed thing to be forgiven?" ah, you can guess the answer. I pray thee, friend, tempt not the terror for thyself. Trifle not with kind entreaty; know that 'tis treason so to do. The pardon spurned will recoil on your own head. You will bewail in everlasting misery the mercy that through your wilfulness was unavailing. Blessed must he be whose sins are forgiven, for it enables him to escape from the horrible doom of the impenitent.

But you shall have a witness nearer at hand. You know, as a fact recorded in the gospels, that the Son of man had power on earth to forgive sins. You know, too, from the testimony of the Acts of the Apostles, that his Name through faith in his Name is invested with the same power. By the ministry of the Holy Spirit one may hear now, as in days of yore, a voice of Divine authority, saying, "Thy sins are forgiven thee; go in peace." It was only last week I met with one who had been forgiven on the previous Sunday. The sweet relief, the calm belief, and the true blessedness of that man was such that you could see it flashing from his eyes and animating every faculty of his being. The whole man was so full of joy that he did not know how to contain himself. The drift of all his conversation was, "I have found Christ, I have laid hold on eternal life! I have trusted in Jesus! I am saved!" His joy, though uttered in part, was unutterable. I sympathized in his ecstasy, remembering that it was so with me when I wanted to tell everybody that Christ was precious and was able to save. Oh, yes, the young convert is a good witness, though the old Christian is quite as good. It is a blessed thing to have had fifty years enjoyment of the forgiveness of sin. I have half a mind to call some of our venerable friends up here to bear their witness. I am sure they would not stammer; or had they lost the power of ready speech through infirmity of the flesh, their testimony would be sound and vigorous, for they would tell you unhesitatingly how blessed is he whose transgression is forgiven, whose sin is covered.

IV. I wish I had time to show you that forgiveness of sin is not only blessed of itself, but ALL ITS CONCOMITANTS HELP TO SWELL THE TIDE OF BLESSING.

A thousand felicities follow in its train. He who is forgiven is justified, acquitted, vindicated, sent forth without a stain or blemish on his reputation; he is regenerated, quickened, invigorated, and brought into newness of life; more still, he is adopted, initiated into a Divine family, introduced into a new relationship, and made heir of a heritage entailed by promise. The work of sanctification begun in him here will one day be completely perfected. He who is forgiven was elected from before the foundation of the world. He was redeemed with the precious blood of Jesus. For him Christ stood as his sponsor, surety, and substitute at the bar of justice. To the forgiven man all things have become new. Our Lord Jesus Christ has raised him up and made him sit in heavenly places with him. He is even now a son and heir, a child of God, a prince of the blood imperial, a priest and a king who shall reign with Christ for ever and ever. He who is washed in the precious blood is favored beyond any words that I can find to express it. Ten thousand blessings are his portion. "How precious," such a pardoned one may exclaim, "how precious are Thy thoughts unto me, O God! How great is the sum of them!"

V. But the BLESSEDNESS OF THE MAN WHOSE TRANSGRESSION IS FORGIVEN, WHOSE SIN IS COVERED, WILL BE MAINLY SEEN IN THE NEXT STATE.

That disembodied spirit, clear of spot or blemish, washed and whitened in the blood of the Lamb, passes without fear into the invisible world. It trembles not, though it appears before the eye of justice. No award can come to the forgiven soul except this—"Come, thou blessed of My Father, inherit the kingdom prepared for thee." We commit the body of the forgiven sinner to the grave in "sure and certain hope of a joyful resurrection." We give his flesh to be the food of the worm and his skin may rot to dust; but though worms destroy his body, yet in his flesh shall he see God, whom his eyes shall see for himself and not another. I was astonished some little time ago when I heard a good pastor, standing by the coffin of an honored minister, say—"There lies nothing of our brother." Not so, thought I. The bodies of the saints were purchased by Christ; though flesh and blood cannot inherit the kingdom of God, neither can corruption inherit incorruption, yet there will be such a marvellous change pass over the body of the forgiven sinner that the same body—changed, but still the same·body—shall be reunited with the disembodied spirit to dwell at God's right hand. Hark, hark! the trumpet sounds! Oh, my brethren, we can but speak in prose. These great scenes we shall all of us see. We shall then think after another fashion. The trumpet sounds. The echo reaches heaven. Hell startles at the sound to its nethermost domains. This trembling earth is all attention. The sea yields up her dead. A great white cloud comes sailing forth in awful majesty. Upon it there is a throne, where Jesus sits in state. But his heart has no cause to quake whose sin is all forgiven. Well may the ransomed soul be calm amidst the pomp and pageantry of that tremendous day; for he who sits upon the throne is the Son of man, in whose blood we have been washed. Lo! this is the same Jesus who said, "I have forgiven thee." He cannot condemn *us.* We shall find him to be our Friend whom others find to be their Judge. Blessed is that man who is forgiven. See him, as with ten thousand times ten thousand others, pure as himself and like to himself, who had washed their robes and made them white in the blood of the Lamb, he ascends to the Celestial City, a perfect man in body and in soul, to dwell forever there! Hark to the acclamations of the ten thousand times ten thousand, the sound of the harpers harping with their harps, and the song that is like great waters. Write, yea, write now—"Blessed are the dead which die in the Lord, for they rest from their labors, and their works do follow them." But doubly blessed are they then that they rise from the dead. Once they were sinners washed in blood; but then, in body and in soul, they shall have come, through the precious blood, to see Jesus face to face.

Oh! how I wish that all of us knew this blessedness! Seek it, friends, seek it. It is to be found. "Seek ye the Lord while he may be found; call ye upon him while he is near." I am specially encouraged in preaching the gospel this evening because I have just been seeing some who have been recently converted. There are hearers of the gospel among you who have been listening to me for many years. Often have I feared that, in your case, I had labored in vain; but I have great hope now concerning some of you. The Lord keeps bringing in the old hearers of eight, nine, and ten years' standing. Oh! I pray the Lord to save every one of you and bring you into the fold. I do long and pant that I may present you all before my Master's face with joy! Even should you go and join other churches, and serve the Lord elsewhere, that will cause me no sorrow or regret. But God forbid that any of you should despise mercy, reject the gospel, and die in your sins. May all of you prove the blessedness of pardon, and then shall we all of us meet, an unbroken congregation, before the Throne.

A Precious Plenitude.

And of his fulness have all we received, and grace for grace.
JOHN i. 16.

ONE Sabbath-day I was staying in an Italian town on the other side of the Alps. Of course, the whole population was Romish. Two or three of us, therefore, being Protestants, held a little service for the worship of God in the simple manner that is our wont. After this I went out for a walk. The weather being hot and sultry, I sought the outskirts of the town to get to as quiet and cool a spot as possible. Presently I came to an archway at the foot of a hill, where there was an announcement that any person who would climb the hill with proper intentions should receive the pardon of his sins and five days' indulgence. I thought I might as well have five days' indulgence as anybody else, and if it were of any advantage to have it laid by in store. I cannot tell you all I saw as I went, first one way and then another, up that hill. Suffice it to say that there was a series of little churches, through the windows of which you might look as one in his boyish days looked through a peep-show. The whole scene and cir-

cumstance of the passion and death of Christ were
thus modelled, beginning with his agony in the
garden, where he was represented in a figure as
large as life, with the drops of bloody sweat falling to the ground; the three disciples a stone's
throw off, and the rest of the apostles outside the
garden wall. Every feature looked as real as if
one had been standing upon the spot. I scruti-
nized each group narrowly, and carefully read the
Latin text which served as an index, till I reached
the top of the hill, where I saw a garden, just like
an English garden, and as I pushed open the door
I faced these words, "Now, there was a garden,
and in the garden there was a new sepulchre."
Walking down a path I came to a sepulchre; so
I stooped down and looked in as Peter had done.
There, instead of seeing a picture of the corpse
of Christ, I read in gilded letters these words—
of course, in the Latin tongue—"He is not here,
for he is risen; come see the place where the Lord
lay." Passing on, I came to a place where his
ascension was represented. On the summit was
a large church, into which I entered. No one was
there, yet the place for me had a marvellous interest.
High up in the ceiling there swung a rude representation of the Lord Jesus Christ, and round it
were statues of the prophets, all with their fingers
pointing up to him. There was Isaiah, with a scroll
in his left hand, on which was written, "He was despised and rejected of men, a man of sorrows, and
acquainted with grief." Further on stood Jere-

miah, and on his scroll was written, " Behold and see if there was ever sorrow like unto my sorrow, which was done unto me." All round the church I read in great words, that were large enough to be seen, though they were blazoned on the top of the ceiling, " Moses and all the prophets spoke and wrote concerning him."

Now, though I cannot take you to see that remarkable sight, which I shall never forget, I would fain bring before your mind's eye something like it. Suppose that all the saints who lived from the days of Adam down to the times when Malachi closed the Old Testament, and that all the saints who lived in Christ's time, and then on through the early ages of the Church in the days of Chrysostom and Augustine, and all the holy men who afterwards gathered around the Reformers, and all who in every place have served God since then—suppose they all stood in one vast circle; to whom do you suppose they would every one point? to whom would they all bear witness? Why, with outstretched arm, every one of them would turn to the Lord Jesus Christ, and speak his praise. Could you then enquire into their individual history, you would find among them characters exceedingly diverse, though all remarkably beautiful; some renowned for courage, others for gentleness; some for patient endurance, others for diligent labor, and yet all inspired by a common faith; all of them aglow with fervent gratitude; all of them looking with steadfast gaze and love intense towards ONE from whom they had received every gift that profited them, every grace that adorned them, every honor that ennobled them; and that One, Jesus Christ, the Son of God, the Saviour of men. The rule would admit of not a single exception. From each man in his own proper position, from every man in his own particular calling, from all the individuals severally in their own personal experience, the innumerable voices, distinct but blending in chorus, would go up from earth to heaven, saying, "Of his fulness have all we received, and grace for grace." Then methinks from the excellent glory would come a response. The inhabitants of heaven would echo back the strain, "Of his fulness have all we, the glorified spirits, received, and grace for grace." This is the testimony of the Church militant and of the Church triumphant; yea, it is the testimony of all who in every place and at every time have come and put their trust under the shadow of his wings.

Our text seems to suggest two thoughts—*the fulness* and *the filling*—upon each of which I will attempt to say a little; a very little. With so infinite a theme we can do no more than children do when they take up a little sea-water in a shell; their tiny scoop cannot embrace the ocean. I stand on the narrow edge of a vast expanse, and leave the boundless depths to your contemplation. *His fulness!* an inexhaustible reservoir. *Our filling!* an illimitable endowment. Beloved, the river of God, which is full of water, can well supply the little canals that are fed from such a fountain with grace for grace.

The fulness, I said. It is his fulness, the fulness of Jesus Christ, the Son of God. Oh, what a fulness he has! The fulness which *belongs to him personally!* Note this well; forget it not. Our Redeemer is essentially God. By nature he is Divine. He has condescendingly taken upon himself our nature, and he is most truly and assuredly man. Very God! for to him belong all the attributes of Jehovah. Very man! for when he took our flesh and blood, he accepted the entire sympathies of our creatureship. In his complex nature he possesses fulness. In him dwelleth all the fulness of the Godhead bodily. He has the fulness of omnipotence, and all power is given unto him as Mediator in heaven and in earth. Omnipresence is his to perfection; "for where two or three are gathered together in my name, there am I (said he) in the midst of them." He has essential wisdom. Even when on earth, "he did not commit himself, because he knew all men, and needed not that any should testify of man: for he knew what was in man." In him is fulness of justice. The Father hath given all judgment unto the Son. Shall not God "judge the world in righteousness by that man whom he hath ordained; whereof he hath given assurance unto all men, in that he hath raised him from the dead"? In him is fulness of mercy, for "through this man is preached unto you the forgiveness of sins." The attributes of God make up a perfect total. The unity, with all its uniqueness, is his. Divisions and subdivisions are ours. The fractional parts of which we take account are but the breaking up of a great fact to our weak understanding. Think as you may, your thought cannot describe or compass God; for God is all that is good and blessed. And as is God so is Christ. All the divine attributes are contained and represented in Christ Jesus in their fulness, not diminished by his humiliation, but resplendent by his triumph.

"In him dwelleth all the fulness of the God-head." He is the express image of the Father's person, the brightness of his Father's glory; not mere glory, but the brightness of his Father's glory. What confidence this ought to inspire in our hearts! The fulness from which you and I derive the grace we receive is none other than the infinite fulness of God over all blessed forever, whose name is Immanuel, God with us. There was a fulness also in Christ in respect to his manhood. Nothing was lacking to him that is involved in being by nature and constitution a perfect man. He was pure; he did not inherit any sin; his disposition did not tend towards any evil. Still, all that pertains to the original creatureship of man as created by God did Christ possess in the fulness of development. Hence, my brethren, there is in him at this moment a fulness of sympathy. He is not such a high-priest as cannot be touched with a feeling of our infirmities, but he was tempted in all points like as we are, yet without sin. Do not suppose that Jesus is less human than you are yourselves; he is fully human. Do not imagine that he is less tender than you would be towards the weak and suffering; he is full of tenderness; his bowels melt with love. A mother has often a tenderness that we do not find in a father. Masculine strength and courage do not always blend with the gentle, sympathetic qualities of woman. Howbeit when God created man in his own image, male and female created he them. The virtues, if I may so say, of both sexes were combined in our Lord; the suavity as well as the staunchness—the feminine as well as the masculine of our common humanity. Human nature in its totality and completeness was fully possessed and thoroughly represented by him. The sympathetic nature which melts at the tear and smiles at the joy of others, was as truly his as the heroic nature that parleys not with fear, but acts with promptitude and suffers with fortitude, like a warrior in the hosts of the Lord. There is thus a fulness of humanity as well as a fulness of Divinity in Christ Jesus, our Saviour—a fulness of perfection in his blessed person, which may well fix your trust and rivet your admiration.

In our Lord, likewise, there is what I may venture to call, for lack of a better word, *an acquired fulness.* He has sojourned on earth, and rendered entire and undeviating obedience to the law of God, having taken upon himself the form of a servant, and by his righteousness earned wages; a fulness, an everlasting wellspring of merit. Throughout his whole life he honored the Divine law, and glorified God on the earth. In doing his Father's will, his action was so voluntary and so vicarious that he has accumulated an inexhaustible fund of merit, which all of us who believe in his name may plead before the Father's throne. More especially did his death consummate the obedience, and constitute its sterling worth, its intrinsic virtue. His death, with all its surroundings—from the bloody sweat in the olive garden to the last cry on the mount of Calvary, "Into thy hands I commend my spirit"—was sublime. All through the scourging and the spitting, the shame, the wounding, the crucifixion, the thirst, the desertion, and the death itself, he was working out an atonement for us,

> **"Bearing, that we might never bear**
> **His Father's righteous ire."**

And now with him risen from the dead, raised to the right hand of the Majesty on high, there is a fulness of prevalence in his intercession when he pleads his blood; a fulness of cleansing power when the Spirit applies the blood to the guilty conscience; a fulness of peace to the heart when his blood speaketh better things than that of Abel. In that fountain filled with blood drawn from Immanuel's veins there is a fulness that never can be exhausted by all the sin of man. He

has finished the work which his Father gave him
to .do. Now the covenant is ratified with him
that he shall see of the travail of his soul and
shall be satisfied. In these respects we are convinced that there is an acquired as well as a
personal fulness in our precious Lord.

No less hath he a fulness of dignity, of high
prerogative. He is a prophet. By him are all
his people taught, warned, counselled, and encouraged with a blessed hope. He is a priest,
and by him they are cleansed from sin, and con-
secrated to God. Moreover, he is also a king,
spreading the ægis of protection over all his liege
subjects, and ordaining peace for them. Under
his beneficent rule they prosper. Thou good Shepherd! Thou great Shepherd of the sheep! there
is no office or obligation that was necessary for
our welfare, but Thou hast taken it, and under-
taken it in our behalf. Thou art to us all that
we require, and all that we could desire. Join
all the qualities involved in name or fame that
commend themselves most closely to your heart,
because they meet your necessities, or draw forth
your sympathies, and you shall find that he com-
prises them all in liberal, lavish fulness. Nor hath
his prerogative any limit. As a priest who hath
once offered a sacrifice of everlasting prevalence,
his absolution or his benediction is final and irre-
vocable. As a prophet his authority is unimpeachable; the authority with which he teaches allows
of no appeal. As a king he has right as well as

might on his side. In the midst of Zion willing subjects yield to his beneficent sway; in the outer world reluctant rebels must submit themselves to his sceptre. He is no priest whose vain pretence has no valid prescript; he is no prophet whose teaching is uncertain in its tone or limited in its range; he is no king whose prerogative is not sanctioned by his wisdom, and whose government awakens no fealty of love. But in the administration of all his offices our Lord Jesus Christ shows a fulness of qualification, and gives a fulness of satisfaction. In such respects he has no rival; nor is there any room for a rival to arise.

And let me say here that the power with which our Lord exercises these offices may well command our devout confidence. Do you want to learn the truth? Oh, come to the Prophet of Nazareth, and you shall find that there is a satiety of truth in his teaching such as was never found in heathen augur or even, to the same extent, in Hebrew seer! Or do you want acceptance before God? Oh then, come ye to the Priest who is not of the tribe of Levi, but a Priest after the order of Melchisedec, whose royalty confers dignity on his sacerdotal office! He can present your sacrifice with the sweet incense of his merit that is acceptable before the throne. Or do you want strength? Do you need one to fight your battles, to take hold of the shield and the buckler, and draw out the spear, and handle the bow? Behold the Hero of Israel whose exploits are told in your songs—Jesus, the King by right of conquest, as well as by right Divine, hath a fulness of power and majesty with which no adversary can cope. He reigneth. His reign is the consolation of his people, the guarantee of their peace. These are bare outlines. Time would fail me to enumerate all his offices. They are very numerous; but, however numerous, Christ possesses them all. He enjoys the prerogatives peculiar to them all in the fullest degree. He possesses the power to exercise them all to the fullest extent.

But in Christ there is verily a blessed fulness *of every kind of perfection.* Whatsoever there may be that is lovely or of good repute is to be found in Christ. All that is virtuous or amiable in the character of men; all that is noble and illustrious in the endowments that Heaven bestows on the most privileged of creatures, our Lord possessed. It was said of Henry the Eighth that if all the likenesses of tyrants had been lost out of history they might have been reproduced out of the one character of that monstrous tyrant-king. So, if all the holy features of patriarchs and prophets, of saints and martyrs, that ever lived were blotted from the canvas of history they all might be painted afresh from the one life of the Divine person of our ever adorable Lord Jesus Christ. In him there was not only one perfection, but all perfections meet and blend to make up one matchless perfection. There was not one sweet alone in him, but in him all sweets combine in a perfect sweetness. John has love, Peter courage, Paul zeal—each saint has his own peculiarity, but in Christ all the qualities of goodness and grace converge. He exhibits them in the highest degree and the purest harmony. After such manner are they incorporated in him as to produce a character the like of which was never known before, nor ever shall be witnessed again.

And never forget that *a fulness of the Holy Spirit* abideth in Christ.

The Lord gives not the Spirit by measure unto him. He hath the residue of the Spirit. His is the head upon which the anointing oil is fully poured. We, who are but as the skirts of his garments, are favored with some droppings thereof, but the fulness of the anointing of the Spirit was bestowed upon Jesus Christ our Lord, and from him his members must receive the portion they enjoy.

His fulness! I linger on the word, for I revel in the meditation. Such a fulness as admits of no diminution, for it is *an abiding* fulness. What though all the saints of every age have come to Christ and drawn their supplies from him, he is just as full as ever! Think not that those who first came drank of a copious fountain that has been partly drained by the myriads who have since slaked their thirst. The Apostles received of his fulness and so do we: they without prejudice to us; we without prejudice to those who shall follow us. When I came to Christ, more than eighteen hundred years after the Apostles came, I received of the fulness at just the same rate as when Peter,

John, or Paul received it. Should this dispensation last another thousand years, and some poor, trembling wretch should come to the foot of the cross to receive mercy, he will not receive of Christ a small quota, but he shall receive of Christ's fulness, for it is an abiding fulness. It is never less than full; it never can be more than full. In him there is an infinity of grace and truth. Such fulness is there in him at all times, under all your circumstances of trial, ay, and under all conditions of sin too. The fulness of Christ to supply will always exceed the faith of the believer to seek. And when you feel your emptiness more than you ever did before, then you will set the most store upon his abounding towards us in all wisdom and prudence. Considering then his abiding fulness, his inexhaustible fulness, his available fulness, I entreat you to avail yourself of this fulness now without demur, without delay.

As there is *a fulness*, so there is *a filling*. This is to be our second part. I must speak of it with brevity.

"Of his fulness have all we received." Surely, then, *all the saints were empty* before. You are empty, my brother, and so was Abraham, so was Paul. Grace, the free grace of God, has made all the difference between Peter and Judas, though the one repented and the other despaired; the one travelled the heavenly road, the other went down quickly to hell. They stood on equal footing in transgression, till grace made them to differ. What radical difference is there between one man and another from a legal point of view?

"All have sinned and come short of the glory of God." All alike have to come to Christ empty of merit, or they would never come at all. That was a pretty tale we heard the other day, and it points a right good moral. A worthy, consistent, industrious woman was married to a low, worthless, dissipated husband. Both of them, however, were alike ignorant of the gospel. They came together to the house of prayer; they heard together the tidings of mercy; they each believed, and each of them received the Saviour, and they both were saved the same way; they both found mercy on the same terms. To the rich, free, sovereign grace of God they vied with one another in ascribing the praise. That is a fact. It occurred last week. I do not know whether this makes it more convincing to you; but I might say as Elihu said to Job, "Lo, all these things worketh God oftentimes with man, to bring back his soul from the pit, to be enlightened with the light of the living."

Observe that *the filling is universal. All the saints partake of it.* "Of his fulness have *all we* received." There are manifold diversities of experience among the Lord's people, but in some things they share and share alike. Some saints do not undergo the stress of trial and tribulation that others pass through. Here, however, there is no partiality. They have, every one of them, received out of Christ's fulness.

Not one of them could do without receiving it; not one of them could receive it from any other hand than that of the Divine Benefactor. They earned it not. They accepted it. They received it of Jesus Christ.

This is peculiar to the saints. While it says, "Of his fulness have all we received," manifestly a certain body of people have become partakers of a privilege which it is no less evident that all men have not received. What thousands and tens of thousands there are who, when invited to the gospel feast, reject the call, "make a wretched choice, and rather starve than come!" "All we!" that is, all of those who have believed. And who are "*we,*" or what are "*we,*" that such grace should be given to us in preference to anybody else? Ah, brethren, little cause enough have we for self-satisfaction! On the score of desert no choice had ever fallen on us. We were the vilest, the least worthy, the least attractive, and, in some respects, the least hopeful! Oh, grace! it is thy wont into unlikeliest hearts to come, and it is the glory of love Divine to find in darkest spots a home! "All we ;" we who were once dead in trespasses and sins; we who were once lost like the prodigal son, lost like the wandering sheep, lost like the piece of money; we who needed seeking, needed finding, needed saving; yet of his fulness have all we received. Recollect that the reception is peculiar to believers; it does not go beyond them.

Be it clear, however, that there is and must be a

personal reception in every case. "Of his fulness have *all* we received." This grace cannot be derived or transmitted from one individual to another. Each one of us must receive it directly from him who is our common Lord. Your Father's grace cannot save you. That was a wise speech of the wise virgins to the foolish virgins who besought them, "Give us of your oil," they replied, "Not so, lest there be not enough for us and you; go rather to them that sell, and buy for yourselves." Family piety involves both privileges and responsibilities, but it cannot stand in the place of personal godliness. Dear hearer, you must go to Christ for yourself. All who ever were saved have done so, and you certainly will not be saved unless you are led to do the same. It is a personal filling. "Of his fulness have all we received."

The bounty is gratuitous. Notice the next words, "*and grace for grace.*" It is not said, "Of his fulness have we all purchased," nor "Of his fulness have we all earned a share;" but being merely passive, we have received. What does the vessel do to fit itself for the water that flows into it? Why, it does nothing. All its doing to fit it to receive is an undoing; that is to say, it empties itself to prepare itself to be filled. Oh, if you desire to find Jesus, the doing must be in the way of undoing. You must be emptied to be filled. The preparation is a consciousness that you are not prepared. In such unpreparedness you are prepared for Christ. This is an enigma and a riddle. Those who think themselves prepared for him are not so, but those who know that they are not prepared are just the souls upon whom his grace will come. Poverty, not riches; blindness, not sight; emptiness, not fulness; sinfulness, not virtue—these are the things Christ looks for. He is come to seek and to save that which was lost; not that which had won victories; not that which was splendid in its own esteem; but that which was defeated, ruined, lost. If thou art lost, he comes to seek and to save such as thou art. Oh thou who wert lost, but now art found, bless his name that thou hast received of his fulness!

"And grace for grace"! What mean these words? We can only just touch them as a swallow with its wing touches the pool; we cannot pretend to enter into their depth. "Grace for grace." Does that mean that those who receive grace under the old dispensation were afterwards led to receive the grace of the new dispensation? Does it mean that we who have the grace of conviction with the Holy Spirit as a spirit of bondage shall receive, by and by, the spirit of liberty, and get out of conviction, through conversion, into full pardon and enjoyment of peace with God? Is that the grace instead of grace; one grace given instead of another? Or does it mean grace by degrees; grace upon grace; a little grace to begin with, and more grace afterwards? "He giveth more grace;" grace following on grace and, further on, superabounding grace, when grace turns into glory and we come

before the throne of grace for ever and ever.
Does it mean that God leads us on step by step,
adding to our spiritual wealth, initiating us first
into simple things, and afterwards leading us into
deeper matters?　"Grace for grace."

Yes, it means all that, but it means more.　God
gives grace to prepare for further grace—the grace
of a broken heart—to make room for deep repentance and abhorrence of sin; the grace of hatred of
sin to make way for the grace of holy and careful
walking, humility, and faith in Jesus; the grace of
careful walking to make room for the grace of
close communion with Christ; the grace of close
communion with the Lord Jesus Christ to make
room for the grace of full conformity to his image;
perhaps the grace of conformity to his image to
make room for the higher grace of brighter views
of himself, and still closer incomings into the very
heart of the Lord Jesus.　It is grace that helps us
on in grace.　When a beggar asks you for a penny,
and you give him one, he does not ask you for a
sixpence; or if you give him a shilling, he would
not consider that an argument why you should
give him a sovereign.　But you may deal thus
with God.　If you have only got, as it were, an
ounce of grace, that is reason why you should then
pray God for a great weight of grace, and afterwards for a far more exceeding and eternal weight
of glory.　Believe that he gives grace for grace;
that is, grace that you may open your mouth for
more grace.　The grace you have expands your

heart, and gives you capacity for receiving yet more grace. Do you not send your child to school to learn A B C? You may call that the grace of learning his alphabet. Yes, but it is preparatory to his learning to read the spelling book. Well, but what does he learn to read the spelling book for? Why, that is a preparation for further acquisition of knowledge. It is preparing him to go on to arithmetic, and geometry, and algebra, and those still higher forms of mathematics. If you begin to teach him Latin, it is generally with a view that you may teach him Greek, and thus one thing is always a preparation for another thing. So one grace gives us a preparation for another grace, and thus as we have more grace we realize the blessedness of this Divine filling out of his fulness.

Or, suppose we read the passage thus—grace answerable to grace—and even this will admit of two constructions. Let God give me grace to be a preacher; he will surely give me grace to discharge the office. Perhaps he has given you grace to teach in a Sabbath-school, then you want a further supply of grace to enable you to be an efficient teacher. Peradventure you have the grace of resignation to suffer for Christ's sake, you will need the grace of patience to support you in the midst of pain or persecution. You are called to pray, and you yield yourself up to be a wrestler with God in prayer. This is a great grace. Oh! may you have grace answerable to that grace, that, when you get with the angel by the brook Jabbok, you may take hold of his strength, plead his promise, his covenant, and his oath, and never let him go until he bless you. Thus a halting, fainting Jacob comes off as a prevailing Israel. May we thus ever have grace answerable to grace. "Grace for grace" may imply grace received by us answerable to the grace that is in Christ. Oh! that we Christians had grace in some measure commensurate with the grace that is treasured up for us in him. All that is in him belongs to you. Then the degree of your daily supplies ought to be proportionate to its ample, unlimited wealth and fulness. A young heir to a large estate, though not of full age, generally gets an allowance made to him by the executors, or the trustees, or the Court of Chancery, suitable to the position he is presently to occupy. If he has £100,000 a year in prospect, he would hardly be limited to a penny a week, like a poor man's child. We cannot suppose that he would have a mean allowance made him or such as would barely enable him to live in a humble cottage on the rich domain he is entitled to. Oh no; that would be a meagre pittance out of all proportion to his position. When I see one child of God always mourning, another always doubting, and yet another always scheming, I feel a kind of disappointment; I see they are living below their privileges. They do not seem to have grace in possession answerable to the grace they have in reversion. We always inculcate the propriety, on the part of all our people, of living within their incomes; but I will defy the child of

God to live beyond his income in a spiritual sense. You that have but little spending-money are like the elder brother in the parable. You say, "Thou never gavest me a kid that I might make merry with my friends;" and your Father replies, "Son, thou art ever with me; and all that I have is thine." If you do not have it, it is your own fault; it is all there, and is freely yours. You have but to ask, and you shall receive; to seek, and you shall find. Oh! could we once get grace in us at all like the grace that is in Christ, what Christians should we be! no longer starlight Christians and moonlight Christians, but sunlight believers, letting our light shine before the sons of men. Oh! to be among the three mighties of our royal David. May each of us covet such a position as this, and God grant it to us for his love's sake!

"Grace for grace" obviously means *grace in abundance.* Like the waves of the sea, when one comes there is another close behind it. Before you can say that one is gone there is another coming to fill its place. There they come. Who shall count them? In long succession wave follows wave. So is God's grace. "Grace for grace." One grace has hardly come into your soul but what there is another one. You have heard the story of Rowland Hill having a hundred pounds entrusted to him for the benefit of a poor minister. He thought that if he sent him the hundred pounds it would be too large a sum to give him all at once; he would scarcely know how to husband it, and perhaps he would not be so thankful for it as if he had it doled out in smaller amounts. So he sent him five pounds, and wrote in the letter, " More to follow." Letters did not come often in those days of ninepenny or eightpenny postage, but in about another week he forwarded another five pounds, and a note with it, " More to follow." After a short interval he did the like again, still saying, " More to follow." So it went on for ever so long, always with " More to follow," till the dear, good man, I should think, must have been at his wit's end to know what could follow when so many good presents came to one who needed them so much. Now, that is just how God has done with me, and I believe he is just doing the same with all of you who are his people. He has sent you a mercy, and when he sent it, you might have seen, if you had looked at the envelope, that it was an earnest of further benefits and benefactions—" More to follow." The mercy you have received to-day has written upon it legibly—" More to follow," and that which will come to-morrow will have upon it —" More to follow." "Grace for grace." Oh! sing unto him a new song. Let him have fresh songs for fresh mercies, and as he multiplies the mercy, so do you multiply the praises you ascribe to his name.

" Grace for grace ! " Does it not mean *grace from him to produce grace in us?* We receive from the fulness of Christ of his grace, in order that it may be a living seed that shall produce grace in us as its natural fruit. The grace of gratitude should be produced in us by the grace of generosity from God. We ought to be gracious with a holy joyfulness for all his goodness. I hope we shall have the grace of patience under all sufferings and the grace of zeal in all our labors. At a time like this, my brethren, when we are seeking the conversion of sinners with special efforts, may we have grace from Jesus that shall make all the graces fruitful and fragrant in us! So shall we be to the Saviour as a garden of olives and pomegranates, of lilies and sweet flowers, and may he take a delight in us! When Cyrus took the Greek ambassador through his garden, he challenged him to admire its charms. The Spartan approved all he saw, but still his admiration was cool and critical. "This garden," said its master, "yields me more pleasure and satisfaction than you can imagine or I can express." "And why?" asked the visitor. "Because," replied Cyrus, "I planted every tree in it myself. I planned all the paths, and all the flowers have I reared. No hand but mine has dug the soil, tended the plants, pruned the trees, or done aught beside but my own." His toil and his trouble thus endeared the place to the king. So, truly, Christ can say when he looks upon his people, "There is a fruitful bough there: I pruned that. He was sick, long laid aside from business, he feared his family would be starved: I was pruning him then; but I love the fruit that is on him because I know how it came there. That plant yonder which is blooming now and shedding such a sweet perfume of love, well do I recollect when it was drooping and ready to die. I came and watered it. She, timid disciple, would say, 'Blessed be the gentle hand that shed the dew and poured nourishment on my poor, parched, and withered root!'" Yes, the Saviour gives us "grace for grace" that we may produce grace. I leave the thought with you for meditation, and the issues for your edification, only praying that his Holy Spirit may work in you "grace for grace."

Oh! that all of you might receive grace from him. You will never get grace anywhere else. Go to him at once by faith, with humble prayer. Plenteous grace with him is found; all the grace you shall ever require between now and glory you shall find stored up in him. His grace is our benediction. Of it may you one and all partake! Amen.

𝔄 𝔐𝔞𝔤𝔫𝔢𝔱𝔦𝔠 𝔉𝔬𝔯𝔠𝔢.

The Lord hath appeared of old unto me, saying, Yea, I have loved thee with an everlasting love: therefore with lovingkindness have I drawn thee.—JEREMIAH xxxi. 3.

FROM the connection it is clear that this passage primarily refers to God's ancient people, the natural descendants of Abraham. He chose them from of old, and separated· them from the nations of the world. Their election fills a large chapter in history, and it shines with resplendent lustre in prophecy. There is an interval during which they have experienced strange vicissitudes, been visited with heavy chastisements, and acquired an ill reputation for the perverseness of their mind and the obstinacy of their heart. Yet a future glory awaits them when they shall turn unto the Lord their God again, be restored to their land, and acknowledge Jesus of Nazareth as the King of the Jews, their own anointed King. Without abating, however, a jot or tittle from the literal significance of these words as they were addressed by the Hebrew prophet to the Hebrew race, we may accept them as an oracle of God referring to the entire church of his redeemed family, and pertaining to every distinct member of that sacred community. Every Christian, therefore, whose faith can grasp the testimony may appropriate it to himself. As many a believer has heard, so every believer may hear the voice of the Holy Spirit sounding in his ear these words, "Yea, I have loved thee with an everlasting love: therefore with lovingkindness have I drawn thee."

There are two things of which we propose to speak briefly to-night—the unspeakable boon, "I have loved thee with an everlasting love," and the unmistakable evidence, "therefore with loving-kindness have I drawn *thee.*"

How exceedingly great and precious this assurance, how priceless this blessing—to be embraced with the love, the everlasting love of God! Our God is a God of infinite benevolence. Towards all his creatures he shows his good will. His tender mercies are over all his works. He wisheth well to all mankind. With what force and with what feeling he asserts it! "As I live, saith the Lord God, I have no pleasure in the death of the wicked; but that the wicked turn from his way and live" (Ezekiel xxxiii. 11). And whosoever of the whole human race, penitent for past sin, will turn to Jesus the Saviour of sinners, he shall find in him pardon for the past and grace for the future. This general truth, which we have always steadfastly maintained, which we never saw any reason to doubt, and which we have proclaimed as widely as our ministry would reach, is not at all inconsistent

with the fact that God hath a chosen people amongst
the children of men who were beloved of him, fore-
known to him, and ordained by him to inherit all
spiritual blessings before the foundation of the
world. As an elect people they are the special
objects of his love. On their behalf the covenant
of grace was made; for them the blood of Christ
was shed on Calvary; in them the Spirit of God
worketh effectually to their salvation. Of them
and to them it is that such words as these are
spoken, "I have loved thee with an everlasting
love;" a love far superior to mere benevolence—
towering above it as the mountain above the sea;
love kindlier, deeper, sweeter far than the bounty
of Providence which gilds the earth with sunshine
or scatters the drops of morning dew; a love that
reveals its preciousness in the drops of blood dis-
tilled from the Saviour's heart, and manifests its
personal, immutable favor to souls beloved in the
gift of the Holy Spirit, which is the seal of their
redemption and the sign of their adoption. So the
Spirit itself beareth witness with our spirit that we
are the children of God.

Now, think for a little while of this inestimable
boon. Let us consider the text word by word.
"I have loved thee." Who is the speaker? "I;"
the great "I am," Jehovah the Lord. There is
but one God, and that God filleth all things. "By
him all things were made, and through him all
things consist." He is not far away, to be spoken
of as though he were at an infinite distance from

us. Though heaven is his throne, yet he is here
with us. We live in him, move in him, and have
our being in him. Imagination's utmost stretch
fails to grasp any true conception of what God is.
The strong wing of reason, though it were stronger than that of the far-famed albatross, would
utterly fail if it should attempt to find out God.
Incomprehensible art thou, O Jehovah! thy being
is too great for mortal mind to compass! Yet this
we understand—Thy voice hath reached us; from
the excellent glory it has broken in tones distinctly
on our ears. "Yea, I have loved thee." Believer
in Christ, hast thou heard it? The love of any
creature is precious. We prize the love of the
beggar in the street. We are flattered by it. We
cannot estimate it by silver or gold. Most men
court the acquaintance or esteem the friendship
of those among their fellow-creatures who are in
anywise distinguished for rank, for learning, or for
wealth. There is a charm in living in the esteem
of those who themselves are estimable; but no
passion of our nature will supply me with an adequate comparison when I ask, what must it be to
be loved with the love of God; to be loved by him
whose dignity is beyond degree, whose power to
bless is infinite, whose faithfulness never varies,
whose immutability standeth fast like the great
mountains? It is the love of him who ever liveth; love that will not fail us when we die; he
changeth not in all our cares, but he will shield
us by his love when we stand at the judgment-

seat and pass the last dread ordeal that as responsible creatures we have to undergo. Oh, to be beloved of God! Had ye the hatred of all mankind, this honey would turn their gall into sweetness. It were enough to make you start up from the dungeon of wretchedness, from the chamber of poverty, ay, or from the bed of death. How like an angel you might feel, and know that such thou art, a prince of the blood Imperial! If this be true of thee, my friend, in joy unspeakable thou mayest emulate the bliss of spirits blest, who see Jehovah, and adore him before his throne. *"I have loved thee."* Drink that in, if thou canst, Christian. Come to that well-head; here is joy for thee indeed. Repeat the words to yourself with fitting emphasis, " Yea, I have loved *thee*."

Is it not a wonder that the Mighty God should love any of the race of Adam—so insignificant, so ephemeral, so soon to pass away? Did an angel love an emmet creeping on an ant-hill it were strange, though the disparity is comparatively trivial between these twain; but for the eternal God to love a finite man is a marvel of marvels! And yet had he loved all men everywhere, save and except myself, it had not so amazed me as when I grasp the truth in relation to myself that he has loved me. Let me hear his voice saying, " Yea, I have loved thee," and forthwith I sit down, abashed with humility and overwhelmed with gratitude, to exclaim with David, " What am I, and what is my father's house, that thou hast brought me hitherto? Why hast thou loved me?" Surely there was nothing in my natural constitution, nothing in my circumstances, nothing in my transient career, that could merit thy esteem or regard, O my God! Wherefore, then, hast thou spoken thus unto thy servant, saying, "I have loved thee"? Oh, how well I could imagine his having rather said to one and another of us, "I have despised thee!" Thou wast, perhaps, once a drunkard, yet he loved thee; a swearer, yet he loved thee; thou hadst a furious temper, yet he loved thee; and thou hast even now infirmities and imperfections that make thee sometimes loathe thyself and lie down in shame, weary of life, chafed with the conflict in which you have to fight with such besetting sins day by day—evil thoughts and evil desires, so degrading to thy nature, so disgusting to thyself, so dishonoring to thy God. Still he saith, "Yea, I have loved thee." Come, brothers and sisters, hear the word and heed it; do not fritter away the sweetness of the text with vexatious questions. Here it is. In large and legible letters it is written. Come to this wellhead and drink. Take your fill and slake your thirst with this love divine. If you believe in Jesus, what though you be poor, obscure, illiterate, and compassed with infirmities, which make you despise yourself, yet he who cannot lie saith, "I have loved thee." These words have been said to a Magdalen, they have been spoken to one possessed with seven devils, they were whispered in the heart of the dying thief. Within the tenfold darkness of despair itself they have sounded their note of cheer. Blessed be the name of the Lord, you and I can hear the voice of his Spirit, as he bears witness with our spirit, " Yea, I have loved thee." What a disparity by nature, what a conjunction by grace between these two, the " I " and the " thee "—the infinite " I " and the insignificant " thee "—the first person so grand, the second person so paltry!

Whenever I attempt to speak about God's love, I feel that I would rather hold my tongue, sit down to muse, and ask believers to be kind enough to join me in meditation, rather than wait upon my feeble expressions. If the love of God utterly surpasseth human knowledge, how much more a mortal's speech? That God should be merciful to us is a theme for praise; that he should pity us is a cause for gratitude; but that he should love us is a subject for constant wonder, as well as praise and gratitude. Love us! Why, the beggars in the street may excite our pity, and towards the criminals in our jails we may be moved with compassion; but we feel we could not love many whom we would cheerfully help. Yet God loves those whom he has saved from their sins and delivered from the wrath to come. Between that great heart in heaven and this poor throbbing, aching heart on earth there is love established—love of the dearest, truest, sweetest, and most faithful kind. In fact, the love of woman, the mother's love, the love

of the spouse, these are but the water; but the love
of God is the wine; these are but the things of the
earth, but the love of God is the celestial. The
mother's love mirrors the love of God as the dewdrop mirrors the sun; but as the dewdrop compas-
seth not that mighty orb, so no love that beats in
human bosom can ever compass it at all by liken-
ing it to the height, depth, length, and breadth
of the love of God which is in Christ Jesus our
Lord. "Yea, I have loved thee." Oh! come thou
near, then, Christian. Thy Father, he that chast-
ened thee yesterday, loves thee; he whom thou
forgettest so often, and against whom thou hast
offended so constantly, yet loves thee. Thou knowest what it is to love. Translate the love thou bear-
est to thy dearest friend, and look at it and say,
"God loves me better than this." Think you there
are some thou couldst die for cheerfully, whose
pain thou wouldst freely take if thou couldst ease
them of it for a while, upon whose weary bed thou
wouldst cheerfully lie down if a night of suffering
could be spared him: but thy Father loves thee
better than that, and Jesus proves it to thee. He
took thy sins, thy sorrows, thy death, thy grave,
that thou mightest be pardoned, accepted, and received into Divine favor, and so mightest live and
be blessed for evermore.

Passing on with our meditation, let us observe
that there is incomparable strength, as well as inexhaustible sweetness in this assurance: "I have
loved thee with an everlasting love." That word

"everlasting" is the very marrow of the gospel. Take it away, and you rob the sacred oracle of its Divinest part. The love of God is "everlasting." The word bears three ideas within it. It has never had a beginning. God never began to love his people. Or ever Adam fell, ere man was made, ere the mountains were brought forth, before the blue heavens were stretched abroad, there were thoughts of love in his heart toward us. He began to create, he began actually to redeem, but he never began to love. It is eternal love which glows in the bosom of God towards every one of his chosen people. Some of our hearers, strange to say, take no delight in this doctrine; but if you know that everlasting love is yours, you will rejoice to hear it proclaimed again and again. You will welcome the joyful sound. Ah! God's love is no mushroom growth. It sprung not up yesterday, nor will it perish to-morrow; but like the eternal hills, it standeth fast. You were loved of your God before he had fashioned Adam's clay. Or ever this round world was rolled from between his palms to spin in its mighty orbit, long ere the stars began to shine, ere time was, when God dwelt in eternity all alone, he loved you then with an everlasting love.

The second idea is, that he loves his people without cessation. It would not be everlasting if it came now and then to a halt; if it were like the Australian rivers, which flow on, become dry, and flow on again. The love of God is not so. It swells and flows on like some mighty river of Europe or America, ever expanding—a mighty, joyous river; returning again into the eternal ocean from whence it came. It never pauses. Christian, thy God loves thee always the same. He cannot love thee more; he will not love thee less. Never, when afflictions multiply, when terrors affright thee, or when thy distresses abound, does God's love falter or flag. Let the rod fall never so heavily upon thee, the hand that moves, like the heart that prompts the stroke, is full of love. Judge not the Lord by feeble sense, but trust him for his grace. Whether he brings thee down into the depths of misery, or lifts thee up into the seventh heaven of delight, his faithful love never varies or fluctuates; it is everlasting in its continuity.

And being everlasting, the third thought is, it never ends. You will grow gray soon, but the love of God shall still have its locks bushy and black as a raven, with the verdure of youth. You will die soon, but the love of God will not expire. Your spirit will mount and traverse tracts unknown, but that love shall encompass you there; and at the bar of judgment, amidst the splendors of the resurrection morning, when there breaks forth the millennial glory, and in the eternity that shall follow, the love of God shall be your unfailing portion. Never shall that love desert thee. A destiny how splendid! For my soul an heritage how boundless! Stand thou to-night on thy Pisgah, and lift up thine eyes to the north and the south, to the east and the west, for the infinite prospective that lieth before thee is all thine own inheritance. God began not to love, nor will he ever cease to love thee. Thou art his, and thou shalt be his when worlds shall pass away and time shall cease to be. There is infinitely more solace and satisfaction here than I can bring out. I must leave it with you, and commend it to your meditation. Sure I am, there is no more delightful manna for the pilgrims in the wilderness to feed upon than this doctrine applied to the heart. The love of God towards us personally in Jesus Christ is an everlasting love.

Now we come to the second point, which is the manifestation by which this love is made known. Good people often get puzzled with the doctrine of election. In their simplicity they sometimes ask, " How can we know whether we are the Lord's chosen, or ascertain if our names are written in the Lamb's Book of Life?" You cannot scan that mystic roll, or pry between those folded leaves. Had you an angel's wing and a seraph's eye, you could not read what God has written in his book. The Lord knoweth them that are his. No man shall know by any revelation, save that which the Holy Spirit gives according to my text. There is a way of knowing, and it is this: "Therefore with loving-kindness have I drawn thee." Were you ever drawn? Have you been drawn with lovingkindness? If so, then there is evidence that the Lord loved you with an everlasting love. Be ready, therefore, to judge yourselves. You are challenged with this pointed question: Were you ever Divinely drawn? Say now, beloved, have you experienced this sacred attraction that made you willing in the day of his power? Were you ever drawn from sin to holiness? You loved sin once: in it you found much pleasure; there were some forms and fashions of vice and folly which were very dear to your heart. Have your tastes been changed and has your track been turned by the sovereign charm of this Divine loving-kindness? Can you say, "The things I once loved I now hate, and what gave me pleasure now causes me a pang"? Is it so? I do not ask you whether you are perfect and upright. Alas! who of us could answer this question otherwise than with blushes of shame? But I do ask if thou dost hate sin in every shape and desire holiness in every form? Wouldst thou be perfect if thou couldst be? If thou couldst live as thou wouldst list, how wouldst thou list to live? Is thy answer, "I would live, were it possible for me to serve God day and night in his temple, without a wandering thought or a rebellious wish"? Ah, then, if you have been thus drawn from sin to holiness by the way of the Cross, no doubt he loved you with an everlasting love, and you need not discredit it. You may be as sure of it as if an angel should come and drop a letter into your hands on which these words should be inscribed. Yea, surer still; for the angel might have missed his way; but God's Word cannot err. If thou art thus drawn, he has loved thee with an everlasting love.

Hearken again. Hast thou ever been drawn from self to Jesus? There was a time when thou thoughtest thyself as good as other men. Had the bottom of thine heart been searched there would have been found written there, " I do not see that I am so great an offender as the most of my neighbors; I am respectable, upright, moral; I should hope it would speed well with me at the last, for if I am not now all that I should be, I shall try to be good, and by earnest endeavors, joined with fervent prayers and repentance, I hope to fit myself for heaven." Oh, that you may be drawn away from all such empty conceit, and led to rest your hope solely on that blessed man who sits at the right hand of God crowned with glory, though he was once fastened to the tree, despised and rejected of men, and made to suffer as a scapegoat for our sins. This, beloved, would be a sure sign that you had renounced yourself and closed in with Christ. You may have been loved with an everlasting love. It is as impossible for any of the elect of God to come to Christ and lay hold on him without Divine drawing as it would be for devils to feel tenderness of heart and repentance towards God. If thou canst say from thy heart:

> " Nothing in my hand I bring,
> Simply to thy cross I cling,"

then his drawing may suffice as the positive proof that he loved thee with an everlasting love.

Have you ever been drawn from sight to faith, from consulting your creature faculties to confidence in God? You used to depend only on what you called your common sense. You walked by the judgment of your own mind. Do you now trust in him who truly is, though he is invisible; who speaks to you, though his voice is inaudible? Have you a sense, day by day, of the presence of One Supreme whom you cannot hear nor see? Does the unseen presence of God affect you in your actions? Do motives drawn from the next world influence you? Say whether do you, in the day of trouble, lean upon an arm of flesh, or cry and pray and make supplications to the Almighty? Have you learnt to walk in dependence upon the living God, even if his providence seem to fail you and give a lie to his promises? Know, then, that a life of faith is a special gift of God; it is the fruit of Divine protection, so that thou art enabled to walk with God, and as he designs to befriend thee, thou mayest humbly but safely conclude that in the records of the chosen thy name stands inscribed. To be drawn into a life of faith is a blessed evidence of Christ's love.

Are you, moreover, day by day, being drawn from earth to heaven? Do you feel as if there were a magnet up there drawing your heart, so that when you are at work in your business, in your family with all its cares, you cannot help darting a prayer up to the Most High? Do you ever feel this onward impulse of something you do not understand, which impels you to have fellowship with God beyond the skies? Oh! if this be so, rest thou assured that it is Christ that draws. There is a link between thee and heaven, and Christ is drawing that link, and lifting thy soul forward towards himself. I love that sweet hymn, and I hope you love the sentiment of it:

> " My heart is with him on his throne,
> And ill can brook delay;
> Each moment listening for the voice,
> ' Rise up, and come away.' "

If your heart is here below, then your treasure is here; but if your heart is up there—if your brightest hopes, your fondest wishes be in the heavenly places, your treasure is manifestly there, and the title-deeds of that treasure will be found in the eternal purpose of God, whereby he ordained you unto himself that you might show forth his praise.

Thus have I tried to show you that those who are thus drawn may be assured that they were loved with an everlasting love. And now will you further observe that it is with lovingkindness they are drawn. Some people are frightened into religion. Beware of any religion that depends upon exciting your terror. Some people's religion consists entirely in doing what they think they must do as a duty, though they do not relish any of the exercises that their conscience enforces on them. They are afraid of punishment or they are anxious for a reward. Such is not the religion of Jesus Christ. It is said that the soldiers of Persia were driven into battle, and that the sound of the whips of the generals could be heard even while the battle was raging, lashing on the unwilling ranks to fulfil their part in the fray. Not so went the Greeks to battle. They rushed like lions amidst a flock of sheep to tear their prey. They fought for their country, for their temples, for their lives, for all that they held dear, and right cheerfully from such an impulse within did they engage in the war. The difference between the Greeks and the Persians is just the difference I want to describe among the professed followers of our Lord. The genuine Christian serves God because he loves him; not that he fears hell, for he knows that he has been delivered from condemnation, being washed in Jesus' blood; not that he expects to earn heaven, he scorns the idea. Heaven is not to be merited by our poor paltry works. And besides, heaven is his inheritance, since Christ has given it to him, having made his title sure. But he serves God because he loves him. He is drawn by a sense of the love of God towards him to love God in return. Who is the best servant? Not, surely, the man who only does what he is paid for; who serves you for his wage, and who would betray your interest to benefit himself: rather is he the true servant who would cling to you in all your fortunes or misfortunes, through good or evil report. Some of the old-fashioned servants were so attached to their masters that they were reckoned on and regarded as members of the family. Those are the true servants of Christ who love him, and render him their services, not menially for the pay they count upon, but loyally, because their hearts are faithful and true to him; they love him so that they could not turn aside from him, or seek another Lord. Say now, are you thus drawn with lovingkindness? What a lovely word this "lovingkindness" is! "Kindness" seems to be like some huge opal or some sparkling diamond, a Koh-i-noor; and love seems to be like fine gold to encircle it. Methinks I could stand and look at that word "lovingkindness" till with sacred enchantment I burst into a song. There is such a charming sweetness and yet such an immutable stability in the grace of God which it reveals, that our rapture is kindled as often as we review it. Of that lovingkindness I have tasted here below, and of that lovingkindness I hope to sing in yonder skies in worthier notes than this weak voice can compass now. The lovingkindness of the Lord, as it beams from his eyes, as it is communicated by his helping hand, as it is expressed by his gentle, tender voice, quickens the soul in the path of duty, and restrains it from falling into sin. How can I do this great wickedness, how can I sin against so almighty a Friend whose kindness to me is so gratuitous, so constant, and so exceedingly generous!

> "Now for the love I bear his name,
>   What was my gain I count my loss;
>   My former pride I call my shame,
>   And nail my glory to his cross.

> " Yes, and I must and will esteem
> All things but loss for Jesus' sake:
> Oh may my soul be found in him,
> And of his righteousness partake ! "

Thus clearly and thus surely may ye judge for yourselves whether ye are God's chosen or not. Are you drawn, and how are you drawn? Is it with lovingkindness? These are the two points that melt and fuse in experience. As before that God whose eyes of fire search you through and through I do adjure you to judge, and righteously judge, now as to your own condition. Be not satisfied to rest peacefully until you can say, " Thanks and praise to God's eternal love, I am drawn: by grace, by grace Divine, I am constrained. Henceforth I freely yield myself up to Christ to be his servant, his disciple, his friend, his brother, forever and forever. The Lord hath appeared unto me, saying, ' Yea, I haved loved thee with an everlasting love.'"

Do I hear a sigh come up from some in this assembly; a sigh which, being interpreted, would say, " Alas for me, this sacred solace was never mine; I never was drawn; I feel no love; no such melting sense of God's favor as your description of lovingkindness ever dawned on me: but, ah, I wish I were drawn; that I had a part amongst that blessed throng who shall forever see his face. Oh that I could believe that I, though the meanest of them all, should find my name written in the Lamb's Book of Life!" Why, friend, with thee, it would seem, the drawing has begun.

Surely God's lovingkindness hath made thy mouth water. I rejoice exceedingly over those who hunger after the bread of life, for they shall speedily be filled. Right well I know my Master will give it to them. If thou desirest Christ, depend upon it, Christ desireth thee. No sinner ever was beforehand with Christ. When you are willing to have him, he is evidently willing to have you. You had not put out one hand towards him if he had not put two hands on you already. Oh! if thou wilt but trust the bleeding Lamb; believe that he can save thee, and trust in him to save thee with unfeigned confidence, then thou art already drawn. This is proof positive that God has loved thee from before the world's beginning. Oh, how I would that some might be drawn to-night; some who have been great and grievous sinners. There be many such among the chosen vessels of mercy. God grant that some of you young people may be drawn. And you, who, though no longer young, are still without the blessing; I cannot bear the thought that you should tarry longer uncalled by sovereign grace. May the Holy Spirit attract you! May you feel in your heart the wish to belong to Christ; the desire to be counted among them when he maketh up his jewels. Turn that wish into a prayer. Bow your head now, and pray with this petition. God will hear your secret sighs. He does not reject sincere prayers, however badly they may be worded. If you can get no further than a sigh, it has its value in his kind esteem. The tear that fell just now upon the floor of the pew was not lost; for an angel tracked and treasured it and carried it on high. God will accept thee if thou wilt accept Christ. If thou trustest Jesus now, 'tis done! Thou art saved. The moment a sinner believes and trusts in Christ, he is saved—saved forever. In that moment his iniquity is blotted out, and he is accepted in the Beloved. From that moment he might sing:

> "'Tis done! the great transaction's done;
> I am my Lord's, and he is mine:
> He drew me, and I follow'd on,
> Glad to obey the voice divine."

The Lord appear to you, speak to you, and bless you, saying to you: "Yea, I have loved thee with an everlasting love: therefore with loving-kindness have I drawn thee." Amen.

A Mournful Defection.

Will ye also go away?—JOHN vi. 67.

NO mischief that ever befalls our Christian communities is more lamentable than that which
comes from the defection of the members. The
heaviest sorrow that can wring a pastor's heart is
such as comes from the perfidy of his most familiar
friend. The direst calamity the Church can dread
is not such as will arise from the assault of enemies
outside, but from false brethren and traitors within
the camp. My eminent predecessor, Benjamin
Keach, though arrested, brought before the magistrates, imprisoned, pilloried, and otherwise made
to suffer by the Government of the times for the
gospel doctrines that he preached and published,
found it easier to brook the rough usage of open
foes than to bear the griefs of wounded love, or sustain the shock of outraged confidence. I should
not think his experience was very exceptional.
Other saints would have perferred the rotten eggs
of the villagers to the rooted animosities of slanderers. Troy could never be taken by the assaults
of the Greeks outside her walls. Only when, by

stratagem, the enemy had been admitted within the citadel was that brave city compelled to yield. The devil himself is not such a subtle foe to the Church as Judas, when, after the sop, Satan entered into him. Judas was a friend of Jesus. Jesus addressed him as such. And Judas said, "Hail, Master," and kissed him. But Judas it was who betrayed him. That is a picture which may well appal you; that is a peril which may well admonish you. · In all our churches, among the many who enlist there are some who desert. They continue awhile, and then they go back to the world. The radical reason why they retract is an obvious incongruity. "They went out from us because they were not of us, for if they had been of us, doubtless they would have continued with us." The unconverted adherents to our fellowship are no loss to the Church when they depart. They are not a real deficit, any more than the scattering of the chaff from the threshing floor is a detriment to the wheat. Christ keeps the winnowing fan always going. His own preaching constantly sifted his hearers. Some were blown away because they were chaff. They did not really believe. By the ministry of the gospel, by the order of Providence, by all the arrangements of Divine government, the precious are separated from the vile, the dross is purged from the silver, so that the good seed and the pure metal may remain and be preserved. The process is always painful. It causes great searching of heart amongst those who abide faithful, and occasions deep anxiety to gentle spirits of tender, sympathetic mould.

I trust, dear friends, that you will not think I harbor any ungenerous suspicions of your fidelity, because my text contains so pointed and so personal an appeal to your conscience. There is more of pathos than of passion in the question as our Lord put it—"Ye will not go away, will ye?" He addressed the favored twelve. I put it to myself; I put it to those who are the officers of the church; I put it to every member without exception: Will ye also go away? But should there be one to whom it is peculiarly applicable, I do not desire to flinch from putting the question most personally to that one—"What! Are you going? Do you mean to turn back? Do you mean to go away?"

Let us approach the inquiry sideways. Will ye *also* go away? "Also" means as well as other people. Why do others go? If they have any good reason, perhaps we may see cause to follow their example. Look narrowly, then, at the various causes or excuses for defection. Why do they renounce the religious profession they once espoused? The fundamental reason is want of grace, a lack of true faith, and absence of vital godliness. It is, however, the outward reasons which expose the inward apostasy of the heart from Christ of which I am anxious to treat.

Some there are in these days, as there were in our Lord's own day, who depart from Christ because *they cannot bear his doctrine.* Our Lord had more explicitly than on any former occasion declared the necessity of the soul's feeding upon himself. They probably misunderstood his language, but they certainly took umbrage at his statement. Hence there were those who said "This is an hard saying; who can hear it?" So they walked no more with him.

There are many points and particulars in which the gospel is offensive to human nature and revolting to the pride of the creature. It was not intended to please man. How can we attribute such a purpose to God? Why should he devise a gospel to suit the whims of our poor fallen human nature? He intended to save men, but he never intended to gratify their depraved tastes. Rather doth he lay the axe to the root of the tree and cut down human pride. When God's servants are led to set forth some humbling doctrine, there are those who say, " Ah, I will not assent to that." They kick against any truth which clashes with their prejudices. What say you, brethren, to the claims of the gospel on your allegiance? Should you discover that God's word rebukes your favorite pleasure or contradicts your cherished convictions, will you forthwith take the huff and go away? Nay; but if your hearts are right with Christ, you will be prepared to welcome all his teaching and yield obedience to all his precepts. Only prove it to be Christ's teaching, and the right-minded professor is ready to receive it. That

which is transparent on the face of Scripture he
will cordially accept, as he says, "To the law and
to the testimony. If they speak not according to
this word, it is because there is no light in them."
As for that which is merely inferred and argued
from the general drift of Scripture, the true heart
will not be hasty to reject, but patient to investigate, like the Bereans, who "were more noble than
the Jews of Thessalonica, in that they searched the
Scriptures daily, whether those things were so."
Oh that the word of Christ may dwell in us richly!
God forbid that any of us should ever turn aside,
being offended because of him, his blessed person,
his holy example, or his sacred teaching! May we
be ever ready to believe what he says, and prompt
to do what he commands! Remember, brethren,
that the gospel commission has three parts to
which the minister has to attend. We are to go
and preach the gospel first. "*Go ye and disciple
all nations.*" The second thing is "*baptizing them;*"
and the third thing is "*teaching them to observe all
things whatsoever I have commanded you.*" As willing disciples of Jesus, let us press forward, heark-
ening to his voice, following in his footsteps, and
accounting his revealed will as our supreme law.
Far be it from us to go back, to repine, or to
desert him then because we are offended at his
doctrines.

Others there are who desert the Saviour *for the
sake of gain.* Many have been entangled in that
snare. Mr. By-ends originally went on pilgrimage

because he thought it would pay. There was a silver mine on the road, and he purposed to survey that, and see whether silver might not be obtained there as well as at the golden city beyond. He came, if I remember rightly, of a family that got its living by the waterman's business, looking one way and pulling another. He was apparently striving for religion, though he had his eye all the while on the world. He was for holding with the hare and running with the hounds. So, when he came to a point where he must part with one or the other, he considered which upon the whole would be most profitable, and he gave up that which appeared to involve loss and self-sacrifice, and kept to that which would, as he called it, help him in the "main chance," and assist him to get on in the present life. Sincerely do I trust there is no one among us but who despises Mr. By-ends and all of his class. If you would make money—and there need be nothing sinful in that—do let it be made honestly; never let riches be pursued under the pretence of religion. Sell your wares and find a market for your merchandise, but do not sell Christ, nor barter a heavenly birthright for a worthless bribe. Put what goods you please into your shop window, but do not put a canting, hypocritical expression on your face, or "wear a holy leer," with a view of turning godliness into gain. God save us from that arrant villainy! May it never have a footing in our midst!

> "Neither man nor angel can discern
> Hypocrisy, tho only evil that walks
> Invisible, except to God alono."

Does any man join a church for the sake of the respectability it implies, or for the standing it may give him, or for the credit he may get? He will soon find that it does not answer his purpose. Then away he will go. The graver probability is that he will be thrust out with shame.

Some leave Christ and go away terrified by persecution. Nowadays it is supposed that there is no such thing. But that is a mistake; for though martyrs are not burned at Smithfield and the Lollards' Tower is a place for show (a memorial of times long ago), yet the harass, the cruelty, and the oppression are far enough from being obsolete. Godless husbands play the part of petty tyrants, and will not permit their wives the enjoyment of religion, but make their lives bitter with a galling bondage. Employers full often wreak malice on servants whose piety towards God is their sole cause of offence. Worse still, there are working men who consider themselves intelligent, who cannot allow their fellow-workman liberty to go to a place of worship without sneers and jeers and cruel mockings. In many cases the mirth of the workshop is never louder than when it is turned against a believer in Christ. They count it rare fun to hunt a man who cares for the salvation of his soul They call themselves " Englishmen," but certainly they are no credit to their country. Look at the base-born, ill-bred cowards. Yonder is an atheist; he is raving about his rights because the magistrate will not believe him on his oath; he claims liberty of conscience to be a heathen himself, but denies his comrade's right to be a Christian.

Look at that little party of British workmen; they belong to the Sabbath Desecration Society. They are petitioning Parliament to open museums and theatres on Sundays, and at the same time they are hounding to death a poor fellow who prefers going to chapel. They air their own self-respect by the oaths they utter, while they betray their self-abasement by the scorn they vent on those who presume to sing a hymn. They hail the drunkard as a chum, and scout the sober man as a fiend. I wonder that there is not more honorable feeling, more good faith and true fellowship among our skilled workmen than to allow of one man being made the butt of a whole community. God give you grace to bear such persecutions as these! If they cut us to the quick, may we learn to bear them with equanimity, and even to rejoice that we are counted worthy to suffer for the Saviour's sake! Some of us have had to run the gauntlet for many years. What we have said has been constantly misrepresented; what we have endeavored to do has been misjudged, and our motives have been mis-understood. Yet here we are, as happy as any-body out of heaven. We have not been injured by any or all the calumnies that have been heaped upon us. Our foes would have crushed us; but blessed be God, he cheered us often when we were cast down. The Lord give you, in like manner, strength of mind and courage of heart to bear the trial manfully! then you will care no more for the laughter and the sneers of men than you do for the noise of those migratory birds high overhead, which you hear on an autumn evening as they are making their weary journey to a distant clime. Take heart, man. Fear God, and face your accusers. True courage grows strong on opposition. Never think of deserting the army of Christ. Least of all should you play the coward because of the insolence of some ill-mannered bully. Let not your faith be vanquished by such scoffing. Alas, that so many a craven spirit has gone away for the sake of carnal ease, and deserted Christ, when his dear name had become the drunkard's jest and the derision of fools.

Anon there are people who forsake true religion out of sheer levity. I know not how to account for some men's defections. If you take up the list of wrecks, you will notice some that have gone down through collisions, and others through striking upon rocks; but sometimes you meet with a vessel "foundered at sea;" how it happened no one knows; the owner himself cannot understand it. It was a calm day and there was a cloudless sky when the vessel sank. There are some professors who, concerning faith, have made shipwreck under such apparently easy circumstances, so free from trial, so exempt from temptation, that we have not seen anything to awaken anxiety on their behalf, yet all of a sud-

den they have foundered. We are startled and
amazed. I remember one that fell into a gross sin,
of whom a brother unwisely said, "If that man is
not a Christian, I am not." His prayers had certainly been sweet. Many a time they have melted me
down before the throne of grace, and yet the life of
God could not have been in his soul, for he lived and
died in flagrant vice, and was impenitent to the last.
Such cases I can only attribute to a sort of levity,
which can be charmed with a sermon or a play; take
a pew at the chapel or a box at the opera with equal
nonchalance; and eagerly follow the excitement of
the hour, "everything by turns and nothing long."
"Unstable as water, they shall not excel." At the
spur of a moment they profess Christianity, though
they do not espouse it; and then, without troubling
themselves to renounce it, they drop off into infidelity. They are soft and malleable enough to be
hammered into any shape. Made of wax, they can
be moulded by any hand that is strong enough to
grip them. The Lord have mercy upon any of you
that may happen to be of that genus! You spring
up soon, and suddenly you wither. Hardly is the
seed sown before the sprout appears. What a wonderful harvest you promise! But ah! no sooner
has the sun risen with a burning heat than, because there is no depth of soil, the good seed withers
away. Pray God that you may be ploughed deep,
that the iron pan of rock underneath may be broken
right up, that you may have plenty of subsoil and
root-hold, that the verdure you produce may be per-

manent. Lack of principle is deadly, but the lack is far too common. Never cease to pray that you may be rooted and grounded, stablished and built up in Christ, so that when the floods come and the winds blow, you may not fall with a great destruction, as that house fell which was built upon the sand.

But oh, what multitudes are tempted aside from following Christ and his Church by evil companions. They do not avoid the society of the wicked; and as a man is known by the company he keeps, we soon discover the direction in which they are drawn. The more intimately we know them, the more readily we perceive their propensities. Have a care, then, with whom you associate. Never confide in those persons of whose principles you have good cause to stand in doubt. Above all, let me admonish you young people not to be unequally yoked together. Marriage without the fear of God is a fearful mistake. Those ill-assorted unions between believers and unbelievers rob our churches of more members than any other popular delinquency that I know of. Seldom—I might almost say never— do I meet with a woman professing godliness who becomes joined in wedlock to a man of the world but what she goes away. She ceases to follow Jesus, and we hear no more of her. Absorbed in the pursuits, the passions, and the pleasures of the life that now is, she is sucked under the stream and drawn into the vortex. In the romance of her courtship, she glibly said, "I shall win him:" but in the reality of their conjugal bonds, he could coolly say, " I have won you." Probably the stronger nature wins the day. In this case, however, a precept of the gospel is violated and a penalty of disobedience is incurred. It is much easier for the one that professes religion to give up the faith after laying down the cross than for another who has no religion to take up the cross and follow the Saviour in whom he has never yet believed. I counsel every young man or woman that contemplates a marriage on the basis of some capricious attractions, without any reference to the sanctity of your relationship before God —such of you as choose to be unequally yoked—that you communicate your intention to your minister, and renounce your membership of the Church before you seal your vows. Give up all profession of religion voluntarily. Do not wait to be excommunicated. Do not sneak away without giving an account of yourself. You had better count the cost and pay the price of your own presumption. This is part of it. Should your sanguine hopes succeed, and could your earnest endeavors to gain the conversion of your helpmeet be requited, that would be an uncovenanted mercy. If God chose to give it you, it would not even then excuse you for tempting him by your waywardness, or provoking him to jealousy by your wilfulness. There is an express command, " Be ye not unequally yoked together with unbelievers." I appeal to every Christian man or woman who has been converted since marriage if you do not find it exceedingly hard to keep up your courage when one pulls one way and one another?

And does it not cut you to the quick to think that your union is but temporary; that, however dear you may be to each other now, you will be parted at the judgment-seat of Christ—parted to meet no more? The Lord make us careful about our associates, about those among whom we stand, by whom we sit, with whom we walk! Their bad morals must harm our good manners. Their influence is momentous. Their virtue might embolden us. Their vice must ensnare us. So, let us choose our acquaintances, and our friends, and our partners for life with great discretion. I am afraid that recklessness is too often the rule. Instead of steering by the chart, you drift with the tide.

And, oh, how many leave Christ for the sake of sensual enjoyments! I will not enlarge upon this. Certain, however, it is that the pleasures of sin for a season fascinate their minds till they sacrifice their souls at the shrine of sordid vanity. For a merry dance, a wanton amusement, or a transient joy that would not bear reflection, they have renounced the pleasures that never pall, the immortal hopes that never fail, and turned their backs upon that blessed Saviour who gives and feeds the tastes for joys unspeakable, for joys of glory full. In our pastoral oversight of a church like this we have painful evidence that a considerable number gradually grow cold. The elders' reports of the absentees reiterate the vain excuses for non-attendance. One has so many children. The distance is too great for another. When they joined the church, their family was just as large, and the distance was just the same. But the household cares become more irksome when the concern for religion begins to flag; and the fatigue of travelling increases when their zeal for the house of God falters. The elders fear they are growing cold. No actual transgression can we detect, but there is a gradual declension over which we grieve. I dread that cold-heartedness; it steals so insensibly yet so surely over the entire frame. I do not say that it is worse than open sin. It cannot be. Yet it is more insidious. A flagrant delinquency would startle one as a fit does a patient; but a slow process of backsliding may steal like paralysis over a person without awakening suspicion. Like the sleep which comes over men in the frozen regions, if they yield to it they will never wake again. You must be aroused, or else this supineness will surely end in death. "Gray hairs were upon him here and there, and he knew it not." Is it so with any of you, dear friends? Are you going aside by slow degrees? He that loses his substance little by little presently becomes a bankrupt, and painful is the discovery when the end is precipitated. How miserable must a spiritual bankruptcy be to him who wastes by degrees his heavenly estate, if he ever had any! No words can describe it. God preserve us from such a catastrophe!

Some have turned aside who allege that they did so through change of circumstances. They were with us when their means of livelihood were competent, if not affluent. From reverses in business they have sunk in their social position. Hence they do not like to come into fellowship with us as they were wont to do. Now, from my inmost soul I can say, if there are any persons that wax poor, I, for one, do not think one atom the less of them, or hold them in less esteem, however impoverished they may become. Do not tell me that you have no clothes fit to come in; for any clothes that you have paid for are creditable. If you have not paid for them, I cannot make excuses for you. Be honest. Frieze or fustian need not shame you; but for fineness or fashion I should certainly blame you. I am always glad to see brethren sitting here, as I sometimes do, in their smock-frocks. One good friend is rather conspicuous in that line. The wholesome whiteness of his rural garb is rather attractive. If he has paid for it, he is a far more respectable man than any one that has run into debt for a suit of broadcloth that he cannot pay for. And I rejoice to think that I am not expressing my own feeling merely, but that which is shared by the whole community. We all delight to see our poor brethren. If there are any of you suffering from a sensitiveness of your own, or a suspicion of our reflections, the sooner you get rid of such foolish pride the happier you will be. You are jealous of being thought respectable. Don't you know that a man is respectable for his character, not for the money he has got in his pocket? Others forsake Christ because they have become rich and increased in goods. They did not scorn the little conventicle when they were plain plodding people; but since fortune has smiled on them, and they have moved their residence from a terrace to a mansion, and they have taken to keep a carriage they feel bound to move in another circle. To their parish church, or to some ritualistic church in their neighborhood, they go once on the Sunday. They patronize the place by their presence; they show themselves among the *élite* of that locality; they bow and bend and face about to the east, as though they had been to the manner born. They are too respectable to go into the little Baptist chapel. They receive visitors in the afternoon, dine late, and dissipate Sabbatic hours in the frivolous pretence of showing off their gentility. Well, I think their departure is not to be lamented. When gone they are certainly no loss to anybody. We sigh for them as we would for Judas or Demas. They have fallen foul of what they thought their good fortune, but of what has proved to be their ruin. Those who have true principle, when they rise in the world, see more reason why they should use their wealth and their influence in aiding a good cause. Principle wonld prevail over policy to the end of their lives if in their hearts they believed the truth as it is in Jesus. It were no dishonor to a prince to go and sit down side by side with a pauper, were they both true followers of Jesus Christ.

In old times, when our sires sought refuge in

caves and dens of the earth, they met the liege an l the lowly, the bond and free; or when, in earlier ages, the Christians gathered in the cata- combs, men out of Cæsar's household—now a chief, then a senator, anon a prince of the blood— came and sat down in those caverns, lighted up with the dim candle, to listen while some uns' od but heaven-taught man declared the gospel of Jes s with the power of the Holy Spirit. That they were illiterate I am quite sure; for on looking over the monuments that are found in the cata- combs, it is rare to find one inscription that is thoroughly well spelt. Though it is evident enough that the early Christians were an un- educated company of men, yet those that were great and noble, learned' and polished, did not disdain to join with them, nor will they ever in any age if the light of heaven shines and the love of God burns in their hearts.

Unsound doctrine occasions many to apostatize. There is always plenty of that about. Deceivers will beguile the weak; some have been laid aside by modern doubt; and positive infidelity has its partisans. They begin cautiously by reading works with a view to answer scientific or intel- lectual scepticism. They read a little more and dive a little deeper into the turbid stream, because they feel well able to stand against the in idious influence. They go on, till at last they are stag- gered. They do not repair to those who could help their scruples, but they continue to flounder on till at last they have lost their footing, and he that said he was a believer has ended in stark atheism, discrediting even the evidence of the existence of God. Oh that those who are well taught would be content with their teaching! Why meddle with heresies? What can they do but pollute your minds! Were I to get black, I imagine that I could wash away all the soils; but I should be sorry to black myself for the sake of washing. Why should you be so unwise as to go through pools of foul teaching merely because you think it easy to cleanse yourself of its pollution? Such trifling is dangerous. When you begin to read a book and find it pernicious, put it aside. Some one may upbraid you for not reading it all through. But why should you? If I have a joint of meat on my table of which the smell and the taste at once convince me that it is putrid and unwholesome, should I show my discretion by *fairly* eating it all before giving my judgment that it is not fit for food? One mouthful is quite enough, and one sentence of some books ought to suffice for a sensible man to reject the whole mass. Let those who can relish such meat feed on it, but I have a taste for better food. Keep to the study of the word of God. If it be your duty to expose those evils, encounter them bravely, with prayer to God to help you. But if not, as a humble believer in Jesus, what business have you to taste and test such noxious fare when it is exposed in the market?

Can you doubt that there are some who turn aside from Christ and his people through sheer laziness? They have nothing whatever to do, and what must a Christian be at who has no part in the service of Christ? Nothing to do for Jesus! A drone in the hive! I do not wonder that you go away. My wonder is that the bees do not drive you out. On the other hand, I fear others have gone aside through having been too busy; they have been so occupied that they have neglected to feed their own souls. I am always pleased to see our dear brothers and sisters diligent in the service of Christ. I am glad to miss many of you on the Lord's-day evening when I know how well you are engaged. I could spare a few more of you if you were intent upon teaching the young, or exhorting those who are out of the way. But I earnestly admonish you never to be negligent of your own souls while you are vigilant for the souls of others. If you do not get nourished with the bread of life yourselves, you cannot grow in grace. This caution, I am fully persuaded, is not uncalled for. There are some who get so absorbed in Christian work that they never listen to the word; they hardly ever read; they only talk. This is sorry work. If you do not take in, you cannot give out. If your own soul is starved, you cannot be strong for the Lord's service. Get at least one good spiritual meal in the day. Then spend all the strength you have for God, and rely on him for frequent renewals. Be constant and consistent, not excursive and erratic in your labors. Keep the fire up, and add fresh fuel to give a more fervent heat. See to it that you are not losing communion with Christ while you think you are getting conversions to Christ. That is a peril you good people must not play with. It is far too serious. But I will not continue in this strain. It is painful to me if not to you. Now let me condense into a few sentences an answer to the second inquiry,—*What becomes of them?* Those that go aside—What becomes of them?

Well, if they are God's children, I will tell you what becomes of them, for I have seen it scores of times. Though they go aside, they are not happy. They cannot rest, for they are miserable even when they try to be cheerful. After awhile they begin to remember their first husband, for then it was better with them than now. They return; but there are scores and scores who, to say nothing of the shame they have to carry with them to their grave, are never afterwards the men they were before. They have to take a second place among their comrades. And even should sovereign grace so wonderfully bless their painful experience that they are fully restored, they can never mention the past without bitter regret. Their by-path serving for others' beacon, they will say to young people, "Never do as I have done; no good, all mischief, comes of it." In the vast majority of cases, however, they are not the Lord's people. So this is what comes of it. Those who prove traitors to a profession they once made are the hardest people in the world to impress. Doubtless some of you, when you lived in the country, used always to be punctual at your usual place of worship, but since you have come to London, where your absence from any sanctuary is unnoticed, you rarely enter the courts of the Lord's house; nor would you have been here to-night but for some special inducement, —some country cousin or some particular friend having brought you. Though unknown to me, God scans your path. Well, here you are, and yet it may be to little profit. You have had counsels and cautions in such profusion that it is like pouring oil down a slab of marble to admonish you. May God of his omnipotent mercy break your obdurate heart, or there will be no hope for you! Such people frequently lose all conscience. They can go a great deal further in talking against religion than anybody else. They will sometimes venture to say they know so much about it that they could expose it. Their boast and their threat are alike unmeaning; but as boys whistle while they walk through the churchyard to keep their courage up, so do their vain talk and their senseless stories betray their stifled fear. They speak contemptuously of God while they justify themselves in a course for which their own conscience upbraids them. They go back—alas! some of them to prove themselves the most abandoned sinners in the world. The raw material out of which the devil constructs the deadliest fabric is that which was presumed to be the most saintly substance.

There could not have been a Judas to betray Christ had he not been first distinguished as a disciple who ventured to kiss his Master. You must pick from among the apostles to find an apostate. As the ringleaders of riotous transgression when converted often make the best revivalist preachers, so those that seem to be the most loyal subjects of Christ, when they become renegades, prove to be the bitterest foes and the blackest sinners.

Painful reminiscences rush over one's mind. Standing here now, in the midst of a great church, I call to mind things that have harrowed up my soul. God grant I may not see the like of them again! They go away!—ah me! full many of them go away to die in blank despair. Did you ever read the life of Francis Spira? If you want to sleep to-night, do not take up that memoir. Did you ever read the life of John Child, a Baptist minister of about two hundred years ago? Mr. Keach gives it in one of his works. He was a man who knew the truth, and to a great extent had felt its power; but he went aside from it, and before he came to die his expressions were too terrible to listen to. The remorse and despair of his spirit chased every one away. At last he laid violent hands upon himself. For a man, after having once looked Christ in the face and kissed him, to betray him and crucify him afresh, to hang himself is not to be wondered at. To eat at the Lord's table, to drink of that cup of blessing, to mingle with the saints, join in their prayers and their hymns, professing

to be a disciple of Christ, and then to go back and
walk no more with him, is to venture on a course
of no ordinary danger. The swing of the pendu-
lum, if it has been lifted high and let go, is so
much the greater on the other side. I marvel not
that any man should be precipitated into flagrant
sin who wilfully renounces his vows of consecration to Jesus. And oh! when his eyes are open
and his conscience is aroused, how he wishes that he
had never been born! Could he terminate his existence and annihilate his anguish-smitten soul, then
the direct act of desperation by which he should
end a life he could not mend might be accounted
wise. But no; that is impossible. The relief he
seeks he cannot find when he takes the dreadful
leap from suffering here to an aggravated form of
misery hereafter, ten thousand times worse. to endure. He seals his doom and makes his own damnation sure as he raises against himself a murder-
ing hand. Do I address any one here who is bereft
of every ray of hope, and shivering on the brink
of cold despair? Hold now! I would cry in your
ears; do thyself no harm. Thou canst do thyself
no good. Think not to cure thy woes by committing another crime.

> " 'Twere madness thus to shun the living light,
> And plunge thy guilty soul in endless night."

While there is life there is hope. Jesus Christ
can forgive you. Return to him. He can wash
you in his blood. He can make you clean, though

your sin be as scarlet. But oh! do not trifle, make
no delay. Tarry no longer in your present condition; else, may be, you will fill up the measure
of your iniquities or ever you are aware, and you
may taste, even in this world, some beginning of
the wrath to come. If not rescued as a trophy
of grace right speedily, you may become a monument of God's wrath; a beacon to deter others
from daring to turn aside. I speak solemnly; I
cannot help it. So intensely do I feel the terror
of that woe, and so confident am I that some of
you are making light of it, that I would go down
on my knees, and entreat you with tears to mind
what you are at. You have got on the inclined
plane, and you are going down, down, down.
Your feet are even now on the slippery places
from which multitudes have been cast down into
destruction. How are they brought into desolation as in a moment! The Lord make haste to
deliver you! May he stretch out his hand and
rescue you! I can only call out to you. You
seem to have get where I cannot reach you. Do
not venture a footstep further in that dangerous
road. Look to Jesus, look to Jesus; he can redeem your life from the pit by his sovereign grace,
and he alone. Then as a wandering sheep, brought
back to the fold, you shall adore his name.

Our third point is this. *Why should not we go
away as they have gone?* Were we left to ourselves,
I cannot tell you any reason why we should not
go as they have gone. Nor, indeed, could I tell

you why the best man here should not be the worst before to-morrow morning if the grace of God left him. John Bradford, you know, as he saw the poor criminals taken away to Tyburn to be executed, used to say, "There goes John Bradford but for the grace of God." Verily, each one of us might say the same. To abide with Christ, however, is our only security, and we trust we shall never depart from him. But how can we make sure of this? The great thing is to have a real foundation in Christ to begin with—genuine faith, vital godliness. The foundation is the first matter to be attended to in building a house. With a bad foundation there cannot be a substantial house. You require a firm bottom, a sound groundwork, before you proceed to the super-structure. Do pray God that if your religion be a sham you may find it out now. Unless your hearts be deeply ploughed with genuine repentance, and unless you are thoroughly rooted and grounded in the faith, you may have some cause to suspect the reality of your conversion and the verity of the Holy Spirit's operation in you. May the Lord work in you a good beginning, and then you may rely upon it he will carry it on to the day of Jesus Christ.

Then remember, dear brethren and sisters, if you would be preserved from falling, you must be schooled in humility and keep very low before the Lord. When you are half-an-inch above the ground, you are that half-inch too high. Your place is to be nothing. Trust Christ, but do not trust yourself. Rely on the Spirit of God, but do not rely on anything that is in yourself; no, not on a grace you have received, or on a gift you possess. Those do not slide that walk humbly with God. They are always safe whose entire dependence is upon the dear Redeemer. Be jealous of your obedience; be circumspect; be careful; take heed to yourselves; your walk and conversation cannot be too cautious. Many are lost through being too remiss, but none through being too scrupulous. The statutes of the Lord are so right that you cannot neglect them without diverging from the path of rectitude. Watch and pray. God help you to watch, or else you will get drowsy. Never neglect prayer. That is at the root of every defection. Retrogression commonly begins at the closet. To restrain prayer is to deaden the very pulse of life. "Watch unto prayer." And I beseech you, dear friends, do shun that company which has led other people astray. Parley not with those whose jokes are profane. Keep right away from them. It is not for you to be seen standing, much less to be found sitting down, with men of loose manners and lewd converse. They can do you no good, but the evil they can bring upon you it would not be easy to estimate. You may have heard the story—but it is so good it will bear repeating—of the lady who advertised for a coachman and was waited upon by three candidates for the situation. She put to the first one this question: "I want a really good coachman to drive my pair of horses, and, therefore, I ask you how near you can drive to danger and yet be safe ? " " Well," he said, " I could drive very near indeed : I could go within a foot of a precipice, without fear of any accident so long as I held the reins." She dismissed him with the remark that he would not do. To the next one who came she put the same question. " How near could you drive to danger?" Being determined to get the place, he said, " I could drive within a hair's breadth, and yet skilfully avoid any mishap." " You will not do," said she. When the third one came in, his mind was cast in another mould, so on the question being put to him, " How near could you drive to danger ? " he said, " Madam, I never tried. It has always been a rule with me to drive as far from danger as I possibly can." The lady engaged him at once. In like manner I believe that the man who is careful to run no risks and to refrain from all equivocal conduct, having the fear of God in his heart, is most to be relied upon. If you are really built upon the Rock of Ages, you may meet the question without dismay, " Will ye also go away ? " and you can reply without presumption, " No, Lord, I cannot and I will not leave thee; for to whom should I go? Thou hast the words of eternal life." So be it. " And the very God of peace sanctify you wholly; and I pray God your whole spirit and soul and body be preserved blameless unto the coming of our Lord Jesus Christ. Faithful is he that calleth you, who also will do it." Amen.

A Solemn Resolution.

I have yet to speak on God's behalf.—JOB xxxvi. 2.

SO said Elihu. And verily many of us might make the like resolve. We have tasted that the Lord is gracious. When first we came to him, laden with guilt and full of woes, we found him ready to pardon—a God with whom there is plenteous redemption.

> "Many days have passed since then,
> Many changes have we seen."

Still we have the same tale to tell. God has been faithful to us under all circumstances. He has passed by our backslidings, he has been patient of our short-comings, and he has borne with our waywardness. To this day his kindness has not abated, his promise has not been forfeited, and his covenant is unbroken; it has never failed us. In bounden duty, yet with cheerful gratitude, we are constrained to say that the Lord is good, and his mercy endureth forever. On God's behalf, then, we will speak. Much reason have we to do so. While the world is scoffing or despising, while some are doubt-

(318)

ing and others are blaspheming, while idolatry
and infidelity have their respective champions, we
will offer our personal testimony in the teeth of all
the Lord's adversaries. Blessed be his name, he
is a faithful and true God, and if all the dwellers
on earth should belie and forsake him, his love
binds us fast. We cannot, neither will we, let our
trust in him be displaced or our witness to him be
silenced. It seems to me that the chief business
of a Christian while here below is to speak on God's
behalf. Why is he placed here? Lower ends or
meaner objects do not appear to me to resolve that
question. Merely to work, to toil, to fulfil his days
as a hireling in common with the rest of his fellow-creatures were a poor account to give of a pil-
grim to the heavenly city bound. Is he not suffered to tarry here that he may glorify his God by
speaking on his behalf? Are we not, each one of
us, appointed to linger in these lowlands, that we
may personally bear witness to what we have heard
and seen, tasted and handled, tested and proved to
be true of the good Word of Life? This sacred obligation may be very heart-searching to some of you.
I am afraid there are dumb tongues that do not
speak on God's behalf; and which of us can escape
a sharp rebuke on this score? for those of us who
do speak, speak not as we should; we are not always giving such evidence and bearing such witness as well becomes us on God's behalf.

I purpose this evening to mention *some of the occasions on which we have yet to speak on God's behalf;*

some prevalent excuses for silence; some imperative reasons for bearing testimony; and some pointed suggestions to those who feel constrained to open their mouths boldly for the honor of God.

I. To my mind it seems obvious that THERE ARE CERTAIN OCCASIONS WHEN EVERY SAVED ONE SHOULD SPEAK ON GOD'S BEHALF. Is it not peculiarly incumbent upon us *immediately after we have found peace by putting our trust in the Lord Jesus Christ?* He that believeth with his heart is bound, according to the gospel, to confess also with his mouth. Hast thou heard the good tidings, the way of salvation thyself, and believed it, and received the fulness of its blessing? Then thou art forbidden to hide thy light under a bushel, thou art admonished to let it be seen by all that are in the house. Thou art not, as a coward, to conceal thine allegiance to thy Lord, but thou art, as a warrior, to put on the King's livery, enter the ranks, and join with the rest of his people.

Is not this the message we are told to circulate— "He that believeth and is baptized shall be saved"? Should you not, therefore, avow your faith and confess your Lord in baptism. Then, having believed his Word and obeyed his precept, ought you not to take up his cross as one who is dead and buried with him in the outward type and symbol, to follow henceforth wherever he leads? This seems to me, as I read the Word of God, to have been the course with all the early Christians. They believed and were baptized. They did not postpone or procrastinate; but no sooner were they Christians by conviction and conversion than they professed their Christianity in baptism. And why is it not so now? Would God that his people would come back to the simple methods of the early churches, and feel that, being saved, their next business is to give the answer of a good conscience toward God, speaking thus on his behalf, and avowing themselves to be the Lord's people.

This is but a fitting preface to a life of testimony. The whole of a Christian's career should be vocal with spiritual power. By the indwelling of God the Holy Ghost within him he should ring out as it were in silver notes, through all his conversation both in the Church and in the world, a goodly, gracious, grateful resolution—" I have yet to speak on God's behalf. Even if I have spoken for the last twenty years, it becomes me yet to speak on God's behalf." I may be gray headed, I may lean upon my staff, I may come near the bounds of man's short span on this poor stage, " I have yet to speak on God's behalf." Even when pillows stay up my aching head, and when my flesh and my heart are failing, until the pulse of life shall flag and the power of speech shall fail, my witness to the sons of men must never falter, much less must it come to an ignoble end. " I have yet to speak." When first I knew him I was constrained to speak. Would that every converted man was moved instantly to avow his Lord. But if we have aught to regret in the past, let us not be hesitant now. Say it, resolve it, ay, vow it. I have, and I shall have, *yet* to speak on God's behalf till speech shall fail me, till, dying, "I clasp my Saviour in my arms, the antidote of death."

And oh, how specially bound the Christian is to speak on God's behalf *when he is cast among ungodly men and women!* There may be in the house where you live no lover of Jesus except yourself. Take care that your conversation makes the rest know that you have been with Jesus and have learned of him. There is no other candle in the house; oh, put not the extinguisher on that one. You only are the salt, take care that you be sprinkled over the mass. Let the savor of your walk and conversation be diffused among your associates. At times the name of Christ will be blasphemed perhaps in your presence; or, it may be, unholy and even lewd conversation will assail your ears. It is for you to express your displeasure at anything which is displeasing to him you serve. You must put in a word, though you do but feebly thrust it in edgeways, for the Christ whom ungodly tongues are slandering. You may not sit still and hear your best friend evil spoken of; that were ungrateful in the extreme. Well might he say, "Is this thy kindness to thy friend?" Should you smile, they will think you are amused; but if you laugh with them over an unseemly jest, they would say you enjoyed it. "Thou also wast as one of them" was a charge made against a professor. Oh, let it never be laid against any of us. If we see our neighbor sin, and rebuke him not when the opportunity offers, we become abettors of his iniquity. Remember this: on such occasions it is our bounden duty to speak on God's behalf.

Yet again, we meet with brethren in affliction. They are mourning and bemoaning themselves and their hardships. God's own people commonly find that in all their trials they are beset with temptations. How apt they are to speak unadvisedly because they think untowardly of the order of God's providence and the manner of his love! I wish this ill condition of the heart and this bad habit of the lips were less prevalent than unhappily it is. They talk as if they served a hard Master, and they murmur as if his providence were peculiarly severe towards them. I beseech you, seize the propitious moment to speak on God's behalf. Daughter of poverty! you who have known the pinch of want, tell of the faithfulness of God that supported you. Child of pain! thou who hast tossed so long upon a bed of affliction, changing thy posture o'er and o'er, till thy bones began to peep through thy skin, speak of the gentleness wherewith thy Lord hath soothed thee. Tell, ye patient sufferers,—and there are many of you whose pangs are smart, whose wounds are incurable,—tell how God has succored you. Be not silent, ye who have gone through fire and water, the furnace and the flood. Testify, you fathers in the Church, and you mothers in Israel—speak on God's behalf of the goodness, the guidance, and the grace

you have proved. Do not let the young recruits
entertain hard thoughts of your Lord and Master.
Tell them that the battle of life, stern though it be,
does not baffle his counsel or his care. He who
has upheld you will bear them through ten thousand billows, keep them alive in the midst of afflictions fiery as a furnace seven times heated, and
even to the end will prove that he is their gracious
God. You have yet to speak on God's behalf.

Now, brethren and sisters, some of you may not
only have so to speak in the chambers where the
afflicted are confined, and in the Sunday-school
where the little children come round your knee,
and in your own families and workshops, but *you
may have a call to speak in the open streets, or in the
pulpits of our sanctuaries.* I pray you, then, if you
have ability for such work in this day of blasphemy
and rebuke, stand not back. I am persuaded that
some of my brethren look for greater talents before
they can speak for Christ than they have a right
to expect at the first. If none are permitted to
speak on God's behalf but those who have ten talents, surely the kingdom of God must be deeply
indebted to the education and scholarship of learned
men. But if I read this Word aright it is not so.
Rather has it pleased God to take weak and foolish
things to confound the mighty and the wise.
Therefore, let not the brother of low degree keep
back his testimony. If thou canst only say a few
good words, say them. Who would withhold a
few drops of moisture from the flowers in the gar-

den because he had no plenteous streams at his
command? Should every twinkling star cease its
shining because it was not a sun, how dark the
night would be! the firmament how bereft of its
beauty! Did each drop of rain refuse to fall because it was but a drop, we had lacked the goodly
showers which cheer the thirsty soil! Do what you
can if you cannot do what you would; for you,
even you, have yet to speak on God's behalf. And,
peradventure, you have more talent than you think;
a little exercise might bring out your latent powers.
Men grow not up to man's estate in a week or a
year. Rome was not built in a day. How can you
expect to be qualified to serve your God with much
success unless you are trained with drill and discipline? If you begin to walk, or even to crawl
on all fours, you may afterwards learn to run. Be
content to use such powers as thou hast to the utmost of thy ability; for he has said, "I will never
leave thee nor forsake thee." Do not reserve thy
strength, but consecrate all thou hast, "for he
giveth more grace;" diligently cultivate every
faculty, knowing that he giveth grace upon grace.
"I have yet to speak on God's behalf."

I know not whether I am just now like the seraph who flew with a live coal, bearing it in the
tongs, from off the altar, to touch some lips, to put
it to any one's mouth, and say, "Lo, this hath
touched thy lips." It may be so. Some child of
God hitherto dumb may be called henceforth to
speak for his Master. If you now hear a voice

saying, "Who will go for us? Whom shall we send?" let your answer be, "Here am I; send me." Respond, in the words of our text, "I have yet to speak on God's behalf."

Turn ye now to THOSE ARGUMENTS WHICH READILY SUGGEST THEMSELVES TO SOME MINDS FOR KEEPING SILENCE.

Have I yet to speak on God's behalf? "Nay," says one, "pardon me, but *speaking out for God cannot be accounted essential to salvation.* Are there not some who come, like Nicodemus, by night? May there not be many believers in Jesus who have not the courage to speak out of the fulness of their heart? Why should not I be one of these secret believers, and yet enter into heaven?" You think to go to the celestial city by a by-road, unseen and unnoticed, hoping to be safe at the last. Suppose it true that to avow your faith is not absolutely essential to salvation, I ask you if it is not absolutely essential to obedience, and I ask again if obedience is not essential to every believer as a vindication of his faith? Though you may tell me that there are many secret believers, I venture to affirm that you never knew one; or do you think you did, the secret must have been ill kept if you knew it. Obviously if it was a genuine secret it must have been beyond your ken or mine either, so we cannot fairly argue about it, and as we do not know that such a thing ever was, we have no fact to build upon. Surely to some one or other that gracious secret must have been made known; or what you tried to conceal some one would have found out. I should think, if your Christian character and conduct were not palpable, your Christianity could scarcely be sterling. Who can conceal fire in his bosom? Will it not sooner or later break out? The more wicked the persons by whom you are surrounded, the more readily will they discover the difference between a Christian and themselves. You can scarcely conceal the light; it must reveal itself. Why, therefore, should you attempt to hide it? Merely to do what is absolutely needful for salvation is a mean, selfish thing. To be always thinking about whether this or that is necessary to your being saved—is this how you would show your allegiance to the Saviour? Should the self-denial of our blessed Lord and Master be requited with the selfishness of followers who are always muttering, "*Cui bono?* What profit can I make of his service?" Oh, that we may be delivered from such an ungenerous disposition! Knowing that Christ has done so much for us, and feeling the constraining power of love, may we rejoice to serve him, whether the service shall be grateful to our taste or mortifying to our pride; so doing, we shall soon find that in keeping his commandments there is great reward.

"*But do you happen to be of a very retiring disposition?*" A beautiful disposition that is, I have no doubt, and rare enough in some select circles to claim admiration, but undesirable indeed on some particular fields at some critical junctures. For a soldier, when the battle is raging, to be of a retiring disposition would be neither patriotic nor praiseworthy. Had this dainty temper been the main virtue of the hosts from whence British heroes leapt forth, the trumpet of fame had long since ceased to resound the deeds of prowess of which every Englishman is proud. A soldier of Christ may well be modest in estimating himself, but he had need be mighty in serving his Lord. If he be too modest to avow his Master, his shameless modesty betrays a craven spirit, at which his comrades well might shudder.

> "Ashamed of Jesus! that dear Friend
> On whom my hopes of heaven depend?
> It must not be; be this my shame,
> That I no more revere his name."

Ashamed of Jesus! Really, the words seem so harsh that they imply an insult. Yet this beautiful, retiring disposition, when translated out of the fine words in which you wrap it up, means nothing more nor less than a disloyalty which verges hard on treason. Ashamed of Jesus, who shed his blood for you! Ah! you must all confess that there is no violation of genuine modesty in avowing one's intense attachment and allegiance to the Lord Jesus Christ. This may be true retirement, after all; for you may renounce thereby the world's praises, repudiate her honors, bring upon yourself her loudest censure, and be requited with the cold shoulder by your companions when you take up your cross and follow him.

But have I not often heard persons say, " Why should I speak on God's behalf, when already some who do speak are hypocrites?" This seems to me a reason why you should speak twice as much in order to counteract their false testimony, and why you should speak with all the more carefulness and integrity, making their example a beacon, lest you fall into the same condemnation. If a friend of mine has an enemy who is a snake in the grass, pretending kindness while he is plotting mischief, am I therefore to say, " I will forsake my friend and not own him, because another is a traitor to him"? Such reasoning would refute itself; let us not therefore delude ourselves with its subtilty. The more hypocrites there are, the more need of honest men to grasp the banner of the cross. The more deceivers, the more cause why the faithful and the true should come and fill up the ranks, and prevent the battle being turned over to the enemy.

Or do you hesitate to speak for God *because you are afraid your testimony would be so very feeble?* But why disquiet yourselves on this ground? Are not all great things the aggregate of little things? and may there not be something great involved in the motion of the little? A good word from your tongue may kindle a thought or a series of thoughts which will issue in the conversion of one whose eloquence shall shake the nation. You emit but a spark, but what a conflagration it may cause heaven only knows. What though you seem tiny and insignificant as the coral insect, yet if you do your fair share of the work with your fellows, you may help to pile up an island that shall be abundant in fertility and transcendent in beauty. Thou art not called upon to do aught that exceeds thy power or thy skill. Enough that ye do what ye can. God requireth not according to what a man hath not, but according to what a man hath. Therefore let it be no excuse for thy silence that thou canst not speak with a voice of thunder.

"But," saith one, "were I to open my mouth on God's behalf, *I should feel ever afterwards a weight of responsibility from which I could not escape.* A man of God standing by that pool not many weeks ago said to me, "I dare not be baptized, though I believe it is a Scriptural ordinance, because I feel that it involves such a solemn profession. I should never be able to live up to it." My reply to him was, "Is not that the very reason why you should yield up yourself to God at once; for the more we feel bound to holiness the better." "Thy vows are upon me." Should the profession of our faith in Christ become a restriction to us, it need not be regretted on that account. We want such restrictions. If we shall feel bound to be more precise, we serve a precise God; and if we feel bound to be more jealous, we serve a jealous God. I like to see men put upon their mettle. Members of this church, whenever the world picks holes in your coat and watches you, I am thankful to the world for so doing. It is good for our welfare to have an eagle eye upon us. What though Argus use all his eyes, let us only be what we should be, and we need not mind who criticises or carps at us. If we are not what we ought to be, but mere hypocrites, then in truth we may well wish to be hidden. Confess the name of Jesus, become a true follower in his blessed footsteps, and walk with all humility and carefulness, as his grace shall enable thee, worthy of thy high calling. Be bold to confess his name all the more—certainly none the less—because such confession will lay thee under solemn obligations to live nearer to him than before.

Still, I can imagine that there are many here who are urging some excuse or other, which they would not like to mention. They say they will wait a little; they will tarry awhile. Others say nothing, but are simply neglecting the duty. Well, I will not stay to argue with them, but I will rather pray that God the Holy Spirit may convince them, if they have been quickened from their spiritual death, and are this day heirs of God, to face their incumbent duty and their blessed privilege in all ways, and on all prudent opportunities to speak on God's behalf.

But THERE ARE COGENT REASONS WHY WE SHOULD SPEAK ON GOD'S BEHALF, to which I will now draw your attention.

Surely *it is demanded of all believers.* We are bidden to confess with the mouth if we have believed with the heart. We have, moreover, the promise that "He that with his heart believeth, and with his mouth confesseth, shall be saved;" and this likewise, "He that confesseth me before men, him will I confess before my Father which is in heaven." The alternative is fraught with judgment, "He that denieth me"—which signifies a non-confession—"He that denieth me before men, him will I deny before my Father which is in heaven." If it be then the Lord's will, it is at your peril that you forget or neglect it. "He that knoweth his Master's will, and doeth it not, shall be beaten with many stripes." Hasten, then, thou backward Christian. Make haste, and delay not to keep his commandment; be convinced that thou hast yet to speak on God's behalf.

Most assuredly such testimony as you can and ought to bear *would be a great comfort to the Lord's people.* You do not know, some of you saved ones who have never confessed your faith, what pleasure it would give the minister. I know of no joy comparable to that of hearing that one has been made the instrument of the conversion of a soul. It keeps our spirits up, and our Master knows that we have good need sometimes of some success to encourage us. He who thinks that the Christian ministry is an easy post, exempt from care and free from trials, had better try it. 'Twere better to be a galley-slave chained to the oar than to be a minister of the gospel if it were not for the strong consolations which support us in the present and for the divine reward in the future which stimulates us. He who diligently discharges this solemn vocation never knows rest or release from anxiety. His mind is always actively exercised in his Master's service, his heart bears about a load which it cannot shake off. He dreams of some who walk disorderly, and wakes to sigh and cry over others who grow cold or lukewarm. He must plough the stony ground, and he can but regret the loss of his seed. He scatters the good seed on the way, and if it come not up by and by, according to the promise, he crieth, "Who hath believed our report, and to whom hath the arm of the Lord been revealed?" As cold water to a thirsty soul, so would the news be of your conversion. You saved ones ought, for that reason, to speak on God's behalf.

And how encouraging it is to the entire Church! In the church assembly I am sure we often have simple music that is more thrilling than any of the anthems in your cathedrals. There is joyful melody in our hearts before the Lord when we hear of a broken-hearted penitent finding peace, of an outcast reclaimed from the wilds, an outrageous sinner led into paths of obedience and holiness. Even the angels account this to be rare music to be exquisitely relished. I believe they strike their golden harps to nobler melody when they learn that prodigals have sought their Father's face. You have yet to speak on God's behalf for his Church's sake, that she may be encouraged.

Greatly too does it behove you to speak on God's behalf, *for the sake of the undecided.* Some of them would probably be fully persuaded if they saw your example. How many people there are in the world who are led by the influence that others exert over them! Thousands have been brought to Jesus just as those early disciples, of whom we read that Andrew followed Jesus, and presently brought his own brother Simon to Jesus; or Philip, who, after being found of Jesus, finds Nathanael, and tells him and draws him to the Saviour. We can all exert an influence of some kind; let us tell what God has wrought in us, and many a one who halteth between two opinions may, by divine grace, be induced to cast in his lot with the people of God.

Look on the great outlying world. What a mass of creatures whose *lives must prove a blessing or a curse!* Will you not speak on God's behalf for their sakes? Do you not feel constrained to bear your testimony against their apathy, their waywardness, or their wilful disobedience of the great Father? With habitual negligence and constant forgetfulness they slight him who never disregards them, but with unslumbering eyes watches for their good. Lay this to heart, my brethren, and come out, I pray you; be ye separate, touch not the unclean thing. You have your Father's promise that he will be a Father to you, and you shall be his children. You are not of the world, even as Christ is not of the world; why, then, should you seek to continue mingled with the world in name? Be distinct and separate; take up the cross daily, and follow your Master.

For your own sake, too, I would venture to press

this upon any of you who are backward in avowing your faith. You cannot conceive what blessing it would bring you were you distinctly and persistently to speak for Jesus. That timidity which now embarrasses you would speedily cease to check your zeal. After you had once openly professed Christ, gifts that now slumber unconsciously to yourself would be developed by exercise. Rich comfort the service of God would then bring you. Were you ever to win a soul for Jesus, you would be happier than the merchantman when he found the goodly pearl. You would think that all the happiness you ever knew before was less than nothing compared with the joy of saving a soul from death, and rescuing a sinner from going down into the pit. Oh, the bliss of speaking a word that affects three worlds, making a change in heaven, and earth, and hell, as devils grind their teeth in wrath because one of their victims is snatched out of their jaws; as men on earth wonder and admire the change that grace has wrought; and as angels rejoice when they hear of sinners saved.

For the sake of him who bought you with his precious blood, seek out others who have been redeemed at the same inestimable price. For the sake of that blessed Spirit who brought you to Jesus, and who now moves in you that you may move others to come to Jesus, be up and doing, steadfast, immovable, always abounding in the work of the Lord, forasmuch as ye know that your labor is not in vain in the Lord. You have yet to speak on God's behalf, and these are the motives that ought to move you.

And now let me close with ONE OR TWO SUGGESTIONS.

Should you feel, dear friends, that you ought to speak on God's behalf—and I hope you do feel it—whether brethren in public ministry or sisters in the privacy of social circles, I would counsel you before you begin to speak to *seek of God guidance as to how you shall speak on his behalf.* There are better words spoken by the ignorant when they wait upon God than by the wise when they speak out of their own heads. It is wonderful to read the answers which some of the martyrs gave to their accusers. Think of that woman, Anne Askew, how, after being racked and tortured, she nonplussed the priests. It is really marvellous to read how she overcame them. There was my Lord Mayor of London— what a fool she made of him! He put to her this question: " Woman, if a mouse were to eat the blessed sacrament, which contains the body and blood of Christ, what dost thou think would become of it?" " My lord," she answered, " that is a deep question; I had rather thou wouldest answer it thyself: my lord mayor, what dost thou think would become of the mouse that should do that?" " I verily believe," said the Lord Mayor, whose ears must have been preternaturally long, " I verily believe the mouse would be damned!" And what said Anne Askew? Why, what could she reply better than this: " Alas! poor mouse!" Often a few short words, even three or four words, have met the case when the martyrs have waited upon God, and they have made their adversaries seem so ridiculous that methinks they might hear a laugh both from heaven and hell at once at their foolery, for God's servants have convicted them of folly and put them to shame. Ask what thou shouldest say, particularly when men would wrest thy words, and when they would catch thee in thy speech. Be like thy Master sometimes—stoop down and write on the ground; wait awhile. Sometimes a question is best answered by another question. Ask your Master to teach you that rhetoric which confounds men who would catch you in your speech.

And if you seek the conversion of others, especially recollect that *it is words from God's mouth rather than words from your own mouth that will effect it;* enquire of the Master, for he knows how to draw the bow when you cannot. You might draw it at a venture, but he can draw it at a certainty, so that the arrows shall surely pierce between the joints of the armor. Here is a prayer for every man and woman that has to speak for Jesus: "Open thou my lips, and my mouth shall show forth thy praise."

And look to *the Holy Ghost, that he would bless what he directs you to say.* 'Twere better to speak five words by the promptings of the Holy Spirit than to utter whole volumes without his guidance. Better be filled with silent musings by the blessed Spirit of God than pour forth floods of words and sentences, however passionate, without his hallowing influence. There is an irresistible power about the man who hath an unction from the Holy One which Demosthenes or Pericles, Cicero or Socrates, Pitt or Burke never dreamed of. Put the man up to speak to his fellow-men who is endowed with this mysterious power, and he will make hearts of stone melt, and force a way for the truth of God through gates of brass and bars of triple steel. Where the Divine Witness attests the word spoken, there is a majesty in the simplest utterances that carries conviction to the heart, while it makes Satan and all his myrmidons tremble. Seek for this might. Tarry at Jerusalem till thou art endowed with power from on high, and then speak boldly on God's behalf. Wherever thy calling may be, and whenever thy opportunity shall arise, speak as one whose heart has been enlarged, as one whose mouth has been opened, as one who is filled with the Spirit.

Very earnestly would I caution you, young Christians, not to put off or delay speaking, otherwise you will lack the facility you might quickly attain by habitually attending to it. An aptitude for speaking to people one by one is very desirable. I know some brethren in the ministry whom I greatly envy for the possession of a talent which I do not possess myself in the same proportion that they do. The genius of conversation —so sanctified that one can be personal and yet prudent; plain and pointed yet withal pleasant; administering a rebuke without endangering a rebuff; winning a man's confidence while wounding his pride, and commending the gospel by the courteousness with which it is stated—that is a power of utterance to be emulated by us all. We are too apt to be ambitious of speaking to the many, and oblivious of the talking power that can adroitly speak to a friend. Begin early, then, after your conversion to speak one by one with your kinsfolk and acquaintance. Keep up the practice. Should you find yourselves getting sluggish, so that it becomes irksome to you, seek unto the Lord, confess your sin before him. The tact of speaking to individuals is worth all the study and attention you can bestow upon it. Ask for wisdom and prudence to know when to speak and how to speak. It is not every fisherman that can catch fish. There is a knack about it, and so there is about speaking for Christ. There is a suitable time and there is a suitable way. Why, there are some people who, if they were to try to speak for Christ, would do mischief. They have got such forbidding faces, such ungainly manners, such a coarse way of expressing themselves, that in spite of good intentions they rather hinder than help. They expect to catch their flies with vinegar, but they will never succeed or be able to do it. If they could learn to be kind and genial, affable and sympathetic, they would be far more likely to succeed. There are men who put the truth in such a shape that it looks like a lie. There are other men who do a good deed with so

little delicacy that they affront those they intend
to oblige. Do let us learn, when we speak for
God, to speak in the best possible manner, exer-
cising all the Christian graces. Of our blessed
Lord it was said, "Never man spake like this
man." Of us who are his humble followers may
it be observed that we have been with Jesus, and
have learned of him.

God grant you believers all grace to speak for
God; and you unbelievers, may you be brought to
trust the Master and to love him, and then to
speak for him; and his shall be the praise, though
yours shall be the profit.   Amen.

A Clear Understanding.

Jesus saith unto them, Have ye understood all these things?
MATT. xiii. 51.

THIS is a question which might often be asked of us when we have been reading the Scriptures, when we have been attending upon the public means of grace, or when we have been partaking of the Lord's Supper—" Have ye understood all these things?" It were well for some one to run up to us, as Philip did to the eunuch, who on his return from Jerusalem was reading in his chariot, and say to us as Philip did to him, " Understandest thou what thou readest?" Or the question might be put to us, " Understandest thou what thou hearest? Understandest thou even that which thou sayest?" I fear there are hundreds of religionists in this country who never think of understanding that which they attend to under the name of religion. They pass through the wonted forms, listening to, and it may be joining in, the liturgy, till at length the service is finished, the day is over, and the thing is done. The language of devotion has thus slipped through the lips, without having leaped from the heart. Among ourselves, I fear, there may be many who are content with listening to the sounds of gracious words, who never pierce through the shell of the words into the kernel of the meaning; satisfied with the external, which is nothing, they miss the internal, which is everything. "Understandest thou these things?" then, is a question which may be asked of every worshipper and should be asked often, for it is only so far as we enter into religious worship, understanding what we are doing, and casting our hearts into it, that it can be at all acceptable to God. The Lord's Prayer is quite as good said backwards as forwards if you do not say it from the heart; there is quite as much likelihood of a benediction in a number of words thrown out pell-mell, without any kind of connection, as there would be in the best arranged sermon, if there be not an attentive ear and an understanding heart. Words that touch not the understanding glide over us as oil over a slab of marble, without effect. Men may perish with the gospel in their houses, they often do perish with the gospel ringing in their ears, for until they understand its import it cannot become a soul-saving word to them.

Nor can it become a sanctifying word to any, except so far as they receive it into the understanding. If we were to hear the gospel in Latin, after a fashion never so orthodox, one might be no more edified by it than by listening to so much blasphemy, because it is not the thing heard, but the thing understood and received into the heart, which blesses the soul. Do let me exhort all of you who are in the habit of going up to the house of God, never to be content unless you feel that you have got a hold upon the thing that is being taught. Oh you Christian people, I beseech you not to be satisfied with merely the terms of theology without getting into the pith and marrow of them. To realize in your own soul, by experience, the meaning of a doctrine is the only way of knowing it. Those men never forget a truth who have had it burned into them as with a hot iron, by feeling the bitterness of their soul for want of it, and the preciousness of that truth to their souls when they receive it. He that does not receive the truth in the very power and force of it hath but a name to live while he is dead.

I think these observations are warranted from the fact that though our Lord preached the mystery of the kingdom of heaven in the plainest parables to the listening crowd, the very plainness of his speech in using familiar metaphor to make spiritual truth common, became, through the hardness of their hearts, embarrassing to them; they stumbled at the mere outward figure, but never learned the inward meaning. It was to his own chosen twelve, his favored and elect ones, he expounded the riddle, when he took them apart, and then afterwards inquired of them, lest they should have missed the meaning of his exposition: " Have ye understood all these things?" The outward testimony of the gospel may be addressed to the multitude, but the understanding of it is conveyed with transparent clearness to his own people. To hear it is a privilege, but such a privilege as may end without the salvation of your soul, and with the aggravation of your doom; but to understand it is the privilege which leads to eternal life, and happy are they who thus find the way to God's right hand.

I. Let us first consider this searching question—"Have ye understood all these things?"—as spoken to those who can humbly, but yet confidently, say, "Yes, I have understood these things."

I believe there are many of us here who, although we should not like to boast of what we know, and could but confess our ignorance before God, yet dare not be so false to our own experience as to deny that we do know the things which make for our eternal peace. We can say with the man whose eyes were opened, "One thing I know; whereas I was blind, now I see." We do understand, at least, as much as this—that we are sinners, lost and ruined in ourselves, and that in Jesus all our help is found. We do understand that we were cast away in the first Adam, and that our rescue is found in the second Adam, to whom we look, and to whom we are now united by a union that never can be broken. We understand this, also, that upon his advent into this world, upon his holy life, his blessed death, his resurrection, his ascension, and the power which he now possesses at the right hand of the Father—upon him in all these respects we rest, and rest entirely. If we have not learned enough to understand all mysteries, and open up all prophecies, yet we do know that Christ is precious to our soul, that he is the appointed Saviour, that he is *our* Saviour, and that we are saved through him. Yes, blessed be his name, we can say that we have understood, in our measure, all these things—not as we shall understand them, not as we shall know them by and by, when clouds and darkness shall all have disappeared, and we shall be in the clear light of the throne of God; but we have understood these things sufficiently to be led to cast ourselves on Jesus, and to be affected in our daily life and conversation by the truths which Jesus Christ has taught us.

If we have thus understood all these things, what then? Let us be thankful to God with all our hearts that we can say as much as this, for this understanding of divine truth is not due to any natural intelligence we possess. We were by nature blind as bats to the things of divine truth. Neither is it by searching that we have found out God, for it was by his searching after us rather than by our searching after him. If we have received an understanding to know him, and the height and depth of his precious love, truly we have received it as a free grace gift from the hand of our Lord. Had he withheld it we had never found the Saviour, but it is because he, out of his own good pleasure, irrespective of anything in us, was pleased to touch our eyes with eye-salve that we should see, and to bring us out of darkness into his marvellous light—it was because of his rich, free, sovereign, distinguishing grace that we have been made what we are. Come, then, let us bless the name of God. Do we feel distressed with remaining sin? Yet remember, "by the grace of God I am what I am." If I have but little grace, let me be thankful for that little; I might have had none at all. And if I am struggling with corruption, let me be thankful that I have grace to struggle with it, for time was when I should have enjoyed my corruptions instead of lamenting and deploring them. Whatever trial may depress my spirit, let me not rob my God of a song; but if, indeed, he has made me to understand the things which save my soul, let me praise him and extol him for his amazing grace towards such an undeserving one, the least deserving of all his family.

Further, brethren, if you have been led to understand these things, *ought not this to encourage you to seek to understand more?* The young beginner in grace should feel that it will not be impossible for him to grow to the stature of a perfect man in Christ Jesus, because grace has quickened him and made him a babe. That is the greatest thing to be made alive at all. When grace has gone so far as to give me life and put me in the family, I need not fear but what grace will nurture that life, and ultimately bring me to perfection. If I find myself growing in God's garden, though I be the tiniest plant in all the bed, yet it is such a mercy to be in the garden at all—I who was a wild rank weed out in the wilderness before—that I will not doubt but what he will water me when I need it, and that he will tend and care for me till I shall come to perfection. Never think, dear Christian friend, that you cannot master the gospel doctrine. Why, you have learned that Christ is yours; that is the secret of the Lord. All other doctrines, after this, are learnable and comparatively easy. Give yourselves up to the teaching of the Divine Spirit. Wait upon him in believing prayer, and he that has led you through the veil will not keep back the keys of any of the chambers of the temple that shall be profitable for you to enter. Having understood so much, it behoves you to hope to understand more, and it becomes you to seek to understand more as an intelligent believer in Christ.

And surely, if you have understood all these things, my dear Christian friend, you should not be backward *to tell them to others.* We are not sent into the divine school to be scholars merely for ourselves. We are to be in this world pupil-teachers—pupils always, but teachers too; pupils learning constantly at the Master's feet; teachers instructing others in the truths we know. Let it never be supposed that the office of teaching in the Christian Church can exclusively belong to one man, or to one class of men. It belongs to every man, and to every woman too. You cannot teach beyond what you have been taught of God, and it is in proportion as you are taught of God that your teaching takes a wider sphere. But you must teach what you do know. You will seldom learn much to your own profit unless you are diligent in imparting knowledge and edifying one another, for it is in the distribution of the good things which God has given you to the rest of the brotherhood that you shall enjoy the blessing of the Lord which maketh rich. If you will not communicate to the backsliding, to the desponding, and to the feeble the comforts which God gives you, you have cause to fear that in your time of trouble you may have those comforts withheld which you once stifled in your own breast, not knowing how to use them for the Church's benefit. Never keep a truth to thyself, my brother. Hast thou found honey? There are other mouths that would fain know its flavor, and there is enough in that Jonathan's wood of the Scripture for all the hosts of Israel to eat; they cannot exhaust it. Thus would I tell to others what a dear Saviour I have found. Let other candles be lit from thy candle, and thy candle shall burn none the less brightly; but the rather in this it may be said, that to enrich yourselves in all knowledge you must enrich others with the knowledge that you have.

"Have ye understood all these things?" There I will leave you, dear people of God. May your hearts glow and your thoughts be stirred when you are alone in pondering this question of the text.

II. But SOME WHO THINK THEY UNDERSTAND ALL THESE THINGS DO NOT UNDERSTAND THEM.

In all our congregations we have many who would say as quickly as the question was heard, " Do you understand all these things?" " Indeed I do; I have been a hearer these thirty years; I tell you, sir, I know the difference between Calvinism and Arminianism; a man is not going to deceive me; as soon as I hear a sermon I can tell at once whether it is sound or unsound." Well then, dear friend, I am glad to hear that you have so much knowledge; but I want to ask you, Is your life in accordance with what you know? Knowing the right from the wrong so well, is your life conformed to the image of Christ Jesus, or are you living for all the world as if you did not know anything about these things? Because, let me say to you, dear friends, it is a very very solemn thing to have a sort of understanding of divine truth, but not to be affected by it so as to repent of sin, so as to live unto God, so as to seek after holiness. All this religion of yours will be a painted pageantry for you to go to hell in; it will be nothing better than a millstone tied about your neck to sink you deeper and deeper. It were better, very likely, for you that you never had known the way of salvation at all than that, having known it, you should have done despite to it, and have lived in opposition to its spirit and its precepts. You had better have been born in the interior of Africa, and never have listened to the missionary telling of the Crucified One, than to have been born in London and fostered under an orthodox ministry, if you befool your soul with a name to live while you are dead; boasting about your knowledge, but never proving your holiness; talking about faith, but having a faith that is lifeless, producing no fruits, resulting in no works answerable to your profession. I charge thee, knowing professor, to remember thy solemn responsibility. I beseech thee, as thou lovest thine own soul, not to make a downy bed out of thy knowledge, for it shall be a thorn in thy dying pillow. I charge thee, man, not to make hell hotter to thyself than it need be by taking all this knowledge in, and panting after more, while you forget that to obey is better than sacrifice, to trust is better than to boast, to love is better than to rival, and to serve out of simple affection is better than to prate, and to discuss, and to criticise, and to censure. It were well if every one who understands the things of the gospel, or who thinks he does, would constantly examine himself about this business—especially those of us who are ministers. It is a very easy thing for us to be self-deceived, probably more easy for us than for any other people, because having a sacred office for a secular vocation we handle these things every day. Assuming it to be our duty to admonish others, we are prone to resent admonition ourselves. If we have not been converted it is the least likely thing in all the world that we ever should be. I have made the remark myself, I have heard it verified by others, that for pew-openers to be converted is a thing probably unheard of. They are busy here and there, till they are wont to forget their own obligation to worship. Unless they are converted before they take that office—concerning which I think we should make strict inquiry—they never will be in all likelihood, because they are so concerned about the pews, and about putting people in them, and I know not what besides, it seems impossible for them to give their ears to hear, their conscience to feel, or that the voice of truth should ever reach them. Next to them comes the preacher, who is always dealing with the shell of truth. When he sits down to read the Bible, he cannot help thinking whether this or that text would make a sermon. When he is praying, the temptation often is to glide into a kind of ministerial prayer, not the prayer of a poor sinner coming near to God. Perhaps the least likely person to get a blessing after all is the knowing professor. I tell you that the drunkard and the harlot are often rescued when such professors are not even reached with the thrilling message. The sermon which is made useful to a man who never heard the gospel before is of no use to the hard-hearted critic, because he knows too much to get any good out of it. Oh! there are some people you cannot preach to aright. If the Holy Ghost himself were to speak, they would accuse him of being heterodox. If an angel from heaven were to deliver the truth fresh from the mouth of God, he would not satisfy them. They are on the lookout for a word amiss. They are always seeking, if they can, to pick holes, detect flaws, and find fault; this is their trade, their craft, the thing at which they are deft, to make the message of mercy a butt that they may fire at, a kind of target into which they may shoot their arrows. These men seldom, I might almost say never, get a blessing. I do not see how they can. The infinite mercy of God can do what it wills, but seldom does God's sovereignty light on these shallow professors who are eaten up with conceit. Oh for a solemn searching, a sincere self-examination of our hearts. Peradventure we may find that our heads are growing and our hearts are shrivelling. Some children die early because they get the rickets. Their heads are too big, poor things. And so there are many professors with big heads and small hearts. Alas, they have not got the life of God in them at all! God save us from this temptation.

III. Are there not some in every congregation WHO WOULD HARDLY KNOW HOW TO ANSWER THIS QUESTION. —"Have ye understood all these things?"

They do understand them, and they do not. They do up to a point theoretically comprehend them, but, spiritually and experimentally they discern them not. Fearing lest there might be such in the present assembly as really do not understand the very first principles of the truth of God, I would pointedly and earnestly address myself to their particular case. My dear friend, it would be a very dreadful thing for your soul to be lost for want of knowledge, and to perish for lack of understanding. Solomon says that for the soul to be without knowledge is not good. You tell me that you do understand the gospel. I reply to you, Then, why do you not accept it? You do know you are lost, you tell me; you do know that Jesus Christ is set forth as the only Saviour; you do know that a simple trust in him will save you. How is it you can continue peaceful and happy while you are not a partaker of the grace of God? How is it you can remain satisfied when, knowing there is but one way of salvation, you have not yet entered upon it; when, acknowledging Christ to be the Son of God, and to be the only way of salvation, you have lived up till now a despiser or a neglecter of him? I would fain hope—for it would be the only excuse I could offer for you—that perhaps, after all, you really do not understand these things which you think you do understand. Let me remind you now: you are an unsaved sinner, you are lost, your sin has condemned you, you fell in Adam, you have sinned personally and actually, and you are condemned to die. It is not that one day you will be condemned: you are condemned already. At this present moment you are spared, and suffered to go about this world, but you are like a criminal in a condemned cell. The sentence has gone out against you, and only God's long-suffering stays that gleaming axe from falling and utterly destroying you. Do you understand that? Have you really got that thought into you? There you are, just like a man to be beheaded, with your neck on the block, and the axe uplifted now, and it may fall. While I am yet speaking, the axe of death may come, and you, soul and body, may be lost forever ere that clock ticks again. You know this, but do you understand it? Will you try to understand it? Will you try to make it real to your thoughts to-night? For methinks, if you would, there might be some hope that now you would escape from your present ruin, and lift up your heart to the great Father of mercies, and say, "Lord, save me, or I perish."

You know another truth, and you say you understand it. Let me put it to you. Jesus Christ came into this world. He was God's only-begotten Son, but he became man, and as man for man he suffered. God must punish sin, but he punished Jesus Christ for the sins of his people, and those who trust him are secure, because Jesus Christ was their substitute, and they go free. Now, there is no other hope of redemption from the fiery wrath of God but by having a part and lot in the substitutionary work of Christ. You know that, but you have not got a part and lot in it, and you must be lost if you continue without that part or lot. How is it that you can be quiet? You sleep soundly at nights; you eat and drink cheerfully and you enjoy sometimes a merry ringing laugh. How can you revel in the pleasures of sense; how can you give sleep to your eyes or slumber to your eyelids until you get the one thing needful, the one thing which alone can make eternity happy, that infinite future upon which you are so soon to enter? If Jesus Christ, standing in heaven, is preached to you to-night, and you are bidden to believe in him, and you do not believe in him, then you do, as far as you can, crucify him afresh, and open his wounds again, and make him bleed. Do you mean to do that? Do you understand that this is what you are doing every day? Would you, dear friend, would you call God a liar? And yet the Apostle John says that he that believeth not hath made God a liar, because he believeth not on the Son of God. Do you understand what this unbelief of yours really is? You doubt Christ; that is to say, you do not think Christ to be truthful, or good, or able, or strong. Oh! but you say, you know better than that. Then, if you do know better, why do you act as if you did not know better? If he be able to save, and willing to save, oh! my dear hearer, why not come to him as thou art, and cast thyself at his feet, and rest in him in whom thine only rest can be found. "Have ye understood all these things?" then, is a question which you cannot answer after all in the right way; but I beseech you never rest until you can.

Should there be, my dear hearers, something which keeps you back from Christ arising, not so much from your want of will as from your want of knowledge, may God the Holy Spirit stir up your desire and never let you rest till you know Christ, till you hear so that your soul shall live. How shall you know? He is a great teacher, but in the use of the means he will teach you. Be constant in attending the house of God where Christ is most preached. Search the Scriptures, for in them ye think ye have eternal life, and these are they that testify of him. Go to the Father of mercy, and plead with him ere you sleep. Say to him thus, " Father, if there is some sin that I do not know to be a sin that I am indulging in that keeps me from Christ, show it to me, and enable me to give it up; or if it be a sin which I do know, but seem to have struggled in vain with, my Father, strengthen me that I may cut off the right arm, and pluck out the right eye, sooner than cherish those vain delights which bode my everlasting destruction." Plead with him thus: "Oh! my God, I want to know thy Son; reveal thy Son in me, for so I read thou dost to thy people; reveal thy Son in me by the Holy Ghost. I am a poor, blind, ignorant thing; but teach thou me, for hast thou not given the Spirit of God on purpose to be the teacher of the ignorant, and the instructor of the babes?" Plead with the Lord, and plead always with the recollection that you cannot ask because you deserve, but you must ask because Christ deserves. Plead his wounds, his blood, his death, his infinite merits, and you shall ere long— I am certain of it—you shall ere long, in answer to your cries, receive light from the Word, and in that light you shall see light, and you shall understand the things which make for your peace.

I am deeply concerned for some of you, especially for such of you as often listen to my voice, that I may not forever keep on talking into your ears, and never reach your hearts. What, am I to rock your cradle and send you to sleep, that you may sleep yourselves into perdition? Is mine to be the voice that is really to increase your responsibility, and not to be the means of bringing you to Jesus? I pray God avert so dreadful a result to all our ministry, but may you be led this very night—for God's people have been praying for you—may you be led this very night to confess that you do not understand what you ought to understand, and go to the great and wise God to teach and instruct you; and as surely as his Word is truth he will instruct you and teach you in the way that you should go, and bring you to himself. "He that believeth on the Lord Jesus Christ shall be saved." Thus saith his own Word. "He that believeth and is baptized shall be saved." Trust—that is the matter. To believe is to trust, to rely on, to depend upon. He that depends upon Jesus trusts him, believes in him, is saved. May we be of that blessed number, and . his shall be the glory. Amen.

Now he that hath wrought us for the selfsame thing is God, who also hath given unto us the earnest of the Spirit.—2 COR. v. 5.

HOW very confidently Paul contemplates the prospect of death! He betrays no trembling apprehensions. With the calmness and serenity, not merely of resignation and submission, but of assurance and courage, he appears joyous and gladsome, and even charmed with the hope of having his body dissolved, and being girt about with the new body which God hath prepared for his saints. He that can talk of the grave and of the hereafter with such intelligence, thoughtfulness, faith, and strong desire as Paul did, is a man to be envied. Princes might well part with their crowns for such a sure and certain hope of immortality. Could emperors exchange their treasures, their honors, and their dominions, to stand side by side with the humble tent-maker in his poverty, they would be great gainers. Were they but able to say with him—"We are always confident, and willing rather to be absent from the body, and to be present with the Lord," they might well barter earthly rank for such a requital. This side heaven what can be more heavenly than to be thoroughly prepared to pass through the river of death? On the other hand, what a dreary and dreadful state of mind must they be in who, with nothing before them but to die, have no hope and see no outlet,—the pall and the shroud their last adorning; the grave and the sod their destination! Without hope of rising again in a better future, or realizing a better heritage than that which shall know us no more ere long, without any prospect of seeing God face to face with rejoicing; well may men dislike any reference to death. So they shrink from the thought of it; far less can they tolerate its being talked of in common conversation. No marvel that they recoil from the shade of mortality when they are so ill-prepared to face the reality of the soul's departure. But, dear friends, since it is so desirable to be ready to depart, it cannot be inexpedient sometimes to talk about it: and on my part the more so, because there is a proneness in all our minds to start aside from that grave topic which, as God shall help us, shall be our subject this evening—preparation for the great hereafter. "For," saith the Apostle, "God hath wrought us for this selfsame thing;" he has prepared us for the dropping of the present body and the putting on of the next, and he has "given us the earnest of his Spirit."

Our three departments of meditation will be— *the work of preparation itself; the Author of it; and the seal which he sets to it, the possession of which may resolve all scruples as to whether we are prepared or not.*

I. The work of preparation stands first. Is it not almost universally admitted that some preparation is absolutely essential? Whenever the death of friend or comrade is announced, you will hear the worst-instructed say, "I hope, poor man, he was prepared." It may be but a passing reflection, or a common saying. Yet everybody will give expression to it—"I hope he was ready." Whether the words be well understood or not I do not know, but the currency given to them proves a unanimous conviction that some preparation is necessary for the next world. And, in truth, this doctrine is in accordance with the most elementary facts of our holy religion. Men by nature need something to be done for them before they can enter heaven, and something to be done in them, something to be done with them, since by nature they are enemies to God. Dispute it as ye will, God knows best. He declares that we are enemies to him, and alienated in our hearts. We need therefore that some ambassador should come to us with terms of peace, and reconcile us to God. We are debtors as well as enemies to our Creator—debtors to his law. We owe him what we cannot pay, and what he cannot pardon. He must exact obedience, and we cannot render it. He must, as God, demand perfection of us, and we as men cannot bring him that perfection. Some mediator, then, must come in to pay the debt for us, for we cannot pay it, neither

can we be exempted from it. There must be a substitute who shall stand between us and God, one
who shall undertake all our liabilities and discharge
them, and so set us free, that the mercy of God may
be extended to us. In addition to this we are all
criminals. Having violated the law of God we are
condemned already. We are not, as some vainly
pretend, introduced to this world on probation; but
our probation is over; we have forfeited all hope;
we have broken the law, and the sentence is gone
out against us; thus we stand by nature as condemned criminals, tenants of this world during the
reprieve of God's mercy, in fear of a certain and
terrible execution, unless some one come in between
us and that punishment; unless some gracious hand
bring us a free pardon; unless some voice divine
plead and prevail for us that we may be acquitted.
If this be not done for us, it is impossible that we
should entertain any well-grounded hope of entering heaven. Say then, brethren and sisters, has
this been done for you? I know that many of you
can answer—" Blessed be God, I have been reconciled to him through the death of his Son; God is
no enemy of mine, nor I of his; there is no distance
now between me and God: I am brought near to
him, and made to feel that he is near to me, and
that I am dear to him." Full many here present
can add—" My debts to God are paid; I have looked
to Christ my Substitute; I have seen him enter
into suretyship engagements for me, and I am persuaded that he has discharged all my liabilities; I

am clean before God's bar; faith tells me I am clean." And, brethren, you know that you are no longer condemned. You have looked to him who bore your condemnation, and you have drunk in the spirit of that verse—"There is therefore now no condemnation to them which are in Christ Jesus, who walk not after the flesh, but after the Spirit." Surely this is a preparation for heaven. How could we enter there if our debts are not discharged? How could we obtain the Divine favor eternally if we were still condemned criminals? How could we dwell forever in the presence of God if we were still his enemies? Come, let us rejoice in this, that he hath wrought us for this selfsame thing, having championed our cause from the cradle to the grave.

Preparation for heaven consists still further in *something that must be wrought in us;* for observe, brethren, that if the Lord were to blot out all our sins we should still be quite incapable of entering heaven unless there was a change wrought in our natures. According to this Book we are dead by nature in trespasses and sins—not some of us, but all of us; the best as well as the worst;—we are all dead in trespasses and sins. Shall dead men sit at the feast of the Eternal God? Shall there be corpses at the celestial banquet? Shall the pure air of the New Jerusalem be defiled with the putrefaction of iniquity? It must not, it cannot be. We must be quickened; we must be taken from the corruption of our old nature into the incorruption of the new nature, receiving the incorruptible seed which liveth and abideth forever. Only the living children can inherit the promises of the living God, for he is not the God of the dead, but of the living; we must be made living creatures by the new-creating power of grace, or else we cannot be made meet for glory. By nature we are all worldly. Our thoughts go after earthly things. We "mind earthly things," as the Apostle says. We seek after the world's joys; the world's maxims govern us; the world's fears alarm us; the world's hopes and ambitions excite us. We are of the earth earthy, for we bear the image of the first Adam. But, brethren, we cannot go to heaven as worldly men; for there would be nothing there to gratify us. The gold of heaven is not for barter to use, nor for covetousness to hoard. The rivers of heaven are not for commerce, neither are they to be defiled by any sensual contaminations. The joys and glories of heaven are all spiritual, all celestial.

> "Pure are the joys above the skies,
> And all the region peace."

Such peace is of a heavenly kind and for heavenly minds. Carnal spirits, greedy, envious spirits— what would they do in heaven? If they were in the place called heaven, they could not be in the state called heaven, and heaven is more a state than a place. Though it is probably both, yet it is mainly the former, a state of happiness, a state of holiness, a state of spirituality which it would not be possible for the worldly to reach. The incongruity of such a thing is palpable. Therefore you see, brethren, the Holy Spirit must come and give us new affections. We must have a fresh object set before us. In fact, instead of minding the things that are seen, we must come to love and to aspire to the things that are not seen. Our affections, instead of going downwards to things of earth, must be allured by things that are above, where Christ sitteth at the right hand of God. In addition to our spiritual death and worldliness we are all unholy by nature. Not one of us is pure in the sight of God. We are all defiled and all defiling, but in heaven they are " without fault before the throne of God." No sin is tolerated there; no sin of thought, or word, or deed. Angels and glorified spirits delight to do God's will without hesitation, without demur, without omission; and we, like them, must be holy, or we cannot enter into their sacred fellowship. But what a change must come over the carnal man to make him holy! Through what washings he must pass! What can wash him white, indeed, but that far-famed blood of the Son of God? Through what purification he must pass! What, indeed, can purify him at all but the refining energy of God the Holy Ghost? He alone can make us what God would have us to be, renewed in his image in righteousness and true holiness.

That a great change must be wrought in us, even ungodly men will confess, since the idea of the heaven of the Scriptures has always been repulsive, never agreeable, to unconverted men and women. When Mahomet would charm the world into the belief that he was the prophet of God, the heaven he pictured was not at all the heaven of holiness and spirituality. His was a heaven of unbridled sensualism, where all the passions were to be enjoyed without let or hindrance for endless years. Such the heaven that sinful men would like; therefore such the heaven that Mahomet painted for them, and promised to them. Men in general, be they courtly or be they coarse in their habits, when they read of heaven in the Scriptures with any understanding of what they read, curl their lips, and ask contemptuously, Who wants to be everlastingly psalm-singing? Who could wish to be always sitting down with these saints talking about the mighty acts of the Lord and the glorious majesty of his kingdom? Such people cannot go to heaven, it is clear; they have not character or capacity to enter into its enjoyment. I think Whitefield was right. Could a wicked man enter into heaven, he would be wretched there; being unholy, he must be unhappy. From sheer distaste for the society of heaven he might fly to hell for shelter. With the tumult of evil passions in his breast he could not brook the triumph of righteousness in the city of the blest. There is no heaven for him who has not been prepared for it by a work of grace in his soul. So necessary is this preparation—a preparation for us, and a preparation in us. And if we have such a preparation, beyond all question we *must have it on this side of our death.* It can only be obtained in this world. The moment one breathes his last it is all fixed and settled. As the tree falleth so it must lie. While the nature is soft and supple it is susceptible of impression, stamp what seal you may upon it; once let it grow cold and hard, fixed and frigid, you can do so no more; it is proof against any change. While the iron is flowing into the mould, you may fashion it into what implement you please; let it grow cold, in vain you strive to alter its form. With pen of liquid ink in your hand, you write what you will on the paper; but the ink dries, the impress remains, and where is the treachery that shall tamper with it? Such is this life of yours. It is over, all over with you for eternity, beyond alteration or emendation, when the breath has gone from the body. We have no intimation in the Word of God that any soul dying in unbelief will afterwards be converted to the faith. Nor have we the slightest reason to believe that our prayers in this world can at all affect those who have departed this life. The masses of priests are fictions, without the shadow of divine authority. Purgatory, or " Pick-purse," as old Latimer used to call it, is an invention for making fat larders for priests and monks, but the Scriptures of truth give it no countenance. The Word of God says, " He that is holy, let him be holy still; he that is filthy, let him be filthy still." Such as you are when death comes to you, such will judgment find you, and such will the eternal reward or the eternal punishment leave you, world without end. Preparation is needed, and the preparation must be found before we die.

Moreover, we ought to know—for it is possible for a man to know whether he is thoroughly prepared. Some have said not; but they have usually been persons very little acquainted with the matter. The writings of those grand old divines of the Puritan period abundantly prove how thoroughly they enjoyed *the assurance of faith.* They did not hesitate to express themselves in such language as the Apostle used: "We *know* that if our earthly house of this tabernacle were dissolved, we have an house not made with hands, eternal in the heavens." They were wont to speak as Job doth when he said: "I *know* that my Redeemer liveth." And, indeed, many of the children of God among us at this present time are favored with a confident, unstaggering confidence that, let their last hour come when it may, or let the Lord himself descend from heaven with a shout, there will be nothing but joy and peace for them—no cause of trembling, nothing that can give them dismay. Why, some of us live from year to year in constant assurance of our preparation for the bliss that awaiteth and the rest that remaineth for God's people.

Beloved, our Lord Jesus Christ has not left us in such a dubious case that we always need to be inquiring, "Am I his, or am I not?" He has given us good substantial grounds to go upon to make sure work of it. He tells us that " He that believeth and is baptized shall be saved;" if we have been obedient to these two commands we shall be saved, for our God keepeth his word. He tells us that such believers, patiently continuing in well-doing, inherit eternal life. If we are kept by his grace, walking in his fear, we may rest assured that we shall come to the appropriate end of such a life, namely, the glory which abideth for the faithful. We need not harbor endless questionings. What miserable work it is to stand in any doubt on this matter. Let us not be satisfied till we are sure and confident that heaven will be ours! Alas! how many put off all thoughts of being prepared to die! They are prepared for almost anything except the one thing for which it is most needful to be ready. If the summons should come to some of you at this moment, how dread it would be! Were we to see an angel hovering in the air, and should we have intelligence by a message from the clouds that some one of us must, on a sudden, leave his body behind him and appear before God, what cowering down, what trembling, what muttering of forgotten prayers there would be with some of you! You are not ready. You never will be ready, I fear. The carelessness in which you have lived so long has become habitual. One would think you had resolved to die in your sins. Have you never heard the story of Archæus, the Grecian despot, who was going to a feast, and on the way a messenger brought

him a letter, and seriously importuned him to read
it. It contained tidings of a conspiracy that had been
formed against him, that he should be killed at the
feast. He took the letter, and put it into his pocket.
In vain the messenger urged that it was concerning serious matters. "Serious matters to-morrow,"
said Archæus, "feasting to-night." That night,
the dagger reached his heart while he had about
him the warning which, had he heeded it, would
have averted the peril. Alas! too many men say,
"Serious things to-morrow!" They have no mis-
giving, but when their sport is over they will have
alike the leisure and the inclination for these weighty
matters. Were it not wiser, sirs, to let these grave
affairs come first? Might ye not, then, find some
sport of nobler character than the froth and friv-
olity to which fashion leads on?—a holy merriment
and a sacred feasting that better far become immortal spirits? How vain and grovelling the mirth
which reduces men to children, pleased with a rattle,
tickled with a straw; then brings them down to
drivelling fools, and degrades them often till they
become worse then brutes. I wish I could imprint
a solemn thought on the mind of some careless individuals. Reck ye not that time is short, that life
is precarious, that opportunities cross your path at
lightning speed, that hope flatters those on whom
the fangs of death are fixed; that there is no vesti-
bule in which to adjust your frame of mind; that
the summons will come with a sudden shock at last.
What sentence more trite; what sentiment more

prevalent; yet what solemnity more neglected than this: "Prepare to meet your God." Propound it, profess it, preach it as we may, the most of men are unprepared. They know the inevitable plight, they see the necessity of preparation, but they postpone and procrastinate instead of preparing. God grant you may not trifle, any of you, until your trembling souls are launched into that sphere unknown, but not unfeared, and read your doom in hell.

II. Now as to the AUTHOR OF THIS PREPARATION FOR DEATH, the text saith, "He that hath wrought us for the selfsame thing *is* God." It is God alone then who makes men fit for heaven. He works them to the selfsame purpose. Who made Adam fit for Paradise but God? And who must make us fit for the better Paradise above but God? That we cannot do it ourselves is evident. According to the Scriptures we are dead in trespasses and sins. Can the dead start from the grave of their own accord? Do ye think to see coffins opened and gravestones uplifted by the natural energy of corpses? Such things were never dreamed of. The dead shall surely rise, but they shall rise because God raises them. They cannot vitalize their inert frames, neither can the dead in sin quicken themselves and make themselves fit for the presence of God. Conversion, which prepares us for heaven, is a new creation. That word "creation" puts all the counsel, the conceit, and the contrivance of man into the background. If any one saith that he can make a new heart, let him first go and make a fly. Not until he has created such a winged insect let him presume to tell us that he can make a man a new creature in Christ Jesus. And yet to make a fly would not demonstrate that a fly could make itself; and it would offer but a feeble pretext for that wonderful creation which is supposed in a man's making himself a new heart. The original creation was the work of God, and the new creation must likewise be of God. To take away a heart of stone and give a heart of flesh is a miracle. Man cannot do it; if he attempts it, it shall be to his own shame and confusion. The Lord must make us anew. Have not we, who know something of the Lord's working in us this selfsame thing, been made to feel that it is all of his grace? What first made us think about eternal things? Did we, the stray sheep, come back to the fold of our own accord? No, far from it:

> " Jesus sought me when a stranger
> Wandering from the fold of God;"

and ever since we have been living men in Christ Jesus, to whom must we ascribe our preservation and our progress? Must we not attribute every victory over sin and every advance in the spiritual life to the operation of God, and nothing at all to ourselves? A poor simpleton once said, " 'Twas God and I did the work." " Well, but Charlie, what part did you take in it?"   "Sure, then," said he, "I did all I could to stop the Lord, and he beat me."   I suppose, did we tell the simple truth we should say much the same.   In the matter of our salvation we do all we can to oppose it—our old nature does—and he overcomes our evil propensities. From first to last Jesus Christ has to be the Author and the Finisher of our salvation, or it never would have been begun and it never would have been completed.

Think, beloved, of what fitness for heaven is. To be fit for heaven a man must be perfect.   Go, you who think you can prepare yourselves, be perfect for a day.   The vanity of your own mind, the provocation of this treacherous world, and the subtle temptation of the devil would make short work of your empty pretensions.   You would be blown about like chaff.   Creature perfection indeed! Was ever anything so absurd?   Men have boasted of attaining it, but their very boastings have proved that they possessed it not.   He that gets nearest to perfection is the very man who sighs and cries over the abiding infirmities of his flesh.   No, if perfection is to be reached—and it must be, or we shall not be fit for heaven—by the operation of God it must be wrought.   Man's work is never perfect; it is always marred on the wheel.   His best machinery may still be improved upon; his finest productions of art might still be excelled.   God alone is perfect, and he alone is the Perfecter.   Blessed be God, we can heartily subscribe to this truth,

"He that hath wrought us for the selfsame thing is God."

But what shall I say to those of you, my friends, who have no acquaintance with God? You certainly cannot be fitted for heaven. Your cause is not committed to him. He is doing nothing for you. He has not begun the good work in you. You live in this world as if there were no God. The thought, the stupendous thought of his "Being" does not affect you. You would not act any differently if there were twenty Gods, or if there were no God. You utterly ignore his claims on your allegiance, and your responsibility to his law. Virtually in thought and deed you are without God in the world. Poor forlorn creature, thou hast forgotten thy Creator. Poor wandering soul, thou hast fallen out of gear with the universe; thou hast become alienated from the great Father who is in heaven. I tremble at the thought. To be on the wide sea without rudder or compass; to be lost in the wilderness, where there is no way! Cheerless as thy condition is, remember this: Though thou seest not God, God sees thee. God sees thee now; he hears thee now. If thou breathe but a desire towards him, that desire shall be accepted and fulfilled. He will yet begin to work in thee that gracious preparation which shall make thee meet to be a partaker of the inheritance of the saints in light.

III. And now, thirdly—let the SEAL OF THIS PREPARATION be briefly but attentively considered.

The Apostle says—"He that hath wrought us for the selfsame thing is God, who also hath given unto us *the earnest of the Spirit.*" Masters frequently pay during the week a part of the wages which will be due on Saturday night. God gives his Holy Spirit, as it were, to be a part of the reward which he intends to give to his people, when, like hirelings, they have fulfilled their day. Our country friends just before harvest go out into the fields, and they pick half a dozen ears that are ripe, braid the ends, and hang them up over the mantle-shelf as a kind of earnest of the harvest. So God gives us his Holy Spirit to be in our hearts as an earnest of heaven; and as the ears of wheat are of the same quality and character as the harvest, so the gift of the Holy Spirit is the antepast of heaven. When you have him you have a plain indication to your soul of what heaven will be. You have a part of heaven—"a young heaven," as Dr. Watts somewhere calls it—within you.

Ask yourself, then, dear hearer, this question—"Have I received the earnest of the Spirit?" If so, you have the preparation for heaven; if not, you are still a stranger to divine things, and you have no reason to believe that the heaven of the saints will be your heritage. Come, now, have you received the Holy Spirit? Do you reply, "How may I know?" Wherever the Holy Spirit is he works certain graces in the soul—repentance, to wit. Hast thou ever repented of sin? I mean, dost thou hate it? Dost thou shun it? Dost thou grieve to think thou shouldst once have loved it? Is thy mind altogether changed with regard to sin, so that what once seemed pleasure now is pain, and all the sweetness of sin is poison to thy taste? Where the Holy Spirit is, repentance is followed by the whole train of graces, all in a measure, not any in perfection, for there is always room to grow in grace and in the knowledge of Jesus Christ. Such is *patience*, which submits to the Lord's will; such, too, the gracious disposition of *forgiveness*, which enables us to bear injuries and to forgive those who vex us; such, likewise, that holy courage which is not ashamed to own our Lord or to defend his cause. In fact, where the Holy Ghost is bestowed, all the graces of the Spirit will be communicated in some degree. Though they will all need to grow, yet there will be the seeds of them all. Where the Holy Spirit is there will be the joy. No delight can be more animating or more elevating than that which springs from the indwelling of God in the soul. Think of God coming to abide in this poor bosom! Why, were a cross of diamonds or pearls glittering on your breast some might envy you the possession of such a treasure; but to have God within your breast is infinitely better. God dwelleth in us, and we in him. Oh, sacred mystery! Oh, birth of joy unspeakable! Oh, well of bliss divine that maketh earth like heaven! Hast thou ever had this joy—the joy of knowing that thou art pardoned; the joy of being sure that thou art a child of God; the joy of being certain that all things work together for thy good; the joy of expecting that ere long, and the sooner the better, thou shalt be forever beyond gunshot of fear, and care, and pain, and want? Where the Spirit of God is there is more or less of this joy, which is the earnest of heaven.

This gift, moreover, will be conspicuously evidenced by a living faith in the Lord Jesus Christ. The Holy Ghost is not in you if you rely on anything but Jesus; but if as a poor guilty sinner you have come to him, partaken of his gracious pardon, kissed his blessed feet, and are now depending upon him alone, you have received the Holy Ghost, and you have got the antepast of heaven.

Brethren and sisters, it is intensely desirable that we should seek more to be consciously filled with the Holy Spirit. We get easily contented with a little spiritual blessedness. Let us grow more covetous of the best gifts. Let us crave to be endued with the Holy Spirit, and to be baptized in the Holy Ghost and in fire. The more we get of him the more assurance we shall have of heaven for our peace, the more foretastes of heaven for our happiness, and the more preparation for heaven in lively hope.

Thus have I shown you the need of preparation, the Author of preparation, and the great seal which proves the verity of that preparation. If your honest conscience allows your humble claim to have received this sacred token of salvation, how happy you should be. Do not be afraid to be happy. Some Christians seem to court the gloom of despondency as if they dared not bask in the sunshine of heaven. I have sometimes heard people say that they have *not enjoyed themselves.* No, dear friends; pity, methinks, if any of us ever should. It would be a poor kind of enjoyment if we merely enjoyed ourselves. But, oh! it is delightful when you can enjoy your God, and when you can enjoy the mercies that are of him, and the promises that are in him, and the blessings which through him come to you. When you gather round the table of the Lord's love do not be afraid to partake of the feast. There is nothing put there to be merely looked at; no confectionery spread out for show. And it will be a blessing to your family if you are always happy. You may find that something has gone wrong while you have been away. But go home as cheerful as you can be, and you will be better able to bear the cares and vexations that must and will befall you. Keep your spirit well worked up to the fear of the Lord, and the enjoyment of his presence. Then if some little cross matter should come to disquiet you, you can say, "Who am I that I should be vexed and chafed, or lose my temper, or be cast down about such a matter as this? This is not my sphere of well-being, this is not my heaven; this is not my God."

But, oh! suppose you feel persuaded and honestly admit that you are not prepared to die, not made meet for heaven. Do not utterly despair, but be grateful that you live where the gospel is preached.

"Faith cometh by hearing, and hearing by the Word of God." Be much in hearing the Word, and be much in earnest prayer that the hearing may be blessed to your soul. Above all, give diligence to that divine command which bids thee trust in Jesus Christ whom he hath sent. Eternal life lies in the nutshell of that one sentence—"Believe in the Lord Jesus Christ, and thou shalt be saved." All that is asked of you—and even that grace gives you—is simply to trust in him who as Son of God died for the sins of men. God give you that faith, and then may you meet death with joy, or look forward to the coming of the Lord with peace, whichever may be your lot.

www.ingramcontent.com/pod-product-compliance
Lightning Source LLC
Chambersburg PA
CBHW021712110726
47902CB00005B/1157